Introductory Lectures
on
Religious Philosophy

Amir Sabzevary, Ph.D.

For information, contact

MSI Press, LLC
1760 Airline Hwy, #203
Hollister, CA 95023

Transcriptions and translations by Brian Fletcher Johnson.

Library of Congress Control Number: 2017945388

ISBN: 978-1-933455-49-5

Contents

Amir Sabzevary

Editor's Introduction

This book is a transcription of lectures that revolve around two questions: How does a person become educated? What does it mean to be a teacher? Without continuously entertaining the problems that these two questions create, no one should be licensed to discuss religion or philosophy. These problems seem to have been forgotten in an age when anyone with the privilege of time, intellect and emotions can buy a PhD or publish a book and be considered "educated." But if not with the privilege of a PhD or with a voluminous collection of information, what qualifies someone as a teacher? Introductory Lectures on Religious Philosophy addresses these questions within the context of five ancient traditions: the Epic of Gilgamesh, Hinduism, Buddhism, Taoism and Confucianism. The language of the lectures, the questions that guide the dialogue, and the social atmosphere of this class also comment directly on these problems of education.

In these lectures, delivered at a summer evening class at Laney College in 2017, perennial religious and philosophical ideas are discussed in the cultural language of Oakland. As such, perhaps one of the most startling aspects of this book is the casual language. There is no scholarly language and no technical jargon. There are no footnotes, no references to any readings, and no intellectual prerequisites of any kind but for the few, necessary translations. By clothing profound ideas in profane language, no one is absolved of the burdens of examination. Larger-than-life ideas act as grand and brilliant mirrors, reflecting the ways in which we are guided by petty emotions, cheap ideas, and juvenile self-images. This book is for those who are seeking to understand and live ideas, not for those who are more attached to the language and containers of religion and philosophy.

The class centers around students' questions, which again, may frustrate a reader that is expecting an eloquent catalog of information. Ideas are tailored to students' questions, a demanding approach which usually inspires an invasive, personal back-and-forth. This is not careless but calculated. In place of linear, systematic answers, students receive stories that relate on many levels to their question, or the question is addressed later in response to a different question. The attentive reader will note that once a student asks a question, each time they re-enter the dialogue, the lecture shifts to revolve around their previous questions. The class rotates around these questions, approaching the same ideas from perspectives other questions create. Education is not the acquisition of information; beautifying one's intellect is not the same as beautifying one's life. In favor of appealing to the intellect, religious and philosophical ideas appeal to less accessible, more profound aspects of the human psyche. Likewise, these lectures are layered, symbolic and frequently self-referential, touching upon the questions behind the question, so to speak.

Children roam freely in this classroom. Food is brought and shared. There are no lecture notes, assigned texts or obvious structure. Many students in this class are not only not enrolled, but seem to have been sitting in these classes for quite some time. Classes begin with a series of questions, some of which are unceremoniously dismissed while others carefully dissected. There is an alternating atmosphere of levity and trauma as humor is used, among other reasons, to release some of the pressure created by extraordinarily difficult ideas. Like any good art, the most pregnant moments are embedded within a seemingly casual context, as this context creates intimacy and trust. Without this trust, without a very personal atmosphere, ideas remain mere information, removed from their ability to transform.

In essence, this is a transcription of a living classroom. The classroom, by any definition, should reflect the world beyond the classroom. Yet could any environment be more sterile and lifeless than the modern classroom, subject as it is to political constraints that often perpetuate the very difficulties education is meant to resolve? It is not difficult to read a book and then discuss the ideas from the book. It is nearly impossible to learn how to live ideas, and moreover to convey this life in a way that inspires others to do the same. This book is essentially a manual to life, and more importantly, how to become a good student of life. As these lectures repeatedly stress, being a good student is not about the accumulation of knowledge, but rather about how to learn how to live with loss, poverty, and pain. If the classroom can sufficiently reflect the troubles and turmoil, the uncertainties and the absurdities of life, then life itself can be turned into a classroom, seen through the lenses of those who ceaselessly struggle with the problems of being human. These are the philosophers whose poverty has earned them the title of "educated."

Chapter One:
Introduction to Religious Philosophy

[Lester: So this is a course on religion. What do you mean exactly by "religion," or by "philosophy"?]

There is this wonderful animal called a salmon fish, which of course begins life as a tiny egg. By the sheer force of the water, this egg soon finds itself at the bottom of a river and after a few weeks, the shell opens and out comes a fish. At the bottom of the river, this fish makes lots of friends, buys a house, has children, and has everything that could possibly make it happy. In other words, life is really good for this salmon. Without any warning though, she gets attacked by her own psychology. Don't ask me how it happens, but one morning the fish says to herself, "I don't belong here. This is not my home. I have a house, but it's no longer livable. I have a relationship, in which I feel profoundly alone. I have children, but they're all like strangers. This is not my home."

Now you would say, "What is wrong with this animal?" She has everything and yet she's unhappy. Maybe she needs therapy or drugs! But the truth is, she doesn't need any of that stuff. She's transitioning from one life to another. The fish just wakes up and says, "I don't know why I am so unhappy. All I know is that this not where I belong." All of a sudden, all the business-minded, socially acceptable things that this fish used to do mean nothing. Her entire faculty shuts down because reason is no longer powerful enough to guide this fish. The fish has sex, but is not happy. Has money, but is not happy. For those of you that have read Dante's Divine Comedy, it opens, "In the middle of my years, I found myself in the dark wood." This is the 14th century when people are religious, there's no pornography, no Internet, and yet there is this man, a beautiful poet, who says, "All people come to this crossroads." You don't have to be forty like Dante. At any time you could wake up and say, "This is not my life. I am more than flesh, more than body, more than my relationship, more than a house, more than my life."

All these awful things happen to this poor fish at the worst time of the year, which is springtime. The bears are out from hibernation and they're sitting at the river, so the fish must do something that it was not designed to do. It must not only go against the current of the river, but it must also begin to fly. This fish begins to be guided by something that you and I have lost, called intuition. Look at the life of Malcolm X. This is a guy who has a wife, a guy who's got kids, a family and so much going for him. But he said, "I want my soul to be nourished, not my intellect. My intellect says, 'Protect your life, protect your kids, protect your wife,' but my intuition, or my soul says, 'Live through your passion. Live for justice and fairness.'" You know what it means to be human, right? We do whatever we possibly can to protect and preserve our bodies, our minds, our wealth, our fame, and our reputation. Rational people are concerned about these things, but for some strange reason, Malcolm X becomes irrational. He says, "I don't need my wife or my children, in fact I don't even need my power. I will live through my intuition. My intuition says, 'The white man, the black man, the yellow man, the brown man, they're all my brothers. Deep down inside them lives this thing called intuition, soul.'"

The fish's feelings become so urgent that it starts to swim upwards. Many of the salmon find themselves in the mouth of the bears, and only a couple are able to get through this wall of hungry predators. Intuitively, somehow they get back to the very top of the river and for some strange reason they know it's time for them to lay their own eggs. And once they do, they die. The next generation is ready to float down, live in forgetfulness for twenty or thirty years, and eventually be condemned by their own psychology and try to journey back home, only to find death, which becomes their salvation.

So for those of you that at times feel grief and you have no idea why you've been condemned, your life is no different than the salmon fish. You don't need to drink or smoke. All these traditions are telling us is that we are wired so that at some point, something about you will turn against itself and you will be forced to make a transformation. It will be profoundly difficult, and you may not be successful. But once this dam cracks and breaks open, there is no turning back.

It seems that all of us are after one, simple thing: a life in which you and I can find no wrinkles or blemishes, or a life that is beautiful. One of the reasons why we desire to fall in love, read good books or watch inspiring movies is because these things remove us from our limited life. All of us in this class are pursuing this thing called Beauty. You don't go to church, or pray, or become a Buddhist because you care about any of these people. You do so because on the inside, believing in the Buddha beautifies the way you feel, think and live. You love the way love makes you feel about yourself.

When, for example, my niece was two days old my sister brought her to my place. She was asleep and I was standing over her, just to see how she looks. And all of a sudden she would smile up at me, or sometimes she would tear up and I would ask myself, "I wonder where she came from, and what she saw there?" I loved these moments, because children have the power to make us believe in worlds unseen and untouched by the rest of us.

Ideas are like my niece – they're magic. But though they have the power to transform, there is a price to be paid for this transformation. For those of you that may assume that ideas have no power, that they're just dead things floating in the air, let me give you a couple of examples of how ideas transform and the price people pay for this transformation.

There was a very unhappy white man around the 19th century named Henry David Thoreau, who was in love with his teacher's wife. Thoreau hated school for what it was doing to people, so he opened a school with his brother, only to watch his brother die soon after. He closed the school, walked away from everything and lived in the woods. In the woods he read a tiny Indian book called the Bhagavad Gita, or "music of the gods." The ideas went inside him, which is noteworthy. You can read the best books and be around the best people but if your environment on the inside is not right, those people will not be able to go inside you. If you're single and looking for the perfect guy or perfect gal but you don't have your act together, the perfect person will walk into your life, and then walk out. Ideas are no different in that they are like guests. Like any guest you can exploit them, or receive them well. If you exploit ideas, you speak about them, but you don't feel them or understand them properly. You use them the way you would use a person for money, or for a good time. But receive them well, and they go inside you like a mustard seed and become gigantic trees.

After reading the Bhagavad Gita, Henry David Thoreau understood that every single human has an obligation, in the sense that when we are born, the gods created our birth for a purpose. Our task is to figure out this purpose. We are like a puzzle. You are not here to write essays for your instructors, you're here to write essays that spell out all the puzzles that live inside you, which have lots of missing pieces. And Thoreau got all of this by reading a tiny book that has less than twenty chapters. He writes On Walden, in which he says, "Do not be deceived by modernity. Don't watch TV or play video games, and don't have useless friends. Go into the woods and let the winds be your friend. Let the leaves dance for you. Let the animals be your theatre. Go back to nature because that's what you and I are."

A brown man named Mahatma Gandhi reads On Walden a few years later, and you have to understand how ridiculous Gandhi was at the beginning of his life. Though he was brown he wanted to be English, both inside and out. He was, in fact, educated in England, then went to South Africa to sell his knowledge, only to realize that it doesn't matter how powerful or eloquent you may be as an Indian, if your skin is brown, the white man will never accept you. And he realized that it doesn't matter what you try to become on the outside, if you're impoverished on the inside, meaning that if you have no self-knowledge and you don't know what you're doing with your life, then the false images that you erect to satisfy other people will shatter. Gandhi was so moved by On Walden that he almost single-handedly drove out the entire British Empire from India.

A few years later, a black man named Martin Luther King Jr. reads the life story of Mahatma Gandhi, and his life is transformed. He is able to inspire millions with his ideas on justice, and ultimately sacrifices his life for these ideas. Do not underestimate ideas, especially if you receive them at the right place and the right time. They will paralyze most of who and what you are. It's devastating, and it's also inspiring. It is far safer for you to be closed to any idea that could potentially change something about you, and it is far easier for you to remain cheap. It is safer, more familiar, and more comfortable. Because if you want to make some changes in your life, let me put it to you like this.

Imagine that I have been addicted to alcohol for twenty years. Sure, I can blame my father and mother for being drunks, and I could blame the entire country for what it has done to me. But ultimately one day I realize that I'm getting old and my life has been lived in bars and bottles so I say, "I've lost my wife because of alcohol and my kids don't respect me because of alcohol, so I need to make some changes." For many years people have been telling me that I'm a drunk and I'm no good, but I keep telling them, "I'm a social drinker! I get buzzed once in a while and I get drunk once in a while, but what's wrong with that?" My friends keep telling me, "Look you don't just drink once a week, you drink every day." I'm not quite sure, but at some point someone comes to me and says, "Look, you've been a drunk for a long time, and these are the reasons." For whatever reason it's the right time and the right place and I look myself in the mirror, psychologically speaking, and I say, "He's right. I'm a drunk." Now I have to summon the courage to sober up. Do you know how difficult it is to remove the habit of going to the bar? What am I going to do with my time now that I want to get rid of this addiction of going to the bar? What am I going to do with all my friends that I've known for decades? What am I going to do with the familiar conversation, where we get drunk and talk and laugh, and then I go home and collapse, only to wake up and repeat the same story? This is part of who and what I am, and all of a sudden I want to create a brand-new life for myself and it's not going to happen.

First you physically distance yourself from the bar and the bottle. But what do you do with the friends with whom you've created emotional bonds? Even if you were to physically remove yourself from friends, what do you do psychologically when you sit home, all alone? What do you think about? How do you protect yourself from the emotional chaos? Something inside you realizes that in order to get over your addiction, you can't do it alone. You pick up your phone and say, "I need the closest AA." You call and once you go in, twenty people are sitting in a circle, and one person is the head. All of you have the following in common: It doesn't matter what your parents did to you or what you've done to other people, the truth is, all of you are drunks that are trying to sober up. The common denominator is the same, in that alcohol has been used to escape the tyranny of life. Because you all share the same story, after two weeks there is so much trust that you stand up and say, "I am Amir. All these things happened to me. I drank and I'm trying to sober up. I need help." And for the first time you understand that if you really want to understand life, or live life, you cannot do it on your own. You need a community. In the ancient world, this used to be a cult. In the Middle Ages, these were the halls of education. This is the relationship between a student and a teacher, but in modernity, none of these exist.

So my recommendation is this. If ideas inspire you but you don't have a support system, don't pursue them. You will just become more of a drunk.

My parents sent me to India to become educated and to make my parents happy I said, "Okay." I went through twenty years of school, thinking that when I finish my degrees I'll finally be free and happy. But despite having all these degrees my mom looks at me and says, "You're twenty five. You need to get married." Apparently, a PhD isn't enough. So I got married, and then after being married for about eight months, my wife looked at me and says, "Children." First I thought school would be the end of it. Then they said it's marriage. Then they convinced me that it's children. Then my father says, "What are you going to do with all these degrees?" So I went into teaching. And for the first few years I enjoyed talking very much, I enjoyed reading books very much, and I enjoyed playing with philosophical and religious ideas. I believed that at last I had achieved a modicum of comfort, happiness and stability. But now I look back and I realize that I'm really not happy. For the past fifty-seven years of my life, I have obeyed, respected and done everything that my society and parents have asked, and I have even followed my own nature to some extent. But once in a while I wake up at two or three in the morning and ask, "Has my life been reduced to coming to classes and talking this nonsense and then going home and looking at my wife and looking at my kids, eating, sleeping then talking? If this is it, it is profoundly dissatisfying!" And the truth is, I've committed no crimes, and this is not something that I deserve. Someone who has worked so hard really deserves much better.

You may think that this is my story but the truth is, it's not. Every single one of you in this class, whether you get an "A" in this class or an "F," whether you get a job that pays you six figures, whether you get married or you're lonely, it doesn't really matter what you do. Because it seems that human beings have forever been condemned to be discontent. And we have tried to silence the unhappiness that we feel at times, yet it refuses to go away. As a black man you will go out with a white woman and consider her a trophy, and you will think that your misery has come to an end because now you have power over the white man. But alas, you sit and look yourself in the mirror and realize you're black and ask, "What exactly does that mean?"

This psychological condemnation has been around for at least seventy thousand years, when Neanderthals buried their people in the fetal position, decorated with ornaments, so that when they came back to a world, maybe not the physical world, they would be happier and more content. The simple fact that humans think is an expression of our tremendous capacity for sadness, unhappiness and discontentment. For the first few weeks that you're in a relationship, you never think. You just feel like this is the person that you're going to marry and have lots of children with. All of your reflective abilities have been put on pause because emotionally, you have been consumed by this thing called love. A tremendous amount of passion lives inside you and thinking shuts down, which is why you and I have the ability to take so much nonsense from our companions. But once this emotion called love dissipates a little, the conversations that used to come about so casually now take effort. Boredom has set it. You need to understand that when we tackle ideas, whether they are from Gilgamesh or the Buddha, they are rooted in human unhappiness. There is no escape from it.

It is only in the last two hundred years or so that you and I have been promised happiness down here in the physical world. They tell us that we can, in fact, find our soulmate, get married, have children, get a job, make lots of money and happiness will forever remain our companion. We now seek happiness for the first time in human history, because for the longest time the only thing that was promised to us was this: "You may find moments of joy, but for the most part, your life will be a struggle." You need to appreciate the cultures that tell you that life is not about happiness because if you know that life is not about happiness, you will never enter into any relationship, romantic or otherwise, imagining that this other person or thing will make you happy. Because at our very core, we are lonely, isolated human beings who have to figure out what it is that makes us come to life. And once alive, no one can accompany us.

Let me remind you of one of the last scenes in the Gospel of Mark. Keep in mind that Jesus Christ is supposed to be a man of wisdom, whose body is like a church in that every time he opened his mouth a sermon came out. He is a man who is at peace. But even Jesus, while he's hanging on the cross, finds something missing inside himself and says, "Eloi eloi lama sabachthani?" or "My God, My God, why have you forsaken me?" Even Jesus on the cross feels alone. Before that in the Garden he says, "Let this cup pass by me. It is tremendously difficult to live as a professional human being. It's too much of a burden, so please let me be like other people."

Of all the philosophies created in the past sixty thousand years or so, religion comes forth and says, "Money doesn't give you happiness. Fame and fortune don't bring you happiness. There is some mysterious entity that lives inside the human being, but it is covered in an avalanche of garbage. Once you get rid of all this garbage on the top, then you'll get to this thing." For those of you in this class who've ever been to therapy, make no mistake why you're there. You're there because you want to bring out the innocence that has been lost. You want to figure out why for the past twenty years you have been abused, in all sorts of ways, and you want to get rid of all these awful emotions that have been imposed upon you from the outside world. Deep down, it's no different than what these traditions are arguing.

[Lester: Can you talk about urgency?]

The human body is designed to be complacent, desiring mostly to sit and have things given to it. This tendency towards sloth makes philosophical transformation nearly impossible, because philosophy goes against pretty much everything that the human body desires, and even goes against life itself. To combat this, in Hinduism there is a concept called tapas. It basically means, "to generate heat." In the relationship between a student and a teacher, the teacher generates heat and this heat infects the student in many different ways.

It's like this. If you watch a good movie all sorts of interesting things happen. You begin as this frozen man and then you slowly thaw. If the movie starts slow, but then becomes more and more engaging, you will become warmer and warmer. A movie pulls you inside its world, and the relationship between the student and the teacher is no different.

There is something about the student, which of course the student doesn't know, and there is something about a teacher; the teacher knows it, and very organically the student gravitates towards the teacher. In order to watch a movie, first there's the desire to watch a movie. Then you want to see more until the desire turns from a want into a need, and the moment it turns into a need, you are physically, emotionally, and mentally very engaged in what you're seeing. You don't have to do anything because without any effort on your part, you are emotionally engaged, and these emotions create urgency. This urgency has generated heat inside you, and whenever there is an emotional need, your entire being is engaged in satisfying this need.

But you can't satisfy it if you're distracted. You can't think about your mom, you can't think about death, you can't think about "Black Lives Matter," and at the same time get sucked into a good movie. A good movie is like a magnifying glass that makes you single-minded, a true monotheist. It's just you and the images, and the function of those images is to grab your attention and arouse emotions. These emotions impact your physical body, and now your mind, like a beautiful calculator, says to itself, "How can I fix this?" Now you seek satisfaction. Urgency demands focus and single-mindedness.

In the relationship between a student and a teacher, love is the only way that this is possible. There is no other way. You don't have to make this into anything spiritual or esoteric, because anyone who's ever been in love knows this. You can be with other people but it won't feel good. You can go to a party and dance, but you're still thinking about this other person. Love baptizes your intellect and emotions. You cannot create philosophical urgency alone, especially in America. America is intensely secular and secular culture doesn't provide images that inspire philosophical arousal.

[Lester: Um, you lost me.]

If you want to put this to test, just drink a lot of water before coming to class. But try not to leave the classroom. And something really interesting will happen. The world shrinks. You won't think anything except, "I need to go to the bathroom."

[Lester: So urgency is only physical?]

No. First it's emotional, and then it's physical.

[Dr. Jefferies: Do you have to transcend the physical to get to the spiritual? I was reading an article on St. Augustine yesterday, and the article said

that St. Augustine's theology was driven by his sexual urges. St. Augustine became upset because he could not control his erection, which drove him to believe that the Fall from Eden describes a human being who falls victim to their physical desires, and that true Godly sex had no lust in it. Is it possible to enjoy physical sensation as well as be truly driven towards a spiritual life, or does the physical distract from the spiritual?]

St. Augustine of Hippo's mother, Monica, was so religious that she almost became a nun. St. Augustine lived in an age and an environment that was extremely religious and as a result, Augustine was infected by the idea that all human beings are born in sin, live in sin, and are in fact sinful. In the 21st century, we don't have that particular narrative. We are liberal, there is democracy, and God has largely been removed from our lives. Everything about our culture is secular, and even churches compete for space. When the humongous church was being built by Lake Merritt, most of the other smaller churches were upset because they were worried that they were going to be driven to bankruptcy. So even churches are subject to the capitalistic environment.

Even if you come from a religious background where, from the moment you are born, you see your parents pray and go to church, you will still do lots of ridiculous things, but in the background of your consciousness there may be a voice that says, "This is wrong." However, in order for this voice to whisper to you, your parents must have created a very religious superego inside of you.

There are some wonderful things about sin. One of the most eloquent and inspiring sayings, which comes from the New Testament, is, "I'm not here for the righteous, I'm here for the sinners." Imagine that Jesus Christ is a flashlight, and imagine the righteous are those that believe that they are in the sun and everything around them is light. And Jesus is saying, "Listen. If you feel that you have light inside you, my flashlight is not going to do anything for you, because you already imagine that you possess light." So, he says that he is here for and enjoys only the sinners, because those are the people he can illumine. The task of any good teacher is to notice a good amount of sin inside the student so that the students will weep and long for some light to be shown inside them. Remember that the word guru in Hinduism means, "Someone who removes darkness, and replaces it with light."

If your psyche is created by a religious or spiritual background, then the more sin that you commit, and the more aware you are of all the sins that you are committing, the better your chances are of understanding God and the meaning of Life. Because what happens when you sin, and you are aware that you sin? You become disgusted with yourself. If you don't believe me, for those of you in this class that think rather highly of yourselves, go home and do something stupid. One of the nice things that happens after you do something dumb is that you say to yourself, "That was stupid." I mean you do all this stuff for just a small amount of pleasure and distraction, and then you reflect and say, "This is ridiculous. What was this for?" If your reflections are serious they create an enormous amount of self-hatred, which unfortunately only lasts for a couple minutes. My recommendation for those of you that come from a religious background: sin. Do a lot of naughty things, and then when you become aware of these naughty things, that awareness bends your back and your knees and you'll find yourself somewhere in the dark, crying.

But for those of you that are not religious . . . I don't know.

Augustine is a very special man and if you come from a similar background, sinning helps you. In the Sufi tradition, the Islamic tradition, the suggestion is that if your heart is not broken then God cannot enter into it. If the door to the classroom is shut and locked, then of course no one can get inside the room. There has to be a crack for someone to walk in. Sin cracks you. The bigger the sin, and the more awareness of the sin, the more self-hatred, which will then create more intense longing and yearning. And that is the only thing that teachers do. Teachers cannot do anything but create longing.

The student's stage in life is irrelevant because all stages in physical life have one thing in common. Whether you are after sex or money or family, the common denominator is that there is something beautiful about sex, there is something beautiful about money, and there is something beautiful about having a family. The teacher, the "Socrates," also has something profoundly beautiful. But as you fall in love with sex, money and school, your family and your kids, so you must also fall in love with the teacher. As there is Beauty in all pursuits, so you must also see Beauty inside this person. The only reason that anyone engages in these pursuits is because the emotions are intense, and that same intensity must exist in order for someone in the physical world to be pulled into the world of philosophy To make this happen, Beauty and Love are created, which carry with them longing and pain, and that's the key. Augustine had that.

Before we talk about the Epic of Gilgamesh, let me say a couple things about how these things take place.

[Elise: Do you think that acts of service and taking care of people, like taking care of your grandparents, can be "philosophical"?]

There is a dervish named Momo, and he's sitting by the Vatican. A young man with all these sincere emotions inside him is about to walk into the church to pray. But this old dervish, or monk, has the power to see what's going on inside people, so he looks at this man and says, "What are you doing here?"

The young man says, "I'm here to worship God."

"But don't you have an old mother who is blind and sick?" asks the monk.

"Yes, but I'm here to worship God."

And the monk says, "No, go home and take care of your mom. It is better for you to take care of your mom than to worship God. You will reap far more benefits."

This is a very strange time for all of us, in the sense that our parents are not around. The culture doesn't nourish us because it doesn't have the right narratives. But if you can do something useful, yes, it's good. I especially think that if you have parents to whom you are not talking, you should attend to them first. Just get over your garbage.

[Rebecca: So, what are your sins?]

[Amir begins reciting Persian poetry, but then quickly stops and just says,]

It depends on where you are in life. If you promise yourself not to drink, every thought about alcohol could be categorized as a sin. The more elevated your self-image, the more difficult it is to protect this self-image. But if your self-image is devolved and degenerate, then you can do whatever. If I were twenty years old, I would have no problem hanging out with twenty-year-olds. But when you approach sixty, you have to ask yourself, "What am I doing?"

[Amir quickly finishes answering this question, then invites a student named David to the front of the class. Through Amir's dictation, David writes "Iron," "Bronze," "Silver," and "Gold" on the whiteboard.]

Iron is pleasure, Bronze is power, and Silver is emotions, and we'll talk about what Gold is in a minute. Or you could also say that Iron is body, Bronze is mind, and Silver is heart. These three are the physical stages in life, in that they can be satisfied through the physical world.

As you graduate from stage to stage, your world shrinks. It's like falling in love. When life and love are casual, you have tons of friends, but when you begin to be sincerely interested in someone or something, your interest is reduced to a few people. And when you're really in love, your interests are reduced to one person.

Our political system is structured around pleasure, so you can find lots of friendship nowadays in the Iron level. When the theme of a culture is pleasure, then whatever power you assume in the Bronze level, you will then bring down to the Iron level and spend on pleasure.

So if you're in the Iron stage and you smoke and drink and watch football on Sunday, the moment you say, "I am done wasting my life down here. I want to go to school and make something of myself. I at least want to get a degree before I die," you will begin to talk to your Iron stage friends about these newfound desires that center around school and making a decent life for yourself and out of a hundred friends, only one of them understands you. But he only understands intellectually, in that he doesn't truly understand why you won't smoke or drink or have fun with him. So you walk into the world of the Bronze level by yourself. With a great amount of difficulty, you find a new, smaller circle of friends. So if you have a hundred friends back in the Iron level, the moment you move up to Bronze you have about twenty.

There is a great amount of emotional and intellectual stress when you go to school. Once in a while you need to come down to the Iron level and decompress. As Freud would say, we are containers full of emotions, but we're not very good at expressing these emotions. For example when you get angry, it's not because your companion has done something wrong all of a sudden, but rather because these emotions have been building up. When you're in Bronze and you're disciplined in your studying, on the weekend somehow you need to eject all these toxic emotions from inside you. So you come down to the level of Iron and go out perhaps, or you drink or smoke, and then after a while you come back to Bronze. The only reason you go down to Iron is to exploit. You don't create any friendships and you don't appreciate or respect people in Iron. It's like Costco. You go in, you get your stuff, and you get out. And you have a membership – it's called a history with your friends.

Then you realize that a person in the Bronze stage is selfish and self-centered, just like the Iron stage but in a different way. You're then in a place where you look at other people and you say, "I see that man holding that woman's hand and they have children. I want something like that." You can't do it in the Iron stage; you're not mature enough. You can't do it in the Bronze stage; you're far too self-centered. At a certain point in your life there is this crack inside you, and you say, "I want a family." Let's say you're 30 or 40, relatively attractive, with a decent amount of power and money and the rest of it, then now you begin to look for a companion.

Where you could sleep with anyone in the Iron stage, when you're at the Bronze stage, you can only sleep with those who don't want obligations, because you want to go back and study and work. When you're at the Silver stage though, you're looking for someone who wants to stick around. And so when people say, "Let's go and make money," you say, "No, I want to go on a date to see if I can find a companion."

In all these three areas, you can see, taste, touch, smell, and hear your pursuits, that is, your senses are profoundly active and engaged. Then something happens. It can come from inside you, or it can come from the outside. If it comes from inside, you're in trouble. If it comes from the outside, you have a support system. I'll explain this in a minute.

It's something James and I used to go back and forth about. I come from a different tradition so when there is a desire for the Gold, the way that we do it in our tradition, which is the right way as far as I am concerned, is the following. Make sure that you have had enough sex, that you have had enough booze, and that you have smoked enough. But you can't just experience these things – you have come to understand the experience. Understand why you had the sex, why you had the booze, why you smoked; understand that every episode has a "why," and understand the explanations that come from these "whys." This understanding gets you a diploma of sorts, in the sense that you never have to go back to your high school teacher and ask, "What is two plus two?" Two plus two equals four. It's finished. If any of your pleasures in Iron remain incomplete, that is, if you haven't saturated your pleasures, then when you make lots of money you will use this money to satisfy your needs in Iron. And so on. So you have to make sure that you have a good amount of healthy sex, and that you have understood it, so that it doesn't catch you later when you do this journey. Make sure that you have enough money and that you have your degrees, that school doesn't come back to haunt you later on in life. All incomplete narratives eventually burden us. You know how sometimes you say, "I broke up with that man" or "I broke up with that woman, but there is no closure. I wanted to tell him what was on my mind but I never did"? Even if you become married or have a wonderful relationship, you will always go back and say, "I'm still seeking closure from my previous relationship." So make sure when you move on, that there is closure and make sure you understand. Understand the function of sex, and understand the reasons for smoking and drinking. If you have difficulties, read Sigmund Freud. When life becomes stressful, he argues, our bodies desire a quick fix. You don't seek pleasure or power because it makes you feel good. No – these things are rooted to specific pains, specific emptinesses. And when you're done with the Iron and the Bronze stages, get yourself a man or a woman, get married and have children. Satisfy the Silver desires. These are your obligations in life. You have to do them.

Once you have satisfied the desires in these three realms, something awful usually happens to all of us. You wake up in the middle of the night, look to your left and there is your companion, and you ask, "What am I doing with you? What happened to my life?" This opening is categorized as The Call.

You don't have to have transgressed. You don't need to have committed any sin. It is part of our psyche. There is a very tragic novel written by Franz Kafka called The Trial, which I'll make a little more contemporary. It's about a young black man who wants to have some Peet's coffee, so he goes in his car and drives to Montclair Village. For those of you that have never been to Montclair Village, let me tell you something. There is no black person in Montclair. They are all white. And there is this sign on a gate outside of Montclair that says, "No person of color allowed." Not joking. And so as this black kid is walking in Montclair, like the first scene in the movie Get Out, and all of a sudden a cop car stops and a police officer walks out, looks at the guy and says, "What are you doing here?" And without being given an opportunity to speak, the office forcefully turns him around, pushes him against the car, cuffs him, and as he is being pushed inside the car, this young black kid asks, "What have I done?"

And the police officer says, "Nothing."

And then they're walking and he screams, "But I'm innocent! What have I done?" No one says anything to him.

He is pushed into a tiny cell and again he screams, "But I haven't committed any crimes!" But no one cares. In the morning he goes before the judge and the judge, who hasn't even heard this man's story, looks at him and says, "Guilty. Life in prison."

Again the guy says, "But what is my crime?" Every single day, he wakes up and tells everyone, "I didn't do anything wrong!" And then, when he's ninety, he's about to die and with his last breath he asks, "What did I do wrong?"

Kafka argues that this is the human condition. You don't have to do anything wrong, in fact you could be a saint. You could have spent your entire life taking care of your parents and children, but you will find yourself condemned because you will ask yourself, "What happened to my life? My time? What has become of me?" And the truth is, you look at your resume and it will say that you've done everything the right way, but you will still feel in all the wrong ways about your life.

If you are young and like the whispers of The Call you will bring these whispers down to the Iron stage. You will find a man or a woman and you will dazzle them with all the questions of The Call. And the person will say, "Oh my God, this person is only twenty-two but he is so mature!" And then you will sleep with him but then when it's done, he or she will walk away. Remember, our business in life is to exploit. We are consumers of sex, power, and people with whom we can create a family. All this is of course masked as love and affection and the rest of it, but make no mistake. In the physical stages of life, we exploit the physical world, and it's alright.

[Casey enters and says, "I can hear you across the street at my house."]

I made you some watermelons.

[Amir points to the table at the front of the room, which is covered in food that students brought, including watermelon.]

Do you know how hard we work to figure things out in this world? Do you know how problematic it is to get a Call that is like a gigantic Socrates, walking into the worlds of Iron, Bronze, and Silver asking, "Why, why, why?" And the trouble is, there are no answers to the "whys" that you and I ask, and if The Call is not supported in the right way, you're going to push it away and go back into the worlds of Iron, Bronze, and Silver.

When you have completed these three worlds as an adult, The Call can come in the form of a mid-life crisis. This means that at the age of thirty or forty you have everything but it's not enough, so you go into the old world to find answers to the questions that The Call arouses. Remember The Call is not attached to anything physical. It's not that I'm unhappy with my wife, it's not that I don't have rent money, or that I am unhealthy. Life down here is really good! But the questions that come out of The Call are emotional, spiritual, and psychological, so your companions can't reach you when you are asking these questions; they can't recognize the emotions that are paired to these questions. You may contemplate divorce, or you may contemplate selling your house and moving to the mountains. The Call, like anything devastating, is like a shock to our system, and we have no idea what to do with it. It's like you're sitting at a traffic light and someone rams into you from behind.

We are not the sorts of animals that do well with questions to which there are no answers. We get depressed. We get confused, frustrated, and agitated. The Call is like a sinkhole that opens everything beneath your feet and you look down, but there is nothing there. If you know anything about black holes, then you know that they take everything and give nothing back. Everything gets lost. The Call is big enough to swallow the Iron,

Bronze, and Silver, and leave you with absolutely nothing. We call this spiritual or philosophical poverty.

Examine homeless people. They don't look good, they don't have any friends, they dress bad, and they smell. In the poverty that comes with The Call, you have a home, but you don't belong there. You have a job, but it doesn't give you meaning or purpose. You have friends but there is no mutual understanding. No one can reach you:

> *Morde ye am meeravam bar rooye khak*
> *Zendeh garden jan ye jan bakhshe pak*

This is the realm of the walking dead. There is nothing inside these people that can be inspired by anything, but we're not even talking about the Gold level yet. When these feelings come about most of us run back to the Iron, Bronze and Silver, and rightly so. You want the confusion and despair to go away, and we want to make sure our life is okay.

Now that's the inner call. No one on the outside imposes him or herself onto you. You just wake up one morning and your life amounts to nothing.

There is another way The Call can come about, and this is the best way. Imagine that you are minding your own business, enjoying one or all three of these worlds, and you turn on the TV and there is a teacher in San Jose giving a talk. Or you go to Peet's coffee and there is this ridiculous-looking man or woman sitting there. Or you journey to Tibet for example and some person just looks relatively interesting so you go and say to them, "I'm lost. I want to go to Peet's coffee shop. Can you tell me how to get there?"

And the guy asks, "Why do you want coffee? I have some coffee right here."

"Yeah, but I want Peet's."

"Oh, I make a very special kind of coffee, and I'll give it to you for free."

You say, "Okay," and you feel a little weird. And soon you realize that a ten-minute cup of coffee suddenly turns into ten hours with this man. And then you leave this person to go home, and you don't know what has happened but there is something very unsettled inside you.

If The Call has happened accidentally, that is, if it has happened as part of your psychological mechanism, you have to look for many years to figure out how to put the pieces back together. If, on the other hand, a mechanic opens the hood and removes parts of the engine, then the very same mechanic who has broken the car can put the car back together. The only thing is, you have to leave your car with him. When you meet someone who has done this to you, it takes time to create a decent relationship so that you can begin to trust him or her. Attraction may be immediate, but trust happens much later on.

Whenever there is a Call, something about us tries to protect itself from falling apart. We call it doubt. "I have no reason to question my relationship, my life, my identity, my purpose, my meaning – everything about my life is good," you say. So you begin to doubt your own intuition, and for good reason. It's immensely frightening to have these three worlds swallowed up into nowhere. When the doubt comes about, The Call gets questioned, and these three areas get protected. If, on the other hand, you have a really good mechanic, he or she welcomes the doubt. Doubt indicates a certain amount of security. But as you grow less attached or identified to these three worlds, you become more attached and identified to the person associated with The Call. As you once found an emotional and psychological home in these three worlds, all of the sudden, your home is rooted in one person and one person alone.

The Call always breaks ethical codes. You can no longer be a conformist, in that you can no longer belong to these three worlds, though all the forces from these worlds will try to pull you to themselves. In the New Testament for example, Jesus is walking and looks at these guys and says, "I see that you are a fisherman. You come and follow me, and I will make you a fisher of men." If this person is legit and there is a good amount of Beauty inside them that is connected to agape, to God, to something esoteric, divine, passionate, creative and sincere, then whoever gets this Call will follow naturally. But just because you follow doesn't mean that you are going to be made. That takes time. First you follow, and then someone makes you a fisherman. First you follow this person, then you begin to fish for divine inspiration, for a wholeness on the inside.

Whenever there is a Call, there is going to be this next stage, called The Search. For those of you in this class that know a few things about, say, the African culture, then you know that they have interesting ways of dealing with life. For example, if you were to ask someone in some African tribe, "What time is it?" they would tell you, "Do you want the time for the dead, the time for the living, or the time for the dead but living?" And you say, "What are you talking about?"

If you happen to be educated in the Western world, you are told that when you ask about A, B will be given to you. But if you go to cultures that are much more creative with questions, you get stories. Like in the New Testament, someone asks, "What is the Truth?" Well, there's a story for you. "How can I be more religious?" Story. "Can you tell me about God?" Another story. But what you find in most parts of Africa, when you ask a question and you're expecting a B, they'll never give you the B. They'll give you C, G, F, H, all the way to Z, and then they say, "We're sure you can find B for yourself."

One of the problems with expecting quick fixes is that whenever there is a Call and The Search that follows, you'll be looking for a quick fix. If questions come up, there need to be answers. Now here's the thing: There are no answers. You have tiny moments of experience. That's it.

And what makes this journey so difficult is that you have to be okay with having questions, having no answers, and in the end having no questions at all. First you have questions and you look for answers. You worship the answers but then realize they're useless. Then you need to ask more questions, only to realize later on that questions are useless as well. And then after a while you do something interesting. You stop talking.

There is this scene in the Phaedrus, one of those books written by Plato, where people ask Socrates to say a few things about Love, and he says all these wonderful things. Then all of a sudden he stops himself and walks away. People say, "Socrates, what are you doing?" And Socrates says, "I'll be back." And he goes outside, cries for hours and asks forgiveness. He goes back and people say, "Can you continue to talk about Love?" And then he closes his eyes and he just talks. But this time people aren't just amazed. Because his speech on Love is so moving, they cry.

Plato is telling us that speech can come from two completely different worlds. One form of speech is all about power. There are these repressed emotions that you have on the inside, and you desperately want to be heard because there is no rest inside you. You want to make yourself visible. And Socrates says, "If you want to talk about Love or religion or education or whatever it is you want to talk about, if it stems from a need you have, it's always wrong. Regardless of how inspirational it may be."

When Socrates speaks about Love the second time, he quiets down and enters the parts of him that live in Sabbath. For those of you who have seen a compass, there is one leg that doesn't move and then the second leg circles around the stable leg. The best way to talk about things, Socrates argues, is to make sure that you have one leg resting in a place where there is no 'you,' where there is this something living inside you. For those of you in this class who are somewhat creative, when you sit and write poetry or play music once in a while, there are moments when you sit in class and say, "I need to write down these lines." As you're driving home you put music to these lines and you have to ask yourself, "Where does this come from?" It certainly doesn't come from you. It comes from a very inspired environment inside you, and this inspiration doesn't belong to you.

So when you read books that talk about relationships between students and teachers, you realize that most students talk endlessly, ask all these questions, and the only thing that the teacher will do is say a few things once in a while. That's it.

Once again what makes The Search so problematic is that you can't find the answers in the Iron, Bronze, or Silver. The nice thing about having been broken by someone in Gold is that once they break you, you don't go to Iron, Bronze, or Silver looking for answers. Instead you go to Gold to look for answers. And usually the answers in Gold are given to you and I in the form of puzzles that we have to figure out. But because we are novices, for the most part we can't understand the stories.

Let me tell you a story.

A student in one of these three worlds who had heard The Call looks at this guy or woman in the Gold and says, "There's something about you that I can't understand. I can't really put my finger on it. I'm just really attracted. Can you tell me what it is?" And the teacher tells the student the following story.

There was once a woman sitting at home watching Seinfeld. All of the sudden she hears a noise, so she opens the sliding door and she hears another woman going, "Oooo, aaaa, mmmm."

And the woman goes back inside but says to herself, "Oh, she's having lots of fun." So she goes to close the sliding door and again the voice says, "AHHH, YES!"

And the woman goes back inside, but says to herself, "Oh this is really exciting, maybe I can watch." So she opens the sliding door again, goes to the backyard, peeks through a hole in the fence, and sees a woman lying on the grass with a donkey. The woman goes back into her house and thinks to herself, "Yes that's what I need to do." So she goes to Trader Joe's and buys herself a donkey, comes home, takes a shower and wears the lingerie, goes to the donkey and says, "I'm ready for you!" I don't know if any of you in this class have ever seen a donkey in full glory. It's like God. It really is. It's like from there to there. [Amir points to either side of the classroom.] They begin and the woman screams, but not in pleasure, but because she's in so much pain and then she loses consciousness. She is rushed to Highland Hospital, the place where people go to die, and when she heals a little, angrily she knocks on the neighbor's door, and says, "You deceived me!"

And the woman says, "What'd I do?"

"Well, a couple days ago I heard you having all this fun with this donkey, and I wanted some! I was jealous! And then the donkey hurt me. All this pain."

And the neighbor kindly looks at her, and gently asks, "Didn't you see the watermelon?"

"What?"

"The watermelon!"

And the story ends.

This is a very sincere student and he or she is asking, "You know what, I want to be like you! Socrates, Plato, the Buddha! Instead of giving me a stupid story, I need you to tell me how I can get there!" And Rumi says, "I just told you. The donkey is Wisdom or God or Understanding. You are a seeker after Truth, but a novice. If too much Wisdom is put inside you, it will destroy you. The watermelon is a buffer, a teacher or a parent who knows how much you should receive. As you move up, your capacity grows and more can be given to you." If you're two years old and you're asking about sex and your father gives you too much information, you'll be destroyed. I had a student in 2004 at Laney College, and his father pushed him to be with a prostitute when he was twelve years old. The last time I saw him he was thirty-five and he still hasn't recovered. Too much was given too early. Just as you and I gradually increase our capacities and abilities in the Iron, Bronze and Silver, so does our capacity for understanding gradually increase in the Gold. This is important because if you just jump in, it can kill you. If it doesn't kill you, you'll just go crazy. You'll become dark and gloomy, your life will be shattered, and like Job, you will curse the day of your birth and you'll want the earth to open up and swallow you.

We don't do well with unknowns and confusion. If The Call comes from inside you, then there is going to be built-up frustration, anger and resentment, and you're going to end your life. If The Call comes from the outside, in that someone has imposed him or herself onto you and then The Call erupts from inside you, then you're going to blame this person for all the things that you think are happening to you.

Any Call automatically comes with The Search, and any Search automatically comes with The Struggle. The problem with The Struggle is that there is still a lot of "you," a lot of your ego, a lot of your expectations about how things should and shouldn't be inside you. You haven't yet surrendered or submitted. You haven't yet become naked. You're still holding onto things, but desperately trying to figure things out.

For those of you in this class that enjoy the Samurai culture, there comes a point at which a warrior realizes that he has brought dishonor to their community. There is no struggle inside them for life. They sit, grab a knife, put it in the proper place in their body and two minutes later they're dead. I can't do that. I will struggle to continue my life as if it means something, as if there is something out there for me to achieve. Struggle indicates that illusions of self-importance still exist. In Struggle, not only do we believe that there are things out there worth pursuing, but this conflict shows that we still possess expectations that the path towards Wisdom should be a certain way.

Now before we move to the fourth stage, something really interesting happens to the student. There is a student, we'll call him Bob, and there is a teacher, we'll call him David. If David happens to be a very young teacher, he looks at every person as having the potential of becoming a good student. If he happens to be a proficient teacher, he's going to look for specific people that have specific qualities. If he has any brains or proper experiences, he won't much care about the student's questions, or care about their fancy language. One of the best examples we have is that Jesus Christ hung out with the most uneducated people. Uneducated people were far worthier of Jesus than the people running the synagogue. The closest disciple of one the greatest poets, named Rumi who is Persian, was a man who didn't know how to read or write and couldn't even speak properly. Muhammad, the prophet of Islam, didn't know how to read or write – he was illiterate:

Ma boron roh nanagereem o qal roh
Ma daroon roh benagereem o hal roh

What the teacher looks for is not how people are on the outside, how many books they've read, how much money they have, or what sort of an exterior life they lead. They look at the inside. Is there enough capacity for the teacher to go inside them? Are they ready? In the movie *The Matrix* there are all these people around, but Morpheus is looking for a single human being and he finds that in Neo. Neo is the only one who is seeking the right way. Neo is the only person who knows that he is working for Metacortex, a company that brainwashes people. Neo is the only person who lives in Room 101, numbers which symbolize a room filled with conflict, chaos and corruption. Neo is the only person who goes to gatherings but stands in a corner and can't find any friendships. Neo is the only person who doesn't sleep. Who doesn't eat. Who's always searching. But just because Neo has those qualities doesn't mean that Neo knows. He has to be trained. And the rest of the movie is about how Morpheus, the Greek god of dreams, brings the dreams down so that they can manifest physically.

But how can David give to Bob what lives inside David?

Buyad gereftarm shavee ta ke gereftarat shavam
Az jun o del yaram shavee ta ke khareedarat shavam

Amir Sabzevary

Man neestam chon deegarun bazeeche ye bazeegarun
Aval be aram toh roh vangeh khareedarat shavam

This poem is saying that if you are a fish and you look at a fisherman and say, "Wow, he is really good-looking and he's got a nice boat. I want to be on his boat and I want to be held by this man," there is something that you must do. You need to take the bait. And you need to have a lot of pain, and you need to struggle, and eventually you'll be pulled up while you're still struggling. But there comes a point where you are exhausted from struggling and you simply submit yourself and like Jesus on the cross, you open your hand and say, "Thy will be done."

These are universal themes. Whether you are African or American or Persian, whether you're black or white or blue or yellow – you have to go through the same journey. It makes no difference. Africans don't love in a special way that Americans can't. If you want to love, you go through the same episode.

For whatever the reasons are, Bob has the capacity to see Beauty inside David. The first thing that happens is that Bob becomes attracted to David. Attraction turns into desire. Now how do you create desire from attraction? Physical presence. There is no emailing, there is no texting. Naturally you want to be around this person, but you have to be there physically.

> The desire turns into a want.
> The want turns into a need.
> The need turns into infatuation.
> Infatuation turns into obsession.
> Obsession turns into Love.
> Love turns into Submission.
> Submission turns into Awe.
> Awe turns into Worship.
> Now you're ready to learn. Your journey has just begun.

[These stages, from desire to Worship, are written on the whiteboard, beside "Iron," "Bronze," "Silver," and "Gold."]

There are no guarantees. This doesn't come with a warranty. It's not like Costco. You can't say, "I've used this for 1,000 years, but now I don't want it and I want my money back."

What exactly is it that you worship? [A circle is drawn on the board.] If you know a thing or two about Buddhism, there is a reason why you begin to worship. Inside David lives the Buddha. Inside David lives the dharma.

Inside David lives the sangha. David has the Beauty that we call agape. The student doesn't yet understand, he or she intimates. And when you submit, Beauty has its own lessons. David comes from his own background, his own culture, and his own tradition. All Wisdoms are the same, but they can't but be expressed differently. Which means that the Wisdom of someone that lives in America is going to be received by someone who is American. They at least have a similar way of looking at things. Remember ultimately that every student has to become a very good part of his or her teacher. He or she must adopt the same culture, the same tradition, and the same etiquette. And the reason why all of this is important is because when we speak about the Epic of Gilgamesh, eventually the only thing that Gilgamesh wants is to satisfy Enkidu's desires. Gilgamesh is a king and Enkidu is a nobody, yet inside this nobody is the wealth that Gilgamesh has been seeking. And you know what Enkidu does? He exploits and manipulates Gilgamesh. Enkidu makes a king fall in love with him, a man who comes from nowhere.

Not only does the Buddha or Wisdom or something profoundly awakened live inside David, but this Wisdom also has its own unique way of expressing itself. We call these expressions teachings, or lessons. When it comes to the point where you are in love with this man, he is your home. He is your friend. He is your lover. But he is also your enemy. He is your community. When he's not there, you have no home, and you have no community. This is what sangha means. A single human being can satisfy your body, your mind and your soul. When you read accounts of student/ teacher relationships, you will find that the student longs to just touch the hand, or massage the feet, of their teacher.

But what takes place in Gold is sometimes brought down to the physical world, and social norms are then imposed onto the experiences in Gold. And that which once beautified the student, now becomes the elements of demonization. People gave their lives for Hitler, David Koresh and Jim Jones, the same way they gave their lives for Jesus, Moses and Muhammad. What all these people have in common is that they loved their teacher. The ethical judgments that we put on leaders and their followers come from the ways that we have been socialized:

Agar bar deedey Majnun nasheenee
Be qeer az khoobe Laylee nabeenee

For example, imagine that you take a man or a woman home. "Majnun" in Persian is a man who is intoxicated, and "Leylee" is a woman who is, symbolically, very attractive. So this man looks at this woman and gets intoxicated by her beauty, and so goes to his mom and says, "Mom, I have found the woman of my life."

And the mom says, "Bring her in, let me have a look at her."

And Majnun brings Leylee home, and one eye is up here and one eye is over here. She has no lips. Everything about her is wrong. And the mother says, "What is this? She is like a beast!" And Majnun, the intoxicated lover, says, "Mom, if you were to look at this woman from my eyes, you would see Beauty."

I'm not really quite sure if students will ever get to the fourth stage. It's very rare, if not impossible. The fourth stage is called Breakthrough, which means something very substantial that lives in the teacher gets transferred into the student. It's what we called lineage, or passing the baton. In most of the traditions, once the Buddha or the teacher dies, there's no one to carry his tradition. He takes everything with him.

If I were to put this mapping within the movie The Ten Commandments with Charlton Heston, Moses begins with a privileged life. But all of a sudden there is a shock to his system: "Moses, you're not who you think you are. You may think that your life is good and you may think that you have the blood of the Pharaoh inside you, but that is not the case. You have a very lowly place in life." Moses is in a place in life where he can actually hear, and it destroys him. So he goes and finds this woman and asks her, "Are you my mom?"

"Well, yeah, I saved you, but you're not my son."

"But I'm not the Pharaoh?"

"No."

"So what's up with you people?"

"We believe in this God."

"What God?"

Moses comes to realize that he doesn't belong to his tribe, so he walks away completely, to the desert. Whenever there is a Call, you have no choice but to be in the desert. In the desert there is the scorching hot sun, the beasts are toxic, poisonous and vicious, and you're all alone. There is no food, there is no shelter, and there is no clothing. No one from these three areas of life is going to find him or herself in the desert. They'd prefer to stay home. So in the desert you're always going to be alone. Always. Out of desperation Moses gets married, out of desperation he has children, and one day he says, "There is something very strange about that particular place on the mountain. I'm going to go check it out." There is a cave on the mountain, but before he can enter, a voice says to him, "Take off your shoes, because you're going to be walking on holy ground." The sandal is symbolic. You can wear your shoes if you want to go to Peet's coffee shop, but if you want to go to church, you have to take off your worldly shoes and you have to walk barefoot. That is Moses' Breakthrough: he sees God. Now whenever there is a genuine Breakthrough, not a fake one like what happens when you read a book for example, or when you have a tiny pathetic dream. When there is a Breakthrough something devastating happens. You turn your back on the journey, you turn your back on God and Wisdom and Truth, and you become a man of the people. It's called The Return.

The Return is the true definition of a social activist. Because when you become a social activist as part of your Return process, you understand why people have pleasure; you understand why people pursue money, and you understand why people want to have families. On your Return you speak the language of the people, but the language is seasoned with Wisdom. And that's why someone like Malcolm X can have such a vast following. People smell something really delicious about Malcolm X. They don't think, they smell.

The Gold symbolizes a Breakthrough; the Gold is understanding. But the difficulty with the Gold is that it lives inside the human body. The human body still desires power, visibility, and social status. If one doesn't go above the Gold, the Gold has the potential to become contaminated.

There has to come a point in the individual's quest where they go above the Gold, which we call Transcendence. This means you no longer care about God or Wisdom or Truth, because when you care about something, you're still profoundly ego-invested, in the sense that it's about you. Transcendence means that you just don't care anymore. And once you get there, something amazing will happen to you. It's called Unification. That means the following. You will begin to season everything down here, in these three areas, with Wisdom. You will be like Rumi. You will tell this raunchy story about a donkey and a woman, but it's not about donkeys, and it has absolutely nothing to do with sex.

That is what students go through, and this is what teachers possess.

[Dr. Jefferies: The followers of Jesus and Muhammad tread the same path as the followers of Hitler and David Koresh, and I'm also aware that our ethical codes are generally just socializations. How do we distinguish between the Jesuses and the Hitlers?]

Whenever anything becomes organized it becomes dangerous. I don't really know, to be honest. I know there came a point where Moses just got tired and left his people. He just said, "Let Aaron, my brother, deal with this stuff, and you can have it become organized if you want." Jesus refused to make this into an organized thing, and he was to some extent like a hippy, he was free-spirited. Lao Tzu left China disappointed, and Confucius died unrecognized. I think of all the people it was Muhammad who was the first person to create this thing called Yathrib, "the city," which was actually an organized environment of which he was the head. Kind of like Plato's Republic, where you have a philosopher king at the top and he becomes the very center of the city, and everything revolves around him.

There is something that I didn't mention about teachers that I haven't put together myself in the right way, and because I haven't written it down I can't express it, but I'll try. I'll tell it to you in this way.

Once in a while when I call my mom, her voice is somewhat nasally and I ask her, "Are you okay? Are you sick?"

And she says, "No."

So I ask her, "What's wrong? You don't have allergies so why is your voice this way?"

And she says, "Well, I just miss my mom."

Her mom passed a couple years ago. There is an eternal and immortal brokenness about my mom. And regardless of who she is and what she is, the memory and the fact that she knows that her mom is not going to come back to life causes her to break down. And in breaking down she becomes human, and in becoming human, she becomes innocent.

Teachers need to have this eternal brokenness about them, because this brokenness creates things like humility. When you're broken, like any student, you become open, and when you become open you become receptive to things. When a teacher tries to organize something, everything becomes domesticated and a sense of infallibility is projected onto the teacher. After a while, the teacher him or herself believes that they are infallible. And that's when problems arise. You see this in someone like Hitler, someone like Mussolini, or David Koresh. I'm sure they had their moments of brokenness in private but I think you need to express this brokenness in public. And you can't manufacture it. You have to have gone through this journey in a very concrete way. You can't assume that you've done this. If Thomas Hobbes argued that humans are born with a twin called "fear," I think that a part of good teachers needs to be aware of this twin, which is their own brokenness. Because when they're broken, poverty exists. In poverty, you kneel, when you kneel you pray, and when you pray it connotes your own insignificance. And you need that. It's something you and I have talked about. You and I go to all these ridiculous meetings and all these people walk around saying, "We have found a way to teach students. We call it Student Learning Outcomes. And if you do A, B, C, D, people will learn." And you walk back to your office saying, "What is wrong with these people? How could supposed educators have such superficial thinking about these things?" It's a very organized way of looking at things and nothing gets done.

[Dr. Jefferies: I agree. It's interesting – the worst teachers are the ones who do not have moments of doubt. Jesus had that, but Hitler did not.]

But also, when you look at the life of someone like Jesus or Moses, there are moments when they become absolutists. Look at the Ten Commandments.

[Ismael: At what point does the student lose their personality?]

There is a lot of struggle, and by the time the student gets to the point of submission, they are like wet clay. Through submission, the teacher can mold the student in any way he or she deems fit. Prior to that you can't really mold anything. I mean, you can confess your love for your teacher, but things only really happen after submission. The problem with submission is that it contains infinite poverty. You are nothing, you have nothing, but yet only at that point can you be made into something.

[Ismael: Is it your personality that you lose or . . . ?]

Personality is basically the stuff that's been manufactured, or socialized, for you. In the movie The Matrix there is this scene where Morpheus says, "Human beings are no longer born, they're made." We have to be made in some ways in order to survive in the physical world. You can't come to this class and be all natural. You need to have some social etiquette so that you can come here, I can talk and you can listen. And vice versa, respectfully.

[Ismael: Is there balance?]

No, there is no balance. You have to understand that urgency and intensity knows no balance. The Buddha only becomes the Buddha when he says, "Forget my kid, forget my parents, forget my wife, and forget my life." It's a very extreme way of doing things. Malcolm X becomes Malcolm X because he says, "Forget Elijah Muhammad, forget all the power given to me by him," and then he goes to Saudi Arabia and who knows what happened there. You have to abandon everything. It won't work otherwise. Initially there is extremism, and then when you mature, you find harmony and balance.

It's like any other relationship. There is a scene in one of the episodes of Friends, where Chandler and Monica are having dinner with Phoebe and Phoebe's new boyfriend. Wherever Phoebe and her new boyfriend go, they are intimate. So when Phoebe says, "I'm going to go to the bathroom," and her boyfriend follows, Monica looks at Chandler and they both know what's really going on. Then Chandler goes to the bathroom and Monica follows him, and Chandler says, "What are you doing here?"

And Monica says, "I want to be like them!"

And he says, "Listen, we've been together for five years. I like where we are now. I like being intimate like once every five years."

After time there is this comfortability where you are intimate once every two weeks and there is nothing wrong with that. But for Phoebe and this new companion it's extreme and intense, because they just met. They are completely drunk on love, and they want to be intimate all the time. But some time passes, and time creates harmony and balance. Intimacy goes into the backseat, then to the trunk, and then sometimes you just leave it home. For weeks. But if you want to get anywhere worth going: extremism. It's the only way.

You've walked away from your boyfriend before, because you realized that common sense did not apply to him, right? Does he have the potential? Absolutely. But you walked away. It's an extreme case. Even though you love him, you walk away. You put certain parts of yourself on the cross and you try to protect the other parts. And you just say, "If you grow up I'll take you back, but if not, screw you." We do it every day.

[Rick: So suppose there are two teachers –]

No. It doesn't work. There's only one.

[Rick: Well in the movie Arrow –]

Okay. Let's pretend I've seen it.

[Rick: He learns how to fight from a lot of different teachers. What do you think of that?]

I haven't seen the show and I'm not going to, but I'm going to correct you nevertheless. Is that okay? [Laughter.] This guy in the movie Arrow doesn't really have two teachers. He just has one. He has this thing inside him that enables him to process all the experiences that are given to him. It's like your body. When you were really young, you only had one teacher and that was called milk, either from your mom or from Costco. But as your body matures, you realize that you can have milk, you can have cake, you can have all sorts of things. The real teacher is something inside you that is able to digest and make into nourishment everything and anything that comes your way. Initially you only have one teacher. That one teacher matures your digestive system. Not so much in terms of physical food, but with the experiences that come your way.

There is a group of people in the world of philosophy called the Stoics. They're not unique, really. Stoicism is something that most of us in the class will learn when we get to be ninety years old, which is that we will become quite indifferent to all the things that are taking place around us. Stoics believe that you should never try to control life. It's impossible. Life assaults you on a daily basis. Life creates emotions, you get drunk with those emotions, and then after a while you sober up and you say, "I was too stupid. Why'd I do that?" The Stoics argue that there must be something inside you that welcomes the experiences of life, and plays with them and engages with them, but Stoics will never allow themselves to be pushed up or down by life. They know that in physical life, what goes up must always come down. You may be happy right now, but ten minutes later you'll be sad. Should you create a savings account on sadness, you will soon realize that ten minutes later you're most happy. If you're in a relationship, you experience this all the time. You have a fight with your companion, and one of you says, "I'm going to break up, it's finished!" Ten minutes later things change. And the Stoics argue that there has to be something about you that is bigger than life.

A small tree tends to move with the wind, but when the wind goes away it stands erect, just as tall as before. The tree doesn't try to fight the wind, because it knows that eventually it'll go back to standing just as straight as it was before. The Stoics argue that if you can somehow cultivate this thing inside you that is aware that life is a constantly changing machine – it creates it destroys, it creates it destroys – then you will never become part of this game. Have fun with life, but don't allow it to push you around. Know who you are. And it's a very difficult thing to become because it's tempting to fall prey to anger and jealousy.

So the movie Arrow is about a man who can learn from everything.

[Rick: Not really.]

Well, it's a bad movie then. There is a reason why I didn't watch it. Any other questions?

[Lester: What is a teacher, and who are they?]

Nobody knows.

[Lester: Okay. So, in what ways could I be a teacher?]

You can't.

[Lester: I was prepared for that.]

Why would you want to become a teacher?

[Lester: I don't, but a moment ago you said that milk could be a teacher. How then do I have the capacity to be a teacher?]

Okay, then go be one, nobody's saying that you can't. If you want to, just go be one. You'll be doing what everybody is doing: print some fliers, staple them up on coffee shops, wear a turban, you already have a beard so part of it is done, smoke a pipe, dress a certain way, smell a certain way and you'll be a teacher. See? What is wrong with you? It's like me asking you, "How do I become black?"

[Lester: I'm trying to get to this point that maybe there's some –]

Money?

[Lester: No, but there would have to be a very special type of person for me to get to the point of submission and worship. For example, I'll never see you in that way. How do I know who is leading who where, kind of like the earlier question?]

Can you ask this in a different way?

[Lester: How do you identify teachers?]

One of the best answers to this question is found in the Gospel of Mark: "A prophet never comes in a way for man to see," or "A prophet is never welcomed in his hometown." The truth is, we don't know. If it were easy to recognize teachers, Jesus would never have been crucified. Moses would never have had to battle the Pharaoh. Muhammad would never have battled the Quraysh tribe. Lao Tzu would have been understood. Your question is good, but the answer is enormously complicated. We don't know how teachers are made or how they're recognized. We don't know how they teach. If you look at the Native American tribe and their tradition, some teachers are just clowns. You ask them serious questions and they just make fun of you. And that's the way they teach. Some of them are wild like Socrates. Some of them are like Kierkegaard, they're very quiet. We don't really know. I mean if was to ask you, "How do you make a Malcolm

X? How do you recognize a Malcolm X?" I mean your own people messed it up. They couldn't realize who Malcolm X was, and he got shot. Why is that? We don't know. Why is it that Mark Twain –

[Lester: You're blaming black people for Malcolm X not being successful?]

No. I'm saying that it's very difficult for us to recognize Wisdom. I mean, your parents have said to you many things that you came to understand later in life. And the question is, What was wrong with you? Why couldn't you understand things the right way the first time around? We have no idea at what stage people come to understand anything.

I mean Van Damme, do you know who he is? The black martial artist –

[Lester: He wasn't black.]

[Rick: Oh, Jean Claude?]

Yeah, Jean Claude, the French martial artist. He was married seven times. His seventh wife was his first wife.

[Lester: Meaning what?]

He married this woman named Jackie, and then he began to hate her guts. He divorced her, married a second time, third, fourth, fifth, sixth, and then he said, "You know what, Jackie's really good!" I don't really know if her name's Jackie, but the point I'm trying to make is, why couldn't he see Jackie for who she was the first time? He was an idiot.

[Lester: So can there be learning without teachers?]

Sure, but it depends on what it you want to learn.

[Lester: So teachers are only required for this "transcendence" stuff?]

If you want to learn math, you go to a math teacher. If you want to learn piano, you take a piano class. But when it comes to learning how to live life, it becomes very complicated. The difficulty is, when you want to learn about Life, you assume that you can apply the same language of buying socks and where I get milk to the big questions of life, like, How can I make my life more meaningful? And from what little I know, Socrates says that these are two different worlds. The world of tables and chairs requires a language that goes to tables and chairs, but when you want the meaning of life, language unfortunately fails, and so it becomes esoteric, metaphorical, and allegorical. It's like Valentine's Day. When you love someone, what do you do? When you really love someone? You buy them flowers and choco-late. You wait for hours by the phone. There is no other way to express it. They say, "I really want you inside me," and you say, "For some strange reason I love you too much. I can't really do it right now."   Language falls apart when you're in love, and you express your emotion towards this other person in all sorts of crazy ways. I mean it's like saying, "Why do you fall in love with this person and not that person?" Who knows? You're ask-ing for a how-to, and I don't know the answer. I don't know how anyone becomes a teacher. I don't know how anyone becomes a student.

[Lester: I wasn't asking for a how-to. I was just looking for a possibility outside of this frame, a possibility for learning, for progress, for meaning, purpose.]

If, for example, you are addicted to sex, you can actually go and see a sex therapist. If you are addicted to drinking, you can go to AA meetings and they have a proper language for that. If you want a degree and you want to go to school and you want to make money, or you want to find a job, there is a language for that. There is a way you can get there, and there are people you can look for. If you want a family, you can ask your mom what sort of qualities you should look for in a woman, and if you have chil-dren, you can ask your people about the best way to raise kids.

But when it comes to this stuff, perhaps you say, "I am forty and my life down here is good, but I feel empty," then you have entered no-man's-land and you're really in trouble. Because nothing here [Amir indicates Iron, Bronze and Silver on the whiteboard] is going to satisfy you. Who knows? It could be a blessing or it could be a curse. I don't like easy answers be-cause I don't think that they exist.

[Lester: I like that answer more than anything you've said so far.]

What'd you say?

[Lester: Not that I trust you or like you, but I liked that answer.]

[Dr. Jefferies goes on a long ramble about the sacredness of all human life.]

[Lester: Am I sacred Amir? I thought that you said that I'm messed up.]

No, you're messed up. We're all messed up, really.

[Elise: Regarding the teacher who plays the role of the fool, do teachers know that they're teachers?]

Teachers are aware that they're teachers, but good teachers usually remain invisible, for a couple of reasons. In the movie K-Pax, there's this guy from a different planet, but no one really knows that he's from a different planet because he looks like a homeless man. He's taken to a therapist, and the therapist asks him, "Do you have families on K-Pax? Do you have children?" And the man says, "We try not to have children." And when he's asked why he says, "Because having children is very difficult."

Initially, I think most of us walk into becoming parents in a very foolish way, in that we exaggerate a lot of things about what it means to be a father or a mother. But then you realize the enormous task ahead. First you realize that you don't really have the proper capacities, you lose your patience, you're ambitious and you want to do A, B, C, D and your kids are taking a lot of your time and your energy. Then when you sacrifice your time and your energy, you say, "I'm going to give myself to this kid for the next eighteen years," and then you realize that you stand no chance against this society. The video games have him, friends have him, this and that has him, and then someone comes to you and says, "You know, I want to have children." And since you've been around for a while as a father or a mother, you sit this person down and say, "Listen. the desire to have kids is good, but I think you should give attention to these areas of yourself, these areas of life and these areas of society. Examine these areas well. If after fully examining them you still want to have children, have children." I think good teachers rarely accept students. And the reason is the following.

Down here [Amir indicates Iron, Bronze and Silver on the whiteboard] you are physical. And most of your emotions, and one could say that your soul, is physical as well. But if you really want to see your own soul, this poor person up here [indicates Gold] has to give birth to your soul. And giving birth to your soul is no different than giving birth to an infant. That soul is going to cry. And you have to give this soul nourishment. The soul can't go to any breast. It needs its mother. The person who broke you and took something out of you – and you like it – he or she is the only person that can take care of it. A teacher is no different than any parent who has to sacrifice his or her life to rear a child. When you are a young teacher and when you have a lot of hubris inside you, you want to have a tribe of students. But as you age and mature, and as you realize how enormously difficult this journey is, you can have people be curious, you can have people be interested, but the moment they go up here [indicates Obsession], you will try to push them away. Because it's called codependency. You're not going to go back home. It's like what Rudolf Steiner suggested in his book about schools. His way of educating people was to have one teacher who educates a group of people from first grade through twelfth grade. And then the teacher goes back and starts over again.

If you liken your emotional, psychological, spiritual and intellectual evolution to a physical infant who has needs, then you would realize that a good teacher doesn't accept students. First, it's too demanding. Second, because the journey is so difficult, most of the people who become pregnant with having a tiny soul will do whatever they can to abort the pregnancy. So the person who makes this happen has no choice but to sit back and watch its demise.

You're a woman, Elise. There has come a point where you realize that your body is sacred. If you used to give your body to any man who walked your way, now you pick and choose very carefully. Teachers are no different. No one will put themselves out there, if they are any good.

There are two kinds of teachers. One kind are the prophets, and the others are the monks or the sages. The prophets always pursue people. That's what they do. But the sages are like temples. They sit and people go to them.

Teachers never pursue.

Chapter Two:
The *Epic of Gilgamesh*

[Norman: Last night we talked about the similarities between following a spiritual leader and following a social or political leader. What are the differences between the two?]

Imagine you are eighteen, and you have a boyfriend who happens to be eighteen. He's not going to expect much from you because he hasn't had much life experience. Because his dreams and goals are rather shallow, the relationship is going to be relatively easy. Have you seen the movie Whiplash? In the movie there's this man that wants to be a drummer, but he also likes this girl. But because this is no cheap man, in that he actually has a goal, tragedy awaits this girl. He wants to be one of the best drummers in the world and eventually he is forced to make a choice. He is not going to choose her – he's going to choose the drums.

It's nice to be with someone who has no goals and has no purpose, and if they do, their goals and purpose are cheap, shallow and superficial. The price that you and I pay for quality is a bit too much.

Rumi has a story about a hunter that goes out and he sees a lion, and he thinks that the lion is almost dead. He pushes the lion a little and the lion doesn't move, so he says, "It's surely dead." He grabs the tail and pulls the lion towards his hometown, thinking that people are going to applaud him and call him a hero. But the people go to him and give him all sorts of warnings. Eventually the son says, "You know Dad, the lion you captured wasn't dead, it's quite alive. And if you don't let it go, it'll devour you." The Lion is the symbol for Truth, the symbol for any student who desires to have a good understanding of life. And initially, when you're just curious about something, it's like an animal that's asleep. But when you keep nourishing this quest, it blossoms to the extent that it overtakes your life. And that doesn't go well with who and what we are, because we are animals filled with fear. We like things to be domesticated, familiar and known and if anything disrupts the flow, we stop and push back. We treat these situations like a tax collector: "Should I go or should I stop?"

Following social and political leaders, like Hitler for example, is less demanding than following philosophical leaders.

I like antique cars and when I was younger I'd buy them. The only problem was that I'm not a very good mechanic and I didn't know how to fix these cars, so they'd just rot. Most of us like to tackle perennial questions, the "Who am I?" and the "What am I?" questions, which are like these exotic things that come into our lives once in a while. But we don't have the tools and the wealth to spend, so we get infected, and then get stuck.

Hitler at least gives you something, and the result is immediate. You go out there and someone kills you and it's finished.

[Norman: When you're in a revolution, nothing really matters anymore but the objective, and that seems to be like something that Hitler offers. Would you say that that is a practical approach to living?]

Social and political leaders give you an experience, and it's a reflection, but a corrupted reflection. It's the promise of a better future, that according to history, rarely comes to fruition. This promise, or reflection, puts thinking on pause and while you're engaged in this image, it's like having an out-of-body experience. Is it not true that you were recently engaged in an experience others would have called "unethical," and it was quite nice, wasn't it? And then all of a sudden you began to think about pros and cons, good and bad, right and wrong, ethical and unethical, moral and immoral. The moment thinking enters, it's finished. Again, you can't go ahead. You're stuck.

Political as well as spiritual leaders have the charisma to stop people from thinking. I think if you're with someone, or if anything gives you an experience and causes a certain kind of reflection, you're in a good place. You walk out of a good movie only when you say, "I'm just not excited." You keep anticipating, but you keep getting betrayed, so you leave.

I agree with you, despite all of my nonsense. The part that bothers me, especially in this culture, is that these things are nearly impossible, and this culture doesn't admit this. There is a plant that usually grows in Italy or Spain called palmetto. It's a humongous shrub that is mostly a waste of leaves, so usually people look at palmetto and pass it by. But one of the nice things about this shrub is that if you take the time to slowly get rid of all the exterior leaves, which takes about a month, there is this delicious juicy fruit at the very center. But it's hidden. How many people have the stamina to remove layer after layer after layer of garbage? Because the truth is, these layers of garbage give our lives meaning: the fact that we're going to school, the fact that you have a job, the fact that you continue desiring to live longer. Imagine if you came to realize that most of these things are superficial, and you really want to get to the heart of who and what you are. What is going to be left of you? In the Middle East we call these people "Majnuns." In other words, there is a line in your quest. Should you cross it, you'll join the ranks of those that are categorized as "intoxicated ones." Once you get intoxicated, your life is no longer your own, your will is no longer your own, and it's frightening.

I think when you read the story of Jesus, you read him as sort of a fantasy. It's a nice little book. And what makes the book so nice is that there are no details. The New Testament doesn't tell us what happens to the life of Matthew when Matthew simply leaves. The book doesn't tell us what happened to his kids. The book doesn't tell us what happens when Nicodemus begins to feel spiritually connected to Jesus, and yet at the same time is a Rabbi who no longer wants to be in the synagogue. He of course eventually leaves and he writes his own book, the Gospel according to Nicodemus, but no one tells us the backstory of how difficult it is to leave. It's similar to when you go to a coffee shop and there are these eighty year olds sitting and they're not even holding hands and if they are, it's because the other is afraid of falling, so one uses their companion as a cane. And so they sit and they look at the menu and they don't talk, or even look at each other. And if you're young, you look at your girlfriend and say, "You and I will never be like that." But if you happen to be in a relationship, then you know the value of sitting with someone and not saying anything and being okay with that. It takes about sixty years.

If most people were given the story behind marriage, having children, behind the desire to really learn and the desire to understand who and what one is, most people would just be okay with life being the way it is.

[Gary: How do you deal with difficult family members?]

They're family. You tolerate them. You want to what, fix them? Forget family . . . family . . . that's just the way things are. You can't do much with family. They're like your hunchback. [Laughter.] And if you want to walk this particular path, you have to make sure your family is not exposed to this stuff. So despite all the sadness that exists inside you, around them you need to be profoundly happy and joyful. They can no longer reach you, so when they see your sadness they wonder what is wrong with you, but the truth is, you're at a stage where you're puzzled, curious, angry, and frightened. You have all these emotions that you yourself don't understand. So it's always nice to wear a thick happy mask around people, especially family. Friends, ah, get rid of them, they're no good. The only friend you really need is – well, anyways, forget family, just leave them alone. If you have a husband or wife, if you have children, if you've got parents who are worrying about you, just wear a mask:

"How was last night?"

"Oh, it was beautiful!"

"Why don't we don't have much conversation?"

"Well, it's just because I'm in awe of you." [Laughter.] There is nothing else you can do. I mean, the whole thing really sucks.

Mantiq ut Tayr is the story of these poor birds. One is enjoying the rose, one is enjoying the cactus, the other is enjoying the lily, and then this bird from the heavens comes down and says, "You guys are wasting your time. The rose will last for a few weeks, the lily will only last two weeks, that flower, five weeks. I'm going to show you something that will never die. It's eternal." And I think the birds are quite wise by saying to this heavenly bird, "You know, get lost. The rose is fine. At least I'm happy for two weeks, and then sing sad songs for a year." The poor ones that get lost in the advertisement follow the big bird, and in the course of their journey one goes blind, the other loses his feathers, the other has no legs, and then they get to Paradise and there is nothing there. They wait and wait and wait and then all of a sudden they realize, "Oh, it was always inside me!" And it's true, it's always inside you, but it's going to take 20 or 30 years and by the time you get there you have no legs, because there is no place to go. No longer is anything fun! You're blind because everything you see disgusts you. You have no nose because everything just smells bad, and you have no ears because everyone is stupid and it's not worth listening to them. Would you like to live like that? Hm?! No, there you go, be happy.

Okay, we will begin the Epic of Gilgamesh.

Stories belong to small people who have little pathetic lives, and by that I mean us and that's okay. However, Epics belong to those who lose themselves in the big questions of life, questions that are indestructible. Next time you want to figure out who and what you are, figure out whether or not you have any worth, you have a couple of options. You could either place yourself in stories that you and your friends have created for yourselves, or you could put yourself in this particular Epic.

If you put yourself within the stories created by the social construct, that is, people around you and your environment, I have no doubt that most of you will feel really good. You would be happy that you have a Bachelor's, a Master's, a PhD, that you have a marriage and children, because these make your life meaningful. You would be happy that you can fight for a cause, that you're gay or you're black or you're white or you're brown. All this stuff, it's really fun.

Or you could put yourself within the context of this grand Epic that's been around for at least 10,000 years, which argues that most of who and what we are, our goals and desires in life are pathetic and insignificant.

So my recommendation, before we go any further, is to insert yourself into the tiny stories of life. Then you can feel good about yourself, because when you put yourself in stories, your emotions, thoughts, and goals matter. But when you place yourself in Epics, your emotions and thoughts mean nothing. Both are small and insignificant, ego-driven and self-centered.

The story is written down in clay tablets, and it's been around, at least in written form, for about 5,000 years. But the truth is, we're talking about oral tradition, prior to writing being invented. I have no doubt that some of you go to Barnes and Nobles and pick up a book, say a self-help book, go to a coffee shop and grab yourself a nice latte, sit in a comfortable corner and you read. And you say, "Wow, this is such a good book, this is exactly how I've been feeling for the past twenty years." And you're inspired, and then you go home and you think and you talk to your friends, and then you watch some TV and go to sleep. Books don't demand much from you and I.

Oral tradition is a completely different story. In Hinduism we call this upanishad, which means "sitting and listening." Every culture creates humongous tales that talk about the human condition, and there is always going to be someone in your tribe who has special insight and unique wisdom about our condition in life. Not only spiritual insight, but insight into physical life as well. This person finds a worthy disciple, and this disciple initially becomes their opponent, because most good disciples fight back. Then something about them eventually gives, they break open, and then they submit.

Oral traditions argue that language deceives and books betray. If you are a seeker after wisdom, language must have power within it. This power comes from genuine and unique experiences, which means that ordinary people don't have this power over and within language. People who have these experiences refuse to write the things we find in books today, for the following reasons. Imagine for a moment that you're married and you read a book that inspires you to ask difficult questions: Why do people get married? What is the nature of love? Can people actually love? Is love, as Krishnamurti would say, about loneliness? Is love about jealousy, about fear and possessiveness? Imagine if you were to take these questions seriously, go home, look at your husband or your wife and think, "I get angry when he or she looks at another human being. But Krishnamurti argued that people shouldn't be jealous when they're in love because love is unconditional!" And then you get punished, not from anyone on the outside but from your own self: "Why can't I love unconditionally?" So what you have is a piece of wisdom, given to you at the wrong time, unprocessed, but instead of helping it begins to destroy your life. That's why in any good book on spiritual traditions, when a student approaches the teacher, the teacher says, "Get lost," or throws obstacles in the student's path.

There is another reason why the Qur'an, the New Testament, the Old Testament, Bhagavad Gita, Rig Veda, and all these other books are failures. These books are about a single human being named Muhammad or Jesus talking to the masses, and talking to the masses is an easy thing to do. I have no doubt many of you have nieces and nephews that you take to the park for a couple hours, but then you give them back to their parents and go home comfortably. Jesus comes to the scene, talks to the masses for an hour, then goes away. With most of the esoteric teachers, like what happens to Gilgamesh, it is one-to-one. It's about giving this man named Gilgamesh lots of leaves, then slowly cutting and removing these leaves so Gilgamesh can experience the heart of this shrub. That takes an enormous amount of energy, both on the part of the teacher as well as the student.

Should you desire to read the New Testament, especially the four Gospels, you probably should walk away full well knowing that Jesus, when it came to transforming his disciples, was a complete failure. He couldn't transform anyone, and neither could Muhammad. None of these people can. These people are made to preach and give sermons to the masses, while the Epic of Gilgamesh is about individual transformation.

Parents should never raise their kids, and parents especially should never name their kids. When a child was born in the ancient world, the parents would take this child to a temple. The priestess would gaze into the eye of this infant, and because she had the power to overlook all the physical components, would go directly to the infant's soul and grab a name. The task of the community was to make sure that this infant grew to live out his name. Imagine, for a moment, this man. His name is Ismael. I don't know why his parents chose that name for him, but imagine this was 10,000 years ago and a priestess went somewhere, grabbed this name, imposed this name onto his soul, then told his parents, "This man is supposed to live out his name." Now what does that mean? That means someone needs to walk into his life with a tremendous passion and desire to know God, but coming to know God demands a sacrifice, at least in the Islamic tradition. How does he live out his name? Someone close to him must ultimately put Ismael's life on the line. This is the story of Abraham, who represents a man that desires to know who and what God is. But it's not going to be given to him cheaply, because what does God demand? The object to which he's intensely attached: Ismael.

The name "Gilgamesh" means "an old man that desires to become young." Let me give you a couple of examples of what that means.

Half of the people in this room are not enrolled in this class. They could have sat home and watched TV or done a thousand and one other things. But something about them doesn't feel comfortable sitting home, so they come into this crummy room. For those of you that are not enrolled and you're here, something about you is old. Old in the sense that your senses no longer gratify you the way they once did. Despite the fact that some of you are young and life still has many things to offer, there are parts of you that are broken. And the truth is, this is the flaw in our creation. All of us are born to grow old quickly, and our quest is to become young.

"Gilgamesh" is a symbolic name that represents every one of us in this room. I have no doubt many of you in this class are in relationships. And I have no doubt that some of you care tremendously for your companions. But it's just no longer fun. And I'm not saying relationships ought to be fun but they just get old, and actually begin to suffocate you.

Another way to look at his name is to understand that Gilgamesh is described as two thirds God and one third mortal. You would think that if you have so much God inside you, naturally most of your journey in life would be about the quest towards Truth or Wisdom. But that's not the case at all. If you have children, or if you've been around children, you know they lose their sense of curiosity and awe very quickly. They get old and sit and look at a cell phone or a video game.

All of us in this class are Gilgamesh. We have two thirds in us that is Godly, or divine, that desires passion and creativity, and to be spontaneous. Then there is this one third of us that is frightened and confused and functions very much like a tax collector: "If I give you ten bucks, what am I going to get back? If I take this class, am I going to get a good grade? If I hold your hand, is it going to be guaranteed that we are going steady?" The two thirds doesn't care about any of that stuff. The two thirds only desires engagement with things that are transformative.

Gilgamesh is a profoundly attractive king, the way all of us want to be. The best teacher in the classroom, perhaps, the best wife or the best husband, the best-looking in a gathering, or when my hand goes up I want to be the most insightful person who speaks in the class. All of us have that desire inside us. Because he has so much power, Gilgamesh lives through the mortal part of him, walking around and exploiting people. Some of you in this class are attractive. When you go to a gathering, no doubt a lot of men or women come your way. And the truth is, you don't really have much to offer them, except perhaps your good looks and some fancy language. Our emotions are raw, our intellect is childish, and in the end people grow tired of us and we grow tired of them, and then we walk away, saying, "Maybe we should have a threesome."

What this Epic ultimately argues, at least when it comes to our name "Gilgamesh," is that not a single one of us in this class will escape this fate. Gilgamesh is the creation of the gods, just like you and I. We are the only animals, according to the Old Testament and the Qur'an, in whom God breathed His spirit. It's not a dog, it's not a cat, it's only us. We are like a palmetto shrub and our senses are like leaves that cover this jewel that every single person has on the inside. We are condemned to grow tired of the senses, and at a certain point we stop blaming other people and say, "You know, the truth is, I'm just no good. I don't have much to offer anyone." Henry David Thoreau was right. Most of us end up leading lives of quiet desperation, and we deserve it.

Gilgamesh has a mother, Ninsun, who lives in Paradise somewhere, and Ninsun always goes to the gods with a single complaint: "Why do I have a son whose heart knows no rest?" Every child is born to be a spiritual and emotional nomad. Our bodies desire comfort and familiarity but emotionally we demand inspiration, and things down here betray us far too quickly. And this Epic suggests, since Gilgamesh represents all of us, that there is a profound restlessness at the very core of every human being.

To cure this restlessness Gilgamesh goes to his friends and says, "I want to make a name for myself." Michael Jackson is no longer with us, but I suppose we'll continue talking about him, not only because he was a little weird, but also because he was a great artist. He has become immortal. Malcolm X has become immortal. There is something really flawed about us human beings, which was discovered thousands of years ago. To some extent, we know that we're going to die, so we do everything in life to avoid being forgotten. We want our names to be in history books.

All of us in this class resent Jesus for being immortal, and the truth is, we want to be like him. So you know what we do? We read the Bible. Not because we like Wisdom, not because we like Jesus, but because we resent him for being more than human, more than us, and we can't feel that without him. This desire to be immortal is a great psychological insight into what it means to be a human being. You know what it means to be immortal? You cannot become immortal if you live a regular city life. You cannot be immortal if you simply say "yes" or "no" to Elijah Muhammad. To be immortal the one-third human cannot continue to conquer the two-thirds God. You have to learn how be honest, how to be innocent, how to be like a child. This is what we talk about when we say counter-cultural. You don't smoke because that's how you define counter-cultural, you don't listen to hip-hop. Counter-cultural means you're finding and resurrecting this innocent part inside you.

Imagine someone likes you, but you don't know that. After many tries, they eventually summon up the courage to say, "Would you like to go out and have a cup of coffee?" You're cornered so you say, "Sure." While you're having coffee you keep looking at your watch, and this person who's been wanting to have coffee with you for months is a little hurt. After an hour or two you say, "I'm sorry, I need to go because of A, B, C, D." Then you leave. And this person, who's liked you for so many weeks, is probably thinking to herself, "Is he thinking about me? Is he writing poetry about me? Is he going back and reading the emails I sent him?" What this person is really saying is, "Am I that easily forgettable? Because I don't really want to be forgotten." All of us in this class desire to be remembered if not in body, definitely in emotions and in spirit. Now you may think that this book goes back 5,000 years and it's no longer really relevant to us, but if you really want to understand who you are, there are so many gems and insights in this book. The Epic of Gilgamesh is about the human condition, about our fears of death, and about being forgotten. It's about how society affects us and how all of us get assaulted by something from our insides that says, "You have lost innocence. Retrieve it."

But according to this Epic we are not abandoned, because eventually we complain. Every single one of us in the room at certain moments will sit and say, "Is that really it? I got my PhD, is that really it?" I remember when I was at San Francisco State University, a professor gave me my diploma, a Master's in, I don't know, some stupid thing. And he looks at me and says, "You should be very, very happy!"

And I said, "Yes, I'm very happy."

He said, "But you don't look happy?"

"No, I'm really happy."

"So what are you going to do?"

"Nothing."

"But you have a Master's now!"

"I know."

"Are you happy?"

"Yeah."

There is this "not-enough-ness," and "is this it-ness," that all of us have no choice but to experience during these moments. I suppose in the West you call it "mid-life crisis"?

Gilgamesh is relatively happy living through his body but it's not enough, because he has a dream. In the dream a rock falls in front of Gilgamesh, and he's puzzled because he wants to lift it but can't. I have known many people who claim to be highly ethical and moral, who claim that they would never leave their marriages, that they would never divorce, they would never hit their kids, whatever the case may be. But when a genuine obstacle is put in front of them, they fall victim to it. I have no doubt that some of us in this class say, "I would never go out with a married man or woman, I would never steal, I would never do this, and I would never do that." But when this rock or obstacle stands before you, and it's full of life, and it's intense, you don't care about your moral codes anymore, you just go all the way forward and fall victim to the thing you once condemned.

This dream puzzles Gilgamesh because he's born of the gods, has the strength and beauty of the gods, yet despite all the powers given to him he can't lift this rock. When you and I encounter a dilemma which we can't escape despite all of our cleverness and cunning, the anguish and frustration and self-doubt is horrible but the humbling fact is, despite all of your powers, there is nothing you can do. Gilgamesh has always believed that he has power over life, but the dream tells him, "Regardless of how you may think about yourself, I am going to bring about an event over which you have no power."

Gilgamesh needs to acknowledge that all his assumed abilities to figure out his life are false because submission happens only when there is poverty. You can be poor in money, you can be poor in emotions, you can be poor in intellect, or you can be poor in spirit. Giving yourself up to someone else's knowledge is to some extent the power that the other person holds, but it also is an indication of the power you have lost.

But Gilgamesh doesn't know what to do with the dream, and doesn't know what to do with the feelings of "not-enoughness," so he returns to getting drunk with his physical power. Because Gilgamesh uses his power to push people around, they too began to complain. There comes a point where they realize they are being exploited and they're not gaining much from being exploited. They lose more than they gain. So they come together and begin to pray, and here is something you need to know about prayers. There are times where you sit on your sofa and you say, "I didn't floss last night. I should really go somewhere and brush my teeth and floss to make sure I don't get a toothache." This, in a way, is a subtle prayer to make sure pain never comes to you. It is a prayer to continue having power. Then after many years of not flossing or brushing, you say, "I really want to fix my tooth." You no longer speak about flossing; you no longer talk about brushing; you're no longer speaking from a position of power. You say, "I really want to fix my tooth." And this is a profound prayer because it is accompanied by so much pain, anguish, and loneliness. Then language is replaced with tears and screaming.

When a profound and intense emotion erupts out of you, the gods have no choice but to listen. This is how Enkidu comes to be. Enkidu is like a dentist. Now you go to the dentist because you think he's actually going to take care of you. Well, that's going to be two hours later. From the moment he starts, he's going to have a jackhammer in your mouth and for the next two hours you're going to be in a tremendous amount of pain. When he is done, you can't eat, you can't talk, and you have this tendency of biting your own tongue or your cheek on the inside. And then when the sensation returns you realize you're bleeding because you kept biting your tongue or your cheek.

The people pray earnestly, and because the prayer contains so much pain, the gods listen. To cure Gilgamesh of his disease, which is being all meat and no spirit, they create Enkidu. But they need to make sure that Enkidu remains uncontaminated and unsocialized. He, as Jean-Jacques Rousseau argued, needs to remain a "noble savage." It's kind of like some of you in this class, you're African Americans, and sometimes you say, "I just want to be African." You still live in America, but you have the emotions of the African. For that to happen, you need to study what it means to be African for 20, 30, 40, 50 years. The desire to be African becomes the Enkidu, and the person that was born here and that has all the American tendencies becomes Gilgamesh. There will always be this battle, and eventually Gilgamesh or Enkidu will win.

If again, this doesn't make sense, to make it more relevant for us, perhaps you say, "My parents have done me wrong." That's your Gilgamesh. But then you have these wonderful moments where you say, "I need to forgive my parents. They are human after all, and we all make mistakes." That's your Enkidu. These two will eventually fight. If you desire a lot of power, stability, and predictability, Gilgamesh will win. Why? Because for the past 20 years you've been saying, "My parents are bad, parents are bad, parents are bad." It's like a pathway created in your head. All of a sudden Enkidu comes forth and says, "Listen, forgive them for they know not what they do." It's beautiful, it's innocent, it's noble, it's naked, it's natural, and yet if you were to embrace the Enkidu about you, all of Gilgamesh would fall apart, and as Jesus would say, you find yourself as a child. You've been reborn. Now you have to find the right clothing for yourself, the right language for yourself, and it is immensely difficult. So, the older you are, the more difficult it's going to be for you to embrace the Enkidu aspect of yourself.

Enkidu was not born to live out his life the way he wants to. He was made only to remind Gilgamesh that he is not made of the city, but Gilgamesh is made of Nature, and Nature goes back to God. Gilgamesh is a man of God, but he has forgotten. Why do you think God, in the Gospel of John, creates Jesus, names him His son, sends him down here, so that we could kill him and through his blood and sacrifice, become more human? Messiahs are sent to emotionally, intellectually, spiritually, baptize us from all the corruption we have inherited from the city life. Messiahs are sacrificial lambs. And should any of you desire this stuff, your teacher must always be sacrificed. Always. It's the only way you can go beyond him or her.

In the Sumerian language, "Enkidu" means "the most innocent of mankind." This is a human being who has not been socialized, similar to Jesus in the Gospel of Judas, where whenever the disciples looked at Jesus, they saw him as a child, not as an adult. This is not someone who would think or reflect, but who would allow the Divine Spirit within him to move his physical body.

Enkidu is born naked, and remains naked. Enkidu lives in the forest, lays with the animals, and talks with the animals. He is one with nature. I have no doubt that when some of you in this class go camping or hiking in Muir Woods or Yosemite, and you see people there and ask them what they do and they say, "Oh, I live here."

"What do you do?"

"Nothing, I just walk around."

And a part of you, I guarantee, resents them because we love being in the presence of something that resembles Enkidu, something that refuses to be socially conditioned. But there are no other human beings in the forest, remember – Enkidu only lives with the animals. This is also very insightful. Someone who has regained innocence on the inside will never desire to mingle with human beings, who are the creation of the city life. Remember the movie The Matrix? Thomas Anderson has no friends down here. When he is a full-fledged Neo, a transformed human being, his only friend, at times, is Morpheus. But even Morpheus tells him, "I can only show you the door. The rest is on you, man." He becomes his only friend, and that's the price we pay for innocence.

Let me also say something else about Enkidu. Mothers are interesting animals. Even if they see a kid that doesn't belong to them fall and suddenly start crying, this woman, who is not blood-related but understands what it means to be a mother and what it means to have the pain of a mother, runs towards this stranger, holds him, hugs him, gives him a napkin to wash away the tears, gives him some food, kisses him on the forehead and walks away. In most parts of the world, it's the most natural thing you do.

Being born of nature and having all these natural emotions means that Enkidu has a tremendous amount of empathy and compassion for anything in nature that gets hurt. Remember the idea, if you slap me on the right cheek, I will offer you my left? Why would you hit someone? There must be part of you, so contaminated with anger, resentment and jealousy. These emotions represent, for the most part, the absence of self-control, and the absence of self-control is an indication of poverty, and poverty is painful! Jesus recognizes that. And instead of returning with aggression, like a good mother, he blesses you with openness and compassion. So to be a human being of Nature, you will have no choice but to carry all the contamination of people who have social emotions. "I am here to carry the sins of the world on my shoulders."

Gilgamesh, on the other hand, lives in the city. The city is the place of corruption, darkness, and sin. Most of the emotions you and I have, the emotions of shame, jealousy, possessiveness, anger, and resentment are all manufactured by the city. They don't really belong to you. If I give you an "F" in this class, some of you will be profoundly sad. You know who gave you that emotion? I did. You know where I belong? To Laney. Laney is an institution, an institution that belongs to America, and America lives in the cradle of capitalism. Ultimately, the emotion you have goes back to poorness of money, physical insecurity. I made that for you. Who becomes your God when you have the emotion of fear or anger or sadness? I am your God, for I birthed those emotions inside you. That's not what Enkidu has, the most natural of men, the man from the forest.

These of course are all symbols. You don't actually have to live in the forest. Outwardly you could live in Oakland, San Francisco, or New York, while inwardly be very spontaneous, as Lao Tzu would say. Anytime any of us in this class fall in love, and we are willing to sacrifice a whole host of things, that is our forest life. You allow things to grow naturally, your reflective abilities shut down, and you're okay with losing everything. When things are created spontaneously, there is no reflection involved. How often is it that you and I go to our garden and pull out the weeds and say, "Well, that's it, they're never going to come back." Two weeks later all the stuff you pulled and threw in the garbage come back to visit. That's what Nature is all about. Enkidu is man who lives from one moment to the next. He doesn't plan. He submits himself completely to his own intuition and instinctual habits. It's a very profound place to be in life. Gilgamesh, on the other hand, has to make plans. I go to my office, for those of you that may not know, I say, "No one needs to visit me for at least twenty minutes. I need to see what I'm going to talk about in my class." I prepare. That's what I do. That's not the way Enkidu functions. Enkidu functions: "I am born out of Nature so I will have a summer, a fall, a winter, a season for each emotion. When it's time to be born, I will give birth to this emotion. When it's time for this emotion to go away, I will just get rid of it. I'm not going to think about it." He is a human being who just "ings" along, always in the present.

What history has revealed though is very interesting. Many, many thousands of years ago Nature created an innocent man named Socrates whose job was quite simple. He wasn't to be a father, he wasn't to be a husband, he wasn't to be a politician. His job was to go into the city, metaphorically naked, and ask the most basic, the most childish questions: "Why do you want to be a politician? What does it mean to be a human being? What does it mean to be a student, to be this, to be that?" Remember in the movie Ratatouille, where this rat creates a dish called "ratatouille," and gives it to a food critic who is the business of tasting food and making awful comments about it? And you know what this rat does when he creates this dish? The moment this old man, this 90-year-old man puts this, like, zucchini, in his mouth, he goes all the way back to when he was 5, when he came home crying to his mother and his mother placed before him a plate and the kid would put this food in his mouth and all of a sudden the pain would go away. The hurt would go away, and he would be very, very happy. That is what Socrates does. He kind of takes us back all the way to the point of innocence. It's devastating because we have to get rid of so much crap. Crap that makes us who we are, gives us identity, purpose, meaning. I know some of you in this class are profoundly angry – just angry! And you may want to go to therapy to give up that anger but you will never give up that anger and you know why? Because anger gives your life purpose and meaning. And you will hold onto it despite saying, "I really want to get over this." You really don't. Unless you are able to live in complete nakedness.

If Enkidu remains in the forest and never meets Gilgamesh, Enkidu will never be sacrificed and Gilgamesh will never be transformed. This Epic argues that eventually every human being will cross paths with someone who is innocent and who reminds us of things that we have lost or forgotten. This meeting is not to make Enkidu more innocent, that'd be ridiculous. He was created only for one function. If you've read the New Testament, Jesus was created for one purpose. To give light to those who can't see. Gilgamesh is blind. Enkidu has eyes, has light, and he's created to give Gilgamesh eyes that see.

You may think things in life happen accidentally, but that's not the case at all. When you read this Epic, every episode has a reason. Enkidu doesn't know, he doesn't need to know it. It's Gilgamesh that doesn't know but wants to know but can't, and is puzzled and confused and frightened. Enkidu doesn't know why he was created. Gilgamesh doesn't know why he was created. Which mean the following: All the pains that they suffer have a purpose, but they just don't understand why just yet.

Let me give you an example. I had a colleague, and at the age of eighteen she went to Hawaii and was assaulted. It took her about twelve years to recover from this experience. When, to some extent, she was able to understand and recover, she opened up a shelter for women who went through the same episode. Every year she has over five hundred women stay with her for about six months. One woman goes through a tragic experience and becomes an oasis for hundreds of women to come. Are we going to think that this woman, at the age of eighteen, fully knew why she had this experience? Of course not. But the truth is, she became who she became because of this particular experience, and because of understanding it and processing it. Now she is able to speak eloquently to women who go through the same experience.

The point I'm trying to make is the following. Should your life be filled with troubles and disappointments, do not make any judgments. Have the feelings, but don't let the feelings become emotions of anger and resentment. Just observe the feelings that you have. Because in ten years, instead of saying, "I'm angry," you may come to realize that this anger, or whatever the feeling was, has given birth to lots of insightful perspectives inside you.

So a couple of things. All of us live in the city and we're corrupt. There is a part of us that desires innocence, creativity, passion, being spontaneous, being free, being able to love, but this Epic argues that it's impossible to do this on your own. You need someone on the outside to walk into your life. But here is the trick. If you want to evolve, if you want to be transformed, you have to be filled with sin. You have to be corrupted. You must have a lot of "city" inside you.

Somehow these two people must meet, and the meeting is arranged in the following way. There is a hunter from the city who goes into the forest, not because he loves Yosemite, not because he loves snow, not because he loves to watch exotic animals, but he goes to capture animals, bring them back to the city and sell them for profit. A hunter from the city goes to the forest and lays traps. Animals fall into the trap because they see food and say, "Ah! Another compassionate thing that Nature has done – providing me with food!" not knowing that it's a trap. They fall into the trap, this hunter comes by, picks them up, takes them to the city and sells them. They're butchered. Is it not true that we read books to get all these grand ideas, then take them to a coffee shop and spit them out as traps so that they make us look more attractive, intelligent and refined as human beings? When, in fact, we have no real intention of understanding what these ideas actually mean. Do you really think that the Bible was written so that people can memorize its verses and spit them out so callously?

On this day, this hunter goes into the forest and looks into all his traps only to realize that no animals have been trapped. No trapped animals means no money for the day. He goes back the second day, the third day, the fourth day, but there's still no animals. And he goes to his father and says, "You know, for some strange reason, these traps just come out empty." The father says, "Just go out there and see what is happening." So the hunter sits out there in hiding and watches this gigantic man going to these traps and when any animal has been trapped, he releases them from the trap and frees them. At first the hunter gets angry and goes to fight Enkidu, but then he looks at the size of this guy and says, "I'm no match for this man. He'll destroy me." So he goes to his father and his father says, "Since you cannot beat up Enkidu, there must be another way to make him understand the value of money and the worthlessness of animals. You have to make him civilized." It's something that Karl Marx talked about: the fetishization of commodity. I'm not going to bring my professor coffee because I think there is something nice about this man and I respect the way he thinks and feels about stuff. I'm going to take him coffee because I want him to give me an "A" as opposed to a "B." The city life and the city person turns everything into either a profit or a loss. You take notes not because you enjoy wisdom but because you want to get an "A" on the essay. You fight Occupy Oakland and other social movements not because you've truly understood what injustice is, but instead someone has pushed an emotion inside you and you react like a machine. It's city life that lacks understanding. So this is what his father says to him: "Go to our king Gilgamesh." The hunter goes to the king because kings dominate society. It's ultimately the politicians that allow advertisements to take place, that allow pornography, tobacco, weed, crack and alcohol to exist in the public domain. It's ultimately the politicians that get us hooked to the stuff that makes life go bad.

For those of you in this class that want to complain because I am a bad teacher, I am a product of a society. You're not really punishing me. If you want to replace me, you can – you'll get another bad teacher just like me. If you really want to fix the situation, go to the roots, and the root is the American philosophy of life, the American definition of success, of happiness, of what it means to be educated. The hunter goes to Gilgamesh because Gilgamesh is a con artist who knows how to exploit Nature, how to exploit people, how to be a criminal but never get caught. If you want to get a good view of this, watch Bernie Sanders, Hillary Clinton, Donald Trump, or any politician. They all function the same way: they all lay traps. And we fall into their traps, and once fallen, they have our votes. And once they get into a place of power, they don't really care for us anymore. It's all advertisement. Karl Marx argued that it's the capitalists who exploit us, but Marx was wrong. Whenever you live in the city, you have no choice but to exploit, and be exploited. It's just the way things are.

The hunter tells Gilgamesh, "There is this man but he can't be tamed by any mortal, by any civilized man." No one could even tempt Malcolm X. There is no one in city life who could ever tempt Martin Luther King Jr, and even if they briefly visited these temptations, they would go behind the podium ten minutes later and give, yet again, a riveting and inspired speech. These are innocent people who refuse to be contaminated. It's like they have this force field around them.

Can I tell you a story?

About thirty years ago I was working at Church's Fried Chicken on Hurley and Arden. I had a boss whose name was Ernie who would always say that my cash register was short. Later on, I realized that he was taking my money, which of course he deducted from my paycheck. Anyways, one day I was feeling a little like a superhero, I had all this childish energy inside me and my friends were there so I was showing off a little as well. A car comes through the drive-through, and way back then there were no microphones, so we just had to look inside the car and say, "What do you want?" And this girl, somewhat attractive, at least I thought way back then, said, "I want a number 2."

"Well, I'll give it to you if you give me your phone number."

"No!"

"No chicken then."

Finally I give her a box of chicken and she gives me a couple of numbers. For some strange reason I begin to really like her, as any 16- or 17-year-old would. And I remember one day I brought her home, and it was my first time bringing this young woman home. And we were laying on the sofa and she says, "Let's make love."

I said, "What?"

"Let's make love."

I said, "No."

"Let's make love – the moon, the lighting, everything is just set."

I said, "No."

She said, "Why?"

"I don't know. The thing is, I love you and I don't want to mess it up with my physical body. Let me just hold you, I don't want to go any further." All of us in this class have had those moments when we don't want the movie to end, we don't want the kiss to go any further. Or, for example, we don't want our child out of the house simply because he's a certain age, instead you want him around and you don't mind caring for him for the rest of your life. These are the moments of innocence that most of us have experienced.

So how does Enkidu, the innocent man, get tempted? There is a man some years ago named the Buddha who got really depressed about everything: spiritual life, having a wife, having a son, having a family, even having money. None of that stuff meant anything to him. So he sat under a tree and said, "I prefer death to life because life is absolutely meaningless." And then before he was given his insight, his Wisdom, this temptress by the name of Mara came down and offered him three temptations. The Buddha said, after he was enlightened, whatever that may mean, "If I was given a fourth and final temptation, the temptation of sex, I would have fallen." This is how Enkidu is trapped.

Gilgamesh says, "The only way that Enkidu could be brought back to the city is for you to get a woman, but not any ordinary woman. She needs to be a temple prostitute, someone who really knows the art of sex." This woman, Shamat, gets commissioned: "Go to the forest. Get Enkidu. Civilize him. Tame him." So hand in hand they go, the hunter and the prostitute. In the forest, the hunter looks at the woman and says, "There is Enkidu. The naked guy who's talking to a goat. Can you tame him? Can you civilize him? We need him in the city."

She goes to this Enkidu-guy, this guy that runs around naked and lays with the animals, who is one with Nature and has a great amount of compassion for anything that's feeling bad. He has never seen a woman, never seen the shape of a woman's body. Shamat only has a lingerie on, one of those robes, and goes to Enkidu and taps him on the shoulder. Enkidu turns around and Shamat goes, "Hello." Enkidu is most amazed, but isn't intimate with her. He simply sits and observes the beauty of this woman. Take any two- or three-year-old on a walk, and every petal, every piece of garbage, everything they see on the road, they stop, bend over, look at it, put it in their mouths, smell it, put it in their noses. And as a parent you say, "What is wrong with you, man?" as you drag this kid along. But here's the beauty of innocence. Everything you see out there deserves careful observation and study. Innocence creates respect for the things out there. That's something children have, but something you and I have lost. Enkidu looks at her, but refuses to be with her. Remember the stages we talked about. Desire has not yet taken a physical manifestation. He first becomes curious, then he becomes interested, then he becomes attracted.

For six days and six nights, Enkidu sits back and watches the naked body of this woman without touching her. On the seventh day they rest, they sleep together, no different than what you'll find in Genesis. God creates the world in six days and six nights and then of course He rests and says, "Everything is perfect." Perfection is not going to be given to any of us through objective observation. Great understanding comes from profound intimacy, and that intimacy and understanding allows for rest. You can't read a book and say, "Now I understand." It will never happen. You can't go to therapy and be filled with bumper stickers and say, "I understand." This will never happen. You can't read the dialogues of Plato and talk about the verses and say you understand philosophy. It never happens. Intimacy, whether it's physical intimacy, emotional intimacy, spiritual intimacy, is the ultimate resting ground. No other path will ever be possible. Remember Malcolm X's ultimate Sabbath, or resting ground, was when he went to Saudi Arabia and understood what it means to be human. Once he understood, he no longer has the emotion of hostility towards the whites. Or the blues. Or the blacks. Or the browns. Intimacy. Six days and six nights of battle, of creativity, excitement, inspiration, varied emotions, but ultimately you are intimate with the thing that bothers you the most. And in intimacy you understand.

After having sex, Enkidu falls asleep. The fruit of intimacy is the most comfortable of sleeps, where nothing bothers you. But you awake from it and you realize that you have lost some of your innocence. I have no doubt that many of us got into our relationships because we had sex with someone. Once, twice, thrice. And after a while you say, "I can't leave now." The ancient world believed that intimacy has a very civilizing force to it and once you are with someone five or ten times, you're stuck. You can't leave. You understand things so much better now so you try to go back to the forest, only to realize that you no longer belong there.

When Enkidu wakes up he can no longer talk with the animals. He can no longer run with the animals, and he no longer feels one with Nature. Something about him has gone bad, has been contaminated, and he doesn't know what it is. Imagine the story of Moses. He leaves the corrupt city and the corrupt city ideas. He finds himself in the forest, called the burning bush, and he tries to stay there but ultimately he can't. There is a shift inside him and he no longer wants to be the man on the mountain. He needs to go back to Egypt, and that's exactly what Enkidu feels.

An innocent man must become corrupt and live with the fact that he was once innocent, but is now corrupt. He must take that understanding into the city, encounter someone who no longer believes in innocence, but is all corrupt. This innocent man must be contaminated by the city life in order to baptize the city man, and the price he pays is ultimately death. Enkidu, the innocent man, must die so that Gilgamesh, the corrupt man, may ultimately become innocent. If I was to make this more contemporary, it would be the following. Malcolm X becomes innocent, then comes back to the corrupted city to remind us what it means to be black, what it means to be white, in fact what it means to be human. And that reminder costs him his life. But what we gain from Malcolm X, though dead, though innocent, is that if you understand things the right way, racism will ultimately go away and equality will reign.

I'm going to tell you a story that's about a half-hour long. It's about this man who's about seventy. He lives in this city called Sam'an, and is a sheikh or teacher of his community, and he has about five or six other disciples. He's never been married and he prays constantly. For those of you that have read these tiny little Christian books, authors anonymous, Imitation of Christ or Cloud of Unknowing or The Interior Castle or The Way of the Pilgrim, you know that these books all argue that a person should make sure that within yourself there is a constant awareness of prayer, and that awareness itself is like a prayer. This man has this ceaseless prayer and awareness, but one night he has a dream and in the dream he sees a young woman with yellow hair and fair skin. He gets excited about the dream, but then wakes up and says, "This can't be. I'm seventy. I'm supposed to dream of saints, of angels, of God. I can't be dreaming about things like this." But he also knows that nothing happens accidentally and in fact, realizes that this dream has been sent to him by the gods. So he says, "Let me see where this dream is going to take me."

So he wakes up the following morning and says to his disciples, "Let's go to the city. I want to figure out the meaning of this dream." He goes to the city and the moment he enters its gates, he looks up and there is a young woman with fair skin, brushing her yellow hair. And all of a sudden he doesn't know what has hit him. He falls madly in love.

There is this story that comes to us from the ancient Greeks, who argue that should you find yourself falling in love, whether slowly or instantly, the hands of Cupid are at play. Cupid, this particular god, walks around with a bow and arrow. If Cupid shoots a lead arrow into your chest, it will be very difficult for you to fall in love. And just in case you want to fall in love but you can't, you don't need therapy – it's Cupid. You're just stuck, for life, and you can't fall in love. If, on the other hand, this Cupid fellow throws a golden-tip arrow into you, you will fall in love. Love, the ancient people believed, was sacred. But the moment you civilize and socialize love, it becomes corrupted and goes away. We call it marriage.

His disciples tell him, "What is wrong with you? You're our teacher, you're seventy, stop coveting a seventeen-year-old." And he says, "Love makes all of us young. I have taught you the wrong things about life. You don't need to read the Qur'an, you don't need to fast, you don't need to pray. You need to fall in love. In love you will find God, in love you will find presence, you will find intoxication. In love you will find yourself coming to life." "And the disciples, because they're on the outside, say, "No, we're not going to do this. This is blasphemy."

So day and night this old man sits under her window and sings and writes poetry. The girl comes down, looks at him and says, "You're old enough to be my great-great-great grandfather, get lost." And the man says, "But I love you. In love all of us are transformed. In love, all of us are young. You're only looking at my exterior. My interior is like this juice filled with life, filled with God." As Rumi says,

Eshq ostrolab asrare khodast

This means that if you fall in love, for whatever the reasons, the Magician, God, made it happen.

Whether you love someone for their body or mind or emotions or spirit, they're all the same. The only difference is, sex will not last that long, intellect will eventually get boring, and emotions will eventually become burdensome. Spirit is the only thing that frees.

Ultimately this woman says, "On one condition will I marry you, or hang out with you."

And the old man says, "Anything."

"The first thing you need to do is burn the Qur'an."

Now the Qur'an happens to be the Bible of the Muslim world. If any of you in this class have ever heard of Salman Rushdie's The Satanic Verses, this book talks about sacred verses that have never been analyzed or examined, unlike the Bible. And because these verses were never put under a microscope, the historical accuracies and facts are less important than the images that the verses inspire. So this young woman says, "You need to burn this book." Now, why would this woman ask this poor man to burn not only a book, but the holiest book? Well, a book contains a set of images about right and wrong, good or bad, ethical or unethical, Satan and God, and this woman says, "You need to burn this book." Because the Qur'an doesn't live outside of you, it lives inside of you. All of us in this class have been socialized by codes we don't truly understand. You don't need Jesus Christ and Satan to have assumptions about right and wrong, what success is, what poverty is, what marriage is, what love is. This young woman says, "You need to get rid of all of that. You cannot serve two Masters. You cannot serve your own assumed moral codes and love at the same time. It does not work that way."

So, the Qur'an is the first sacrificial lamb in this story. It's put on the cross and it will not resurrect.

The second is that the woman asks him to burn his jacket. In the Islamic tradition usually teachers have a robe. We call it khede, and usually your teacher gives you this jacket. Your teacher received it from his teacher, which means that the khede goes all the way back to Muhammad. So, this woman says, "You need to get rid of this jacket that goes all the way back to Muhammad."

And the man says, "Fine, I don't really care. I'd rather belong to you than Muhammad, and I'd rather belong to you than to my tradition. I don't need to be Muslim to submit. If I can love you, in love I will submit."

He's accomplished two tasks, and for the last one the woman says, "You need to come with me. You need to worship the things that I worship." And in her case, it's fire, a thing that illuminates. If you've read one of these Gospels, Jesus says, "If you want to sit next to me, you know that you sit next to fire." Fire turns all moral and ethical concepts into ash. And that's what the old man does, he submits himself completely to this woman.

While they are sitting in this room, the man says, "I'm a little bit tired, I need to take a nap." He has a dream, in which Muhammad comes to him and says, "Go back home." So he picks up his stuff and goes back home. While he is sleeping the woman also takes a nap, and she also has a dream. In her dream, someone says, "We gave you an innocent man so that you could be reminded of who you are. Go to him, thank him, and ask for forgiveness." So this young woman runs after this old man, but before she gets to him, she runs out of gas, it's the Middle East, she gets exhausted, she passes out and ultimately dies in the arms of this old man. And the old man looks to the heavens and says, "An innocent man had to become corrupt so that someone who lived in unawareness could become aware."

If that doesn't make any sense, I'll give it to you in this way. Virginity used to be a big deal, it no longer is and it's okay. For the longest time, when a woman wanted to be with someone, she had to be married. In certain parts of Africa and the Middle East, the first night a woman sleeps with her man her mother in-law would sit in the room next door, waiting to come and examine the white sheet. If there is no blood, you've had sex before, and the marriage is annulled. If there is blood, it's a blessing.

For those of you who fell in love and lost your virginity to a man, and if you've come from a very traditional background, go back and examine the journey you went through to sacrifice your body, your tradition, the religion, and the fact that your parents could be profoundly disappointed in you. You sacrificed all of it for love. Remember from last class, submission comes after love. And when someone has fully submitted, then they're allowed to learn.

Back to the Epic. Enkidu is contaminated. If you happen to have become interested in this stuff for a while, your dreams have immense significance. Do not take them lightly. The only problem is, for the most part, you can't interpret your dreams. But before we continue, does anyone have any questions?

[Gary: I'm a little bit confused and I may be interpreting the story wrong, but it seems like the woman is a corrupting force.]

She is.

[Gary: Can you talk more about that?]

You can take women literally or metaphorically. Women have always held a very sacred position in not so much philosophy, but definitely in the religious traditions, for the following reasons.

Women know without knowing. The life of a woman becomes problematic when she wants to know how she knows. And because of those qualities, women have always been, among other things, a gateway for man's inspiration. One of the reasons why the temples housed women is because one of the fastest, easiest and safest ways for a man to get a glimpse of God, or his own nature, is through having intercourse with a woman who is very proficient in the art of sex. You may think that prostitution is a bad thing, and the way we have made it in the modern day, it is really bad. But in the ancient times a temple prostitute was perhaps the only way that someone in the city could get a small taste of God. The Sumerian world has a sun-god whose name is Shamash, and it is no accident that the name of the prostitute and the God are almost the same. The woman is a mini-god, an expression of a god above. Like when Jesus says in the Gospel of John, "You see me, you see God," the temple prostitute could say, "You see me, you see Shamash." Remember that a temple prostitute is in a temple, and temple is in the middle of the city. It is the sun of the city, and all the houses and shops are built around the temple. You know that in a bicycle wheel there are the spokes that go out, but all of them go back to the center? The temple is a hub of the city, and this city is blessed because the temple sends out energy and the person who ultimately controls this temple is a woman. Not a man. The ancients believed that no man is ever worthy of being housed in a temple. A temple is profoundly sacred, and men are anything but. Now, why the prostitution?

A woman sits at this temple, but doesn't go to the city because she refuses to be contaminated. Her business takes place solely in the temple, and she has one task in life. A man knocks on this door. She opens the door, and asks the right questions to make sure that this is a mature man who has come to realize that city life doesn't offer him much. He's about spiritual stuff now, intellectual and emotional stuff. And there she sits and slowly trains him in the art of seduction. Ultimately they are intimate, but they do not have the sort of intimacy to which you and I are accustomed. This woman gives this man a taste of what it means to be holy. Now you need to understand how dangerous this is, because once the man gets a taste of what it means to be holy, it's very hard for him to go back to city life. This is how Messiahs are created. They are filled with contradictions.

But the temple prostitute doesn't have sex with the man, she makes love. It sounds like semantics but it is not. When I ask you, for example, "Do you know how to make chicken noodle soup? Can you tell me the steps to make it?" then you take me through this process step-by-step. The prostitute doesn't accidentally give a man inspiration, she creates it, step-by-step.

I'm going to give you this in a way that many of you can grasp better, without making it too esoteric or spiritual. That would be nonsense. Imagine you look at someone and your eyes say, "He or she is very attractive." But the way we have been designed, it is not enough to simply look at someone. After a while, your body says, "Go speak to them." And so you go and speak with them. But again it's not enough. So then, you say, "Would you like to have dinner?" And then as you sit, your shoulders begin to touch. That's something that you've always wanted, but it had to go through stages. And then you say, "Touching shoulders is not enough. I want to hold his or her hand." And then after two weeks you say, "That is not enough. I want to put my mouth to his or hers." And then you do and you say, "Well, that is not enough," after a few weeks. And then you say, "I really want to be intimate with them." Then slowly you get to the ultimate stage, which is you lay next to them. And then when it comes to intimacy, if you happen to be somewhat mature, you go through it very, very slowly. And the man goes through all of this simply because of a woman. This thing we call sex, it's really a gateway towards love expressing itself physically. It really isn't sex at all. In casual sex the feelings are accidental, but when you make love, the acts and emotions are deliberate. For the ancient temple prostitutes, this is the art of making love.

But if you were to take the word "woman" metaphorically, it would simply mean a creative force. Right now you have a woman, yes? [Gary nods.] Let's call her Julie and let's say you love her. The truth is, depending on your temperament, depending on your needs and your life, it doesn't take very much for another woman who knows her art well to walk into your life, and within a couple of meetings, have you fall in love with her.

And afterwards you'll stay with Julie, but you'll be with Julie with a tremendous amount of guilt. Women are a creative force, but it creates guilt, and that guilt baptizes you. You know you shouldn't be there, but you are nevertheless. The socialized part of you, the Gilgamesh part, likes stability, but this other part of you, the Enkidu part of you, wants to be inspired. This struggle is always going to be inside us, no matter what.

In the Old Testament, in the Garden of Eden, the serpent doesn't speak to Adam. Adam represents the body. If you read the story, you realize that God creates man first, then the man gets bored and unhappy, goes to sleep, God makes a woman, all of a sudden the man gets excited. His life has meaning, and then comes the serpent. The only way for this man to be educated, the serpent, who is known to represent healing and health, has to talk to Eve, i.e. the creative part of us.

I mean, don't you sometimes ask, "Why am I here?" It happens to me all the time. My marriage is okay, my kids are okay, my job is okay, everything about me is okay, but nevertheless this serpent comes by once in a while and whispers into my ears, the ears that hear creativity, passion, authenticity, "You need to leave. This is no good." Now the reason why I stay is that the one third of me, the Gilgamesh part, the Adam part, is far too frightened to leave. But once the serpent whispers into Eve's ears and once Eve tempts Adam, it's like when you're with Julie, but isn't it true that sometimes you think about another woman? You've been expelled already from a relationship that has handcuffs you never asked for, and yet after a couple weeks it's not enough. And then when Adam gets expelled, he has a memory of Paradise, but it belongs to a place that requires toil and effort, and if you come from the Islamic tradition, this man works and works until he finds his way back to Paradise.

I'll address this following statement towards women. Men are too stupid for this, myself included. When a woman feels a bit too much, when she likes someone a bit too much, she wants her body to be respected. And she waits for a man who's aware of what it means to be human, and aware of how to treat a human body. Because remember what the body and the senses do. The senses create emotions, emotions create reflections, and these reflections could either be positive or negative in that they can either inspire or deflate the human spirit. If you're a woman and a man leaves you, you're devastated and forced to sit and think. If you're a man, you're too stupid so you just have more sex.

[Andrew: To continue with the last question, how should women approach these stories?]

They shouldn't.

[Andrew: Because every model for them is allegorical or metaphorical. They're not the subject, they're there to provide an experience for the guy. And I think that's frustrating for a woman. I mean, is a woman meant to identify with Gilgamesh, Enkidu, Shamat, I mean what are the models for the story, what are women meant to take as a lesson?]

Since women have been secularized they have become psychologically like men, so now the story now applies to everyone, man and woman. It makes no difference anymore. You may be a woman, but I'm sure you are male, psychologically speaking.

For those of you who believe in reincarnation and all that nonsense, traditionally it's believed that you must have lived many, many, many different lives to have come to this life as a woman. If you've come back as a woman, chances are, this could be your last life. The body of a woman is perhaps the most noble vehicle that a soul occupies. If you're a man, unless you're turned into a woman, God help you.

Somehow, Gilgamesh needs to be made aware of the fact that though he has God on the inside, his desires have been corrupted. Gilgamesh enjoys sex, but his sex is filled with aggression. He enjoys beauty, but one that's purchased with money. He enjoys power, but he uses it to exploit. So Shamat, the temple prostitute, tells Enkidu, who is now corrupted, "Since you can't go back to being the man that you used to be, why not just come with me and I'll introduce you to my king Gilgamesh. You guys look the same, talk the same, you have the same strength and the same beauty." Enkidu says, "Fine." But as they're journeying towards Uruk, the place that Gilgamesh owns, Enkidu keeps hearing these statements from people, "Gilgamesh is corrupt, Gilgamesh has forgotten." So Enkidu says to himself, "I'm going to meet Gilgamesh and I'm going to remind him what it means to be human." Eventually they come upon a party in honor of Gilgamesh, and because Gilgamesh is the king, everyone removes him or herself from his path, and allows Gilgamesh to walk back and forth freely. Enkidu enters the city, enters this gathering, and refuses to move from Gilgamesh's path. Remember Gilgamesh's dream about the rock? And they fight, for six days and six nights.

This is something that our good friend in this class, Casey, does often. Casey creates inspiring movies about social activism. If any of you in this class have ever experienced anything innocent, if an Enkidu has walked into your life, whether it's an inspiring movie about justice, a book about love, or a nice conversation or relationship with anyone – after inspiration, when you go home, there is an inner struggle. You keep going back to the conversation or the relationship, and though your body demands sleep, emotionally and spiritually you say, "No," because the memories are far too delicious. Whenever there is an Enkidu in our lives, there is going to be a battleground. And like any other battle, it's either Gilgamesh the socialized man who will win, or Enkidu, the forest-life, who will win.

I had this friend, I still see him once every four or five years. In the 1980's he made about $180,000 a year as the manager at PacBell, but he had a wife who was a shopaholic. She was an awful human being. I'm sure it wasn't her fault, in fact her parents were alcoholics. But she had a miserable life and so she made life for other people mostly miserable. And I remember all of us came together when his wife was out and told him, "Hussein, you need to divorce this woman and free yourself." While we were having this conversation, he brings out a book and shows us the math he had done to calculate what would happen as a result of this divorce, should it happen. "I will lose everything," he said. So the socialized part of him extinguished the emotional, the spiritual, more intuitive part of him. Thirty years have passed. He rarely leaves his room. He has two kids. One is addicted to cocaine, one to alcohol. His wife is over 500 pounds and they live in a mansion. All of us in this class know, if you've seen the movie V for Vendetta, when he comes on this big jumbotron, "If you really want to know who the guilty party is, look yourself in the mirror, and there you will see it." Enkidu walked into his life, the voice of conscience, the voice of God. Where some of you are in life, you know this class is boring, and that you want to go home and be with your family. The Enkidu-part says, "Get up, pack your stuff, and leave." But the socialized part says, "Grade, future, graduation, all that stuff."

The innocent part of us will always meet the not-so-innocent, and jihad al akbar, the greater battle, will take place. And either your body will win, or your spirit. In the case of our good friend Gilgamesh, he had always beaten up people, conquered, and dominated. But when he met Enkidu, he couldn't win and the only thing he could do was be friends. It's like when you go to your husband or your wife and you say, "I don't really love you, I like you. I don't really want to be married to you, but I will nevertheless." You serve both worlds harmoniously, and your husband or your wife knows exactly why you're there.

The battlefield creates an intimacy and remember, without intimacy, there is no journey towards transformation. Enkidu touches Gilgamesh, Gilgamesh touches Enkidu. Through touching, emotions are created, through emotions attachments are created, through attachments there is focus, intensity, and sacrifice. Gilgamesh can come to realize something profoundly significant. No matter what he does, he can't get Enkidu out of his life, so he devotes himself to Enkidu. Here is a king who has all the power and who can do whatever he pleases, but these six days and six nights of battle force him to fall in love with Enkidu, a man who is naked, unsocialized, and who lives in complete poverty. And yet a king bows to him.

There is this group of people in the Sufi tradition called the Malamatis. "Malamat" are those who favor pain and hardship as opposed to comfort. They make fun of themselves and make sure they are the fool at the center of every stage. In other words, they want to tarnish their own reputation and deflate the notion or concept of "self" or "ego" that lives inside them. One of the fastest ways, this Epic tells us, that your grandiose, but false, sense of self can be conquered is by falling in love with someone called "Enkidu." Because look: What does Malcolm X offer us? He doesn't show us how to make money, or how to buy a car, or how to get a PhD. He gives us nothing except ideas. These people don't enrich our physical lives. They don't make our relationships better, and they don't make our relationships with our children better. They make us poor, and yet there is something rich about the poverty that they give us.

There is a story that comes from Arabian Nights about a man with a tremendous amount of power and beauty. Every night he has a different woman in his bed, and the next day he has the woman executed because after she's been used she's no longer attractive. You may think it's funny, but every time you and I go to a buffet, that's exactly what we do. You get rid of a plate that's full of food, just to get a new plate and new food. One night a strange woman comes to his bedroom. Her name is Scheherazade, which means, "someone who has the power to birth a city inside you." Not a room, but a city with lots of houses. And the king says, "Disrobe."

The woman says, "I want to tell you a story."

And the king says, "Okay."

Then she tells a story for four or five hours, but she grows tired and says to the king, "Can I tell the rest of it to you tomorrow?" And then she passes out on the bed.

The next day she continues with the story, and again passes out. And this happens over and over and over again for a thousand and one nights. Imagine the worlds that the woman creates with language, with ideas, with words, with stories. As the nights go on, the king thinks less about his town, his kingdom, his power, and more about the stories. Remember the steps I mentioned? It begins with the simple notion of attraction, which creates desire. Then a desire turns into a want, and when it comes to a need you're emotionally entangled with the story. Then the need becomes infatuation: "I long for tomorrow night, 6 p.m. to come, so that this woman can enter my chambers, not for intimacy – I just want to know how the story ends!" Through language the woman forces the king to overlook her body. Through the woman, the king transcends his senses and then after a thousand and one nights, the story comes to an end, and the king doesn't want to have sex with her. He's in love. He marries her.

The battlefield between Enkidu and Gilgamesh is a marriage. This marriage is not given by the State, but given by Paradise and by the gods. There is something about the spirit of Enkidu and something about the spirit of Gilgamesh that mesh really well together.

So one day as Gilgamesh comes home, he finds Enkidu, the most innocent of mankind, in his bedroom on his bed, weeping. And Gilgamesh asks, "Why are you crying? What's wrong with you?"

"Your world, your society, your life, how can you live this way? When I lived in the forest I could be free! I could sing whatever song, I could walk around naked, without shame." You know how when you like someone, you want to hold their hand but you say, "No, no, I don't know what he or she is going to think." You're frightened, you imagine being embarrassed or ashamed, but as you get more intimate, what happens? The fear and the shame go away. The more attracted and in love you become, the less shame and embarrassment there is because you know everything is coming from the right place.

And again, remember, put these concepts within your own life. If there are moments when you wake up and whisper secret things to yourself, that's the innocence, that's the Enkidu part of you demanding justice and shamelessness.

There was this movie in the 1980's with Rob Lowe and Demi Moore. She was a virgin, he was a kind of playboy, and he would repeatedly ask, "Sleep with me, sleep with me!"

And she would repeatedly say, "No, no, no – only when I get married!" But she was in love with him and he was about to leave for good. So that night she couldn't sleep, and she goes to him and she says, "I want you." And Rob Lowe, I don't know who his character was, says to her, "I can't stay. I leave in the morning and I won't be back. Don't you want to save yourself for a man who will stay?"

And she says, "No. Your body may leave me, but the love that I have for you will always stay with me, and that's enough for me. Be with me tonight."

So to satisfy Enkidu, because the king must now serve this humble man Enkidu, Gilgamesh says, "Okay there is a place over there. Let's go and steal some wood." The only problem is there's this monster out there.

And Enkidu says, "I don't want to die. How big is this monster?"

And Gilgamesh says, "Well, it's ten feet and ten inches tall." In every spiritual quest, there is going to be a monster, there is going to be a battle, someone is going to die and someone is going to be exiled, for a long, long, long time.

The name of the monster who lives in the cedar woods is Humbaba. This monster gets killed, but this monster wasn't an ordinary monster – it was the pet of the goddess Ishtar. Ishtar says, "Since they killed my pet, either Gilgamesh or Enkidu must die." Now remember, Enkidu has nothing to lose. Being innocent, he was a dead man already. Though he was brought to the city, he never forgot, so he will die a happy man. The gods decided, "It's Gilgamesh who is to be transformed, it's Gilgamesh who's to supposed to become a human being, it's Gilgamesh who has forgotten. So let us do this. Let Gilgamesh intensely fall in love with Enkidu, and then let us get Enkidu really, really sick, and then let us make him die so that for the first time in his life, Gilgamesh can understand the intensity of love and loss." If you can replace a love with another love, you haven't yet suffered a loss that could result in complete transformation. What's so unique about Gilgamesh and Enkidu, or the relationship between a student and a teacher, is that this relationship must somehow consummate. If not physically, then definitely spiritually. The teacher must go inside the student, and the student inside the teacher. Enkidu is the teacher and Gilgamesh is the student.

Eventually Enkidu gets sick, wakes up one morning, looks at Gilgamesh and says, "I have seen the House of Dust and Darkness, the place where people go when they die. Kings and slaves, whites and blacks, rich and poor, slave and master, they're all the same. Death is the grand equalizer." Next time you want to respect someone when you go to an interview, look at them as if they are corpses. In death we are all equal. Do not respect their sociability, do not respect their social status. Always put them in this Epic, and in this Epic all of us are insignificant. If you do this, you will have one of the best interviews of your life. You'll make fun of them, you'll tell them that their questions are cheap and stupid. You'll be blunt, they'll love you for it, and then when you become a trouble-maker, they'll say, "Why did we hire this person at all?"

On his deathbed, Enkidu begins to say all these nasty things about women, particularly about Shamat. "If it wasn't for her, I'd still be in the forest. If it wasn't for her, I'd still be running around with the animals." And all of a sudden the sun-god Shamash comes down and says, "Why do you curse this woman? If it wasn't for her, you would never had known friendship in Gilgamesh. Not friendship in body, but friendship in spirit. You would never know the wisdom that comes from death. You would never know the shortness of life, so you would never know its value. Through this woman your life became valuable." For those of you that go home tonight and may be inspired to play some music, or to write a couple of lines of poetry, it's those two minutes that make the rest of your evening meaningless and futile. But that two minutes of inspiration will make you profoundly sad, because inspiration lasts only for a couple of moments and then it goes away, leaving behind a memory that ultimately serves only to torment you.

All this is what Gilgamesh and Enkidu find in women, in passion, in the feminine. Gilgamesh holds his friend Enkidu as he dies. Though he weeps because he knows he can no longer find anyone like him, something even worse begins to happen. First you feel bad because you've lost a friend, and you know no one can replace him. But then as you sit with this grief of losing your friend, because death initially was something social, it quickly turns into something personal. Death swallows time and it shrinks life. All of a sudden Gilgamesh says, "I too can die. I too can get sick at any time. If life is so short, how should I really live? If life can take away the person I loved, the person around whom all of my emotions and reflections revolved, if love can be taken by life, if my identity and meaning can be taken, if everything that I hold valuable can be taken by life, is there anything out there that life cannot touch?"

I had a friend. She had gone to this man's house and this man had done some strange things to her. Not physically, but philosophical, religious, and spiritual stuff. Her name was Semiot, and she got a little overwhelmed and frightened because she had three kids and it was just too much for her. So she stopped going to this man. And she had imagined that when she stopped going she would forget, but something within her had already woken up. She was physically in the marriage and physically with her kids, but she really wasn't there. Seven years later, she divorced and went back to this man.

Gilgamesh had tasted something profoundly genuine, authentic, and real. He couldn't go back to Uruk and simply be a king, drink, smoke and have sex. Something about him, some alchemy, had changed the Iron, Bronze, and Silver into this passionate quest for Gold. He couldn't go back to the Iron or the Silver or the Bronze. Now see what has happened. The innocence that lived in Enkidu was somehow transferred into Gilgamesh. Enkidu is no longer needed. All good students come to a place where they no longer need a teacher who lives on the outside, but for this to happen, intense love, devotion, and sacrifice need to have happened. Your teacher serves you. Whatever he or she has goes inside you, and then you will nail him or her to the cross. You will not pick him up, you will not bury him, you will not desire to find him, because now you're looking for the things that he or she had on the inside. You are on your own, and your journey has just begun. You thought your journey began when you found a teacher. No. A teacher is nothing but a stepping-stone, but a very necessary one. Gilgamesh will never be able to forget. Have you ever had a really bad toothache and take all this medication but it doesn't help?

Since he can't go back, Gilgamesh must go forward, but he has no idea what forward is. He has no idea where things are going to lead. Imagine for a moment a man who knew everything about himself, everything about his life, a man who's immensely attractive, a man who has the beauties of the gods on the inside and out, but for him mostly out. Imagine a man who's no longer willing to go back and take advantage of the physical prowess that he has. Imagine the fear, confusion, and depression that lives inside this man. The immense loneliness! To be loved by so many people and yet be in a place where there is only hatred for himself – the self-disgust is so layered, and so pregnant, and so intense! This is a man who grows his hair long, never shaves, never showers. His quest has begun, and the gods are far, far away. He's no longer a king.

For those of you who may one day go through a divorce; for those of you who may experience a break up; for those of you who may think that you're going to get an A in a class, but end up with an F; for those of you who think that your job is secure and then the next thing you realize you're fired: You have experienced a death no different from Gilgamesh. With death comes awareness. In awareness, you can't go back to thinking that your job is waiting for you, your wife or husband is waiting for you, or your kids are waiting for you. In awareness, you have absolutely nothing. When you have nothing your emotions are intense, there is despair, there is depression, there is anger, there is confusion, there is frustration, and above all there is a loneliness that no one will ever understand about you. And the nice thing about this Epic is that it doesn't say that you need to go towards alcohol or towards drugs or sex, or talk to people about ridiculous things. This is what we call the human condition. *It is normal.* Things down here must always get old, sick, and they must always die! We lose interest in them and it's *natural.* Loneliness is an innate part of who and what we are. So don't talk to people about drinking or smoking or watching movies, talk to them instead about the loneliness that lives inside us. Aristotle used to call this "friendship in excellence," in which language is peppered with the human condition. For Gilgamesh, Enkidu is his home. In the physical body of Enkidu he finds rest, emotionally, intellectually, and spiritually. In that body he's willing to sacrifice everything about himself, and the moment this body dies, all that remains is a memory. This process is rooted in death: "I too will die. How should I live?"

Be omre kheeshtan ta yaddaran
Ze hejrat naleh o afqan bar lab

These are a couple of lines by a man named Abu Said Abul Khayr, a 9th century Sufi mystic. If I were to put these lines within the context of this moment in Gilgamesh's life, they would mean the following. As Gilgamesh sits in the ruins of his life, he sits back and reviews everything that he has done. And he gets disappointed. How could I have had such meaningless sex? Why did I drink and smoke? Why did I have those crummy friends? Why was I so *stupid*? And he wants to change a little, but he doesn't know how – he doesn't know towards what. And the lines say, "When I think about my life, all I see is ruins. When I look at my emotions, all I see is depression. When I see my future, it is grey and bleak. There is nothing but tears that I weep." You need to understand when you read the *Epic of Gilgamesh*, whenever you see the name "Gilgamesh," you're dealing with a container of sadness. There is no king. Next time you see a couple holding hands, have lots of fun watching them, but also know that the clock is ticking. Eventually they will stop holding hands. Eventually they will kiss not because it's fun, but because it's an obligation. As the Buddha once argued, "With every birth, see next to it a tomb."

Gilgamesh is now intoxicated with the big questions of life: "If I'm going to die, how should I live my life?" The first thing he does is he says, "Maybe the gods will give me some answers," because after all, the gods live in the mountains, in his case Mount Mashu. But the mountain is guarded by these things called the Scorpion Men. It's a long tradition that I won't get into, but the Scorpion Men ask Gilgamesh, "What are you doing here?"

And Gilgamesh says, "I was a king but my friend Enkidu died. I can't go back because my life is awful. I want to understand the truth."

And the Scorpion Men say, "Gilgamesh, go home. This is sacred ground. This stuff is talked about only by the gods, not mortals. You have to be a god if you're on a quest to find God. Are you one?"

And Gilgamesh says, "I don't really know. But I can't go back."

There is this story that comes to us from Iraq. It's about a man who goes to Safeway, buys three pounds of meat, takes it home, gives it to his wife and says, "Woman, make me some kabobs, three pounds of them."

After a couple minutes the woman comes out and says, "I'm sorry, my king, my cat ate it."

"Ate what?"

"The meat."

"How much?"

"Three pounds."

"All three pounds?"

"The cat ate all three pounds."

The man goes into the kitchen, picks up the cat, puts the cat on the scale, and the cat weighs exactly three pounds. The man looks at the woman and asks, "If this is the cat, then where is the meat? But if this is the meat, then where is the cat?"

When a human being begins to ask spiritual questions, this is no longer a human being with a body. This is a human being without senses. This is why when the Scorpion Men say to him, "Only gods can find God, not human beings. Are you sure you're a God or on your way to becoming one?" he replies, "I don't know, but I'm no longer a human being," and that's enough for them. In other words, if you can turn around and go back and be happy in your old life, you're not yet ready for the quest. Moses, Muhammad, Jesus – none of these people invite us to go into the caves and meditate and love God the way they did. They tell us to become social activists, because they know the path of Love is enormously difficult, and not very many people can traverse it. Just feed the hungry, clothe the naked, shelter the homeless. Don't go on a quest to figure out where Yahweh is. Don't sit in a cave so that the angel Gabriel can come down. Don't go the forest or the desert and be tempted by Satan. It's far too grand for you and I, so just go back home and take care of your people. Gilgamesh is a very unique human being, who doesn't fear being intoxicated with the big questions of life.

Next he goes to this woman whose name is Siduri. Siduri is a goddess who makes divine wine, it's like truth-telling-drink. And Siduri asks Gilgamesh, "What are you doing here? This is a cosmic tavern. Only special people can come here and drink. You have no business here."

And again he goes on telling the same story, and Siduri says, "Why don't you drink a little?"

I'm sure many of you know this, but just in case you don't, one of the reasons alcohol has always been important in the religious traditions is because it is believed that there is this spirit in alcohol, and this spirit has the ability to free certain things. When you consume the alcohol, the spirit that lives inside the alcohol paralyzes the body and the reflective abilities, and then you can act naturally. It's very much like when you get intoxicated by the Holy Ghost, for example. Both have the same spirit in them, but when it comes to Siduri, she has divine wine. When you drink this, you don't say stupid human stuff and you don't do stupid human things. So when Gilgamesh is intoxicated, Siduri asks, "What are you doing here?"

And Gilgamesh says, "I'm here because I have no home. I'm here because I want to be a human being." This man, whether awake and aware or intoxicated, always gives the same responses.

And then Siduri says, "There is only one person who can help you. His name is King Utnapishtim." In the Sumerian language this name means, "He who has found Life," with a capital "L." Not "life" as in coming to life from movies, music or literature. This is something that's permanent, immortal, and eternal, something that no one can take away from you.

"How do I find him?" Gilgamesh asks.

"Well, you have to go sit by this river. There is this Boatman that comes there named Urshanabi. You get on his boat and go past across the Waters of Death, but once you pass there is no return. As you get closer to Utnapishtim, this boat is going to shrink so by the time you get to King Utnapishtim, you will have absolutely nothing of yourself left." When he gets there, Utnapishtim asks, "What's your business here?"

Gilgamesh says, "I know that you're immortal, death doesn't frighten you, and you don't want to live in society. You live in complete detachment and I want to be like you."

He says, "No, this is what the gods gave me. The gods need to give that to you. I can't give that to you." All along Gilgamesh has this idea that someone from the outside can give him wisdom, but that's not the case at all. Everybody's a stepping stone. Everybody's a tool, an instrument.

Ultimately Utnapishtim says, "There is this plant in the river at the very bottom. If you can find it, dive down. Grab the plant and eat it. And then you will have eternal life."

He finds it, but he doesn't eat it. He puts it in his pocket and he travels back home, and he says, "I'm not going to go back home just yet. I look stinky and messy." Remember what we said the other night. Once you complete the journey to a certain extent, the quest itself becomes irrelevant. You turn your back to the journey and instead face society. Gilgamesh doesn't eat the plant because immortality is far too burdensome. For those of you in this class who have seen the movie The Green Mile, it's about a man who was given a gift and just lives and lives and lives. And one day he looks at someone and says, "I want to die. Do you know how many wives I've had? Do you know how many brothers and sisters I've buried? I know how everything unfolds." Being immortal is a burden. The Buddhists have a saying, "Whenever a child is born, never be happy. Always grieve the confusion and the mistakes that this child is going to commit. Grieve the regrets that the child will have, for all the awful things the child will do. Because the child at a certain point will sit back, review their life and say, 'Oh my God, this is all bad.' They may want to change some things about their life, but realizes that they're far too habituated in the old life so lives the remainder of their life in regret."

Gilgamesh does not want to be immortal. He in fact cherishes death and runs towards it. And he says, "I'm not going to eat a plant and become immortal, because that would mean watching people suffer for eternity. That's too much for me. Instead I'm going to go back to my hometown and talk to people about my experiences. I will tell them, 'Money is good, but it's not the meaning of life. Love is good, marriage is good, children are good, all this stuff is good, but they just won't make you happy the way that you want to be happy.'" He comes to realize nobody listens, nobody understands, "The Allegory of the Cave" by Plato? Gilgamesh then says, "Since nobody listens, it seems I've become even more lonely. I have all this wisdom and insight, but no one has the capacity to grasp what I've gone through."

So he builds a wall and he writes his stories on the wall. You can't convey wisdom to anyone because no one will understand it. Your wisdom has been obtained through experience and you want to tell it to someone, but your speech is going to go into someone's ears and the gap is the lived experience. So Gilgamesh just says, "I pray that every person has an Enkidu in his or her life, because wisdom accompanies experience."

[Steven: I'm reading a book but I don't really understand it. Should I wait to read it until I understand it, or should I read it now and not understand it?]

Everything can be helpful but when you read too much, most often it becomes an obstacle. When you have information about whatever the case may be, when something new walks into your life, you begin to compare and contrast. And because the new ideas or experiences don't fit into the structure that you already imagine to be accurate, you dismiss it. I've gone to one of the leading universities on the West Coast to talk a couple of times and it's an awful place to be. There is an overwhelming atmosphere of smugness and hubris because most of the people there have read tons of books but have little experience or understanding. Anytime you say something, a hand goes up, "BUT!" so after a while you say, "It's a complete waste of time."

Books are good to a certain point, and then you need real experience. In The Matrix there is this scene where Tank is inserting combat training into Thomas Anderson/Neo, who then wakes up and says, "I know kung fu." All the software inside him is like all this stuff he's read. Lucky for him, when he says, "I know kung fu," Morpheus is standing above him and says,

"Show me." And then they find themselves in the Construct, this room where they can fight. And despite all the things that Neo knows, he gets a really good whupping by Morpheus.

Books can give you experiences, but most of those experiences live in your head. Ask any of us in this class who've been in long-term relationships. Some of us have read lots of books about relationships, but when it comes to the real stuff of the relationship, books are no good. "I thought that if I cook every night, he'd just be happy!" "I thought that if I just buy you a car, you'll be happy!" "I've done all of this, you're still miserable!" You can't condense life to a paragraph, or to a book. I go back to what Rumi always used to say, "The best teachers or books are those who will remove information, or empty you more, as opposed to fill you with more stuff."

So if a book is able to get rid of the stuff that you thought to be good, it's a good book. The emptier you become, the more painful it'll be, but the more useful you'll become. It's like going out with a woman or a man who's still stuck on their ex. If they're not empty they'll just use you for food and money and this and that. So go out with someone who is empty.

[Norman: I think there are parallels between Enkidu's forest and the Garden of Eden, but for them, these places seem like prisons. Only when they are corrupted do they start looking for meaning. So is the only way to go forward on your quest, is the only way to mature, to be corrupted?]

No, corruption comes naturally. That's not a problem. Becoming aware of the corruption at the right stage in life is difficult. Then being able to have a sufficient amount of will to un-corrupt yourself, that also becomes tricky. All of us get corrupted; we have to be socialized. The deception is that once that you learn how to speak, you'll be able to express yourself. That's what they tell us. Then things happen to you on an emotional level, and now you know how to speak, but you just can't express yourself. And when you do, other people can't understand you, so language has betrayed you. The moments in life where you're really understood, and moments when you can understand, happen when no word is spoken. The most intimate moments, the most sexual moments you will ever have in your life are when there is no sex involved. It's a very strange thing. I mean all of us are under the assumption that intimacy is about your body going somewhere. But that's really the stage where intimacy vanishes. There comes a point where your body messes everything up. If you want to be intimate, never have sex. And if you want to have it, have it carefully.

Most of the things that are given to us are eventually useless. But Gilgamesh has to be made aware of that. How? By falling in love with Enkidu, and then everything about Gilgamesh is Enkidu. It's like when you look yourself in the mirror and the mirror reflects back you, that's what Enkidu is to Gilgamesh. But when Enkidu dies, he has nothing. And no one back home can reflect back to him the way Enkidu did. He's completely lost. And that's how you make someone aware. In Hinduism and in certain parts of the Islamic tradition, and in Jesus Christ, not so much Judaism, love happens to be the only tool with which alchemy becomes possible. There is no other tool. Usually for us, love is a two-way street, you give a little, then I give a little, then you give a little, and I give a little. But that's not the way it works. Gilgamesh must give, and give, and give, and give, and give, and once in a while Enkidu says, "Thank you." Then when Enkidu goes away there is no one else to give to, so the only person to give to becomes God. But for that to happen, you need the love component inside.

Anyone else? Yes, Lester.

[Lester: No questions.]

What happened to you, man?

[Lester: I decided I'd try without questions today.]

Why?

[Lester: Try a new experience.]

Mm. Anyone else?

[Lester: I'll have more for you soon, though.]

Okay, man, calm down.

[Alex: My question is about exploring things for the first time. My friend likes to jump in, but I'm more cautious.]

It depends what it is. I made a mistake a long time ago. My brother went to buy a house, so I went with him. There were these model homes in Roseville, but instead of starting with the smallest and the least expensive, I said, "Let's not waste our time on that. Let's start with the biggest, the most expensive, and then come back." So, we started with this house that was $320,000, five stories, 25 bedrooms, 90 bathrooms, and the backyard was, I don't know, like 90 acres. And then we went to the next one down. That was like a two-bedroom with no backyard. And it had no bathrooms. And then we went to the one to the left. It was just a vacant lot. So, the first one was $320,000, the next one was $300,000, and the last one was $290,000. And my brother says to me, "Which one should I buy?"

"Well, you have to buy the best one."

If you're eighteen, and all of the sudden you go out with a forty-year-old man – I mean a emotionally, intellectually, physically, and spiritually responsible man – and you stay with him for two or three years, and then eventually things don't work out, by the time you guys go your own ways, you're a twenty-nine year-old woman and that man has ruined your poor life, because you've gone out with a mansion. But if, however, you start going out with an 18-year-old, the 18-year-old will dump on you, and you will say, "This is no good." After five years you leave. Then you'll find another twenty five-year-old slash 18-year-old. He'll dump on you some more. And then after being damaged for a few years, you find a really good man. But this man says, "What's wrong with you? Why do you behave this way? You're like fifty now, grow up." Though you've gone out with so many eighteen-year-olds, and though these are beautiful experiences, you were never given a chance to really grow up. So at the age of fifty you have to start growing up. However, usually it's too much for an eighteen-year-old to go out with a forty-year-old, unless the eighteen-year-old can be trained properly.

If you're talking about the big stuff of life, it's usually best to go with the best. I used to go to the dollar store across from our carwash. You buy a hammer for a buck, use it for a second, then it breaks. But then I just went to Costco and spent two thousand dollars on a set of tools. That was forty years ago and I still have them. If you're talking about booze, knock yourself out. If you're talking about sex, whatever. If you're talking about video games, it doesn't really matter. I think eventually you'll just outgrow them, but for that to happen, it'll take like another ten or fifteen years. Were you talking about something specific?

[Alex: No, just in general.]

Are you sure?

[Alex: Yeah.]

Positive?

[Alex: Like 90% positive.]

Well the 10% doubt. What is that?

[Alex: Was I questioning things that I haven't jumped into or –]

You shouldn't jump into anything. Anyways, tomorrow we'll talk about something else. Have a good evening and thank you for all the food that you brought.

Chapter Three: Hinduism

[Dr. Jefferies: You say Alan Watts, the guy who was primarily responsible for bringing Buddhism to America, was married seven or eight times. If someone who is all about awareness and wisdom, as you say, could have difficulties with human relationships, then it seems that the skills needed for a quest towards wisdom are different that the skills necessary for marriage. Are the two incompatible?]

Nowadays, marriage is like climbing Mount Everest. Society itself doesn't allow marriages to stay together, because not only do traditional values no longer apply, there are also so many hidden forces that oppose marriage. Once upon a time we would go to the altar and make all these promises before one another, more importantly before God if there is such a thing, but society has changed. Consider what has happened to technology in the past decade. We've changed more in ten years than agrarian societies changed in five or six hundred years.

The truth is, maybe fifty or sixty years ago, no one would get married because they were needy, depressed and confused. But today, for many reasons, family life isn't intact so we become contaminated early. An intact home life is a place where parents are there and so you're relatively mentally and emotionally functional. This is a place where you're not hooked up to video games, you haven't suffered too much from loneliness and you haven't done too many drugs or too much alcohol. Without a stable home life, eventually we get to a place where we've made a lot of mistakes and imagine that a relationship can put us back together. If you enter into a relationship with too many needs inside you, your companion becomes your babysitter, you're her babysitter, and it won't work. It might not be a bad idea for people to say, "Maybe we should just scratch marriage." I don't really know how it should be done. It wasn't that people in traditional cultures had tremendously happy marriages, but at least there were some boundaries. Shame, embarrassment, your reputation, your name – all these components protected marriage by dissuading you from doing certain things that perhaps you shouldn't do. But those components are gone today. There is nothing holding marriages together anymore.

Someone asked yesterday, "How do you have a beautiful marriage?" And I think for the first few decades of your life with someone, it's going to be a struggle because we're coming from such different places in life, especially these days. We have different experiences, we want different things than what we have, and we have different needs. Plato once argued that we're like apples cut in half with a very dull knife, and to smooth these edges, these two halves have to grind against one another for about forty years so that they can fit together. And the truth is, we are stuck in old age for a long, long time. I have no idea how I got to be sixty, and I'm sure you have no idea how you got to be forty-five [Amir points to an older student]. We don't really know how we got to be so old so sometimes we'll say, "Is there any way that I can go and get some of my youthfulness back?" And the truth is, the answer is "no." Perhaps it's not a bad idea to go into a marriage knowing full well that's it's going to be crap for the first twenty years. And the last maybe thirty years of your life, she can change your diapers, he can change your diapers, and you guys can go to the hospital together holding hands.

Also keep in mind the recommendations from all the religious philosophies. Remember Buddhism: All things are new and in newness they're very exciting, inspiring, and creative. Slowly things live out their lives, and when they get old they get boring. And when you're bored, you're looking for ways out. I don't think it's a bad idea to go into a relationship saying, "Listen, right now things are really good, but just in case you bore me or I bore you, if there are things you need to do, do them. It's okay." One of the nice things about this culture is that we're trained to be emotionally detached. It begins when we're young with our parents. And then we lose the communication skills because of technology, then society is so fragmented that we can't be in relationships that have much substance. So even if we end up in a divorce, we're not going to be broken for too long. All of us in this class have a Black List and the moment something doesn't go well, we can call someone. That's how it is. Every culture creates its own diseases, and then it also produces the remedies. Since marriages are not going to last and since loneliness is widespread, this culture just gives people things with which they can entertain themselves. It's done a good job so far. Sure there is lots of depression and medication, but at least there's a remedy. Not the best types, but what can you do?

In Buddhism, when a child is born, there really is not much of a celebration because in that particular philosophy, life is not to be looked at as a journey where people can find success, fulfillment, and contentment. Life is always going to be a struggle because there will always be self-deception. If you happen to be a relatively mindful parent, you can love your kid, but at the same time, when no one is looking you shed lots of tears because you know there is nothing you can do to protect them. Buddhism comes to this realization through simply examining desires: how desire is created, what is their function, how long desires last, ultimately what happens to desires. Not the desire for sex, not the desire to take a class, not the desire to buy a car or get into a relationship, but the anatomy of desire itself, because all desires all the same. In the end, this tradition argues, the conclusion as well is the same.

[Denise: When you're younger, it seems that you want to give your all to a person, but as time goes by, how do you love yourself, give your all to the relationship, and still love another person? Like when you break up with someone and you feel like you lose your identity . . .]

A couple of things. First, I don't know if you've ever seen concrete being poured. When you're young, you're liquid. You haven't yet formed or dried, you're not yet solid. When you watch these big trucks pouring concrete, usually the concrete sits for about three weeks in order to set. When it sets, then they bring the lumber and the house is built. What you're saying is, "I'm eighteen, there are a lot of components in me that are moving all over the place." Like in the New Testament, "Don't build a house on sand." From the age zero to about fifty, especially in this culture, we're all like sand. And yet, for some reason, we assume that instead of sand we're solid rock and we can actually build a house on this rock. So you grab another human being and you want to build a life with him, but he's also soft and hasn't yet gelled or formed. And eventually this is going to crumble. It's the natural way of doing things. I would say, without offending you, that if you want to be in relationships for the next twenty years, all different kinds, you're going to have no choice but to witness these relationships crumbling, for many reasons.

First, your ideas about yourself are going to change. Life is going to give you experiences that you have never known, and you'll have no idea what to do with the emotions that these experiences inspire. Then you'll have no idea how to express these emotions, and once you express them you have no idea if your companion is going to understand you. So the time you have right now, which may be fun and good and pleasant, is going to be overwhelmed by all these different experiences.

Remember Dante's wonderful line, "At the age thirty-nine, I saw myself in the middle of the woods, and it's dark and gloomy and frightening." What he's basically saying about the human condition is that no matter how comfortable you may be, how much you may know about yourself, life is always going to throw you into this new place. It's going to be dark, it's going to be dangerous, and it's going to be frightening. And then you will feel lonely. You could be married or not married, you could have a girlfriend or boyfriend, but when you're put into this dark place, psychologically and emotionally speaking, you become single. In more traditional cultures, relationships were more protected because your life wouldn't revolve around your wife or your husband or children. In this culture, however, because we are broken into so many different pieces and the elements of loneliness are so pronounced, most of our relationships revolve around needs. If that is a little difficult to grasp, let me give it to you this way.

The divorce rate is much lower, usually non-existent, in other cultures. Parents know how to pretend well. They argue and fight in private. In these cultures, you're always going to have a busy house so you learn how to be a social animal. You're never allowed to express your feelings or emotions because they don't mean anything. Your tribe is more important than your individual feelings, and this is the narrative you're told from a very young age. You have aunts and uncles and grandparents, an entire tribe, that protects you. There are no needs inside you and nothing about you is broken, and if there is anything broken inside you, the culture has narratives to put you back together. There are no therapists, and there are no drugs unless you're going on a vision quest.

When it comes time for you to get into a relationship, you can't choose your partner. It's a taboo because as a young kid, you have no idea what love is, you have no idea who you are, and you have no idea what a marriage is. The elders of a community choose for you. You don't get married because you love. Instead, you get married because you're fifteen, and by the time you're twenty-five you need to have three kids and then you raise them and send them out into society. When you start relationships this way, you never talk about your feelings with your husband. You talk about in-laws, you talk about children, you talk about society, you talk about this, you talk about that. It's never about you, and your language is never personal Then you get to be 50, and you realize that your son is getting married now. You don't go into a marriage because you don't have friends. You don't go into a marriage because you're lonely, or depressed. You go into a marriage because you're full, and because you're full you don't demand ridiculous things from your husband.

These cultures create human beings who are, for the most part, depressed in a very philosophical way. Not socially depressed, but culturally depressed.

[Denise: How so?]

When a culture goes through famine, war, and a tremendous amount of loss and grief, if the culture doesn't produce the proper stories, the culture and its people will simply be erased from history. For all these different reasons, if a group of people need to migrate and change their scenery, psychologically and physically, somehow the culture creates the right stories and those stories protect the psyches of people.

Nowadays, especially here, the story is different. To understand this, go back in time and figure out what exactly happened to us. It's just part of how cultures evolve. If you live in a village in the South, you're exposed to only ten or twenty pieces of advertisements every day. And most of those advertisements are going to be organic: buy milk, or buy this car. Simple stuff. When you enter big cities such as Oakland, it's vulturous and there are half a million people occupying a tiny space. Remove time so that all of life is about speed. Remove parents, and there's abandonment and all these broken pieces on the inside. Remove relationships, and all of a sudden you realize you're amongst strangers. That's how big cities function. Add capitalism, which is in the business of selling images and emotions. Then keep people immature so they have to live in the eyes of other people, condemned by advertisements, Hollywood stars, and their friends. If people have low self-esteem, then capitalism can sell them things. Now they're broken.

Because we are social animals, because of simple evolution, you need to find someone out there. You need to hold hands; your body demands intimacy. You mind demands expression, and your emotions desire to be seen and felt. So what do you do? You have no choice but to find someone, and once you find someone, you're going to give him or her 110% of everything that you are. You know what happens when you invest all of your money in a single thing? You better hope that your investment doesn't go bankrupt. And I'll tell you: every guy you're going to encounter is bankrupt. So if you want to be wise, give this person 20%, and keep 80% in the savings account. When he has proven himself, give him another 10%. And I assure you, with the passage of time, you'll realize the 20% is too much. You will remove 15%, and you will only give him 5%.

There is nothing wrong with having open relationships, as long as you know that the undercurrent is loneliness and depression, absence of visibility and lack of relevance. As long as you know those things, whenever you move into those relationships, you also take guilt with you as a sibling. Guilt and awareness go hand-in-hand: "I'm not sleeping with people because I love sex or other people. I'm sleeping with this person because I'm looking for significance and I want to be seen, but in the eyes of my companion I'm not being seen in the way that I want to be, so I go to another human being."

Add to it the fact that sex is one of those things that brings us to life so quickly. Do you know how many hours you need to sit and read the Bible to feel something? Do you know how many conversations you need to have with your friends to feel something substantial? Do you know how many movies you have to sit through to have an Al Pacino shake your soul? But when it comes to the senses, we can come to life comparatively quickly. Though we don't know how we become attracted to certain people, when you see certain people there is an element of attraction, and like a good con-artist you create the right environment. Soon you're in bed with them and you feel alive, but it's not that you ever wanted the person in the first place. No: you want the feeling of aliveness to stay. And that's the thing – it can never stay for us. There is this movie Like Water For Chocolate, which says, "Inasmuch as we want to be around the sun all the time, we don't have the capacity to be near the sun. That's why we created candles." You can't be in love for more than a few weeks, because it'll destroy your psychology. You have to sober up. Our own psyche, in order to protect itself, removes love from our biology and psychology, and then you have to work really hard. In that struggle, insights and wisdom and all that stuff come about. And when you have the right wisdom, you become like the Buddha who says,"Life sucks," but in the right way.

But these days we're far too contaminated, so we get to a place where we've made a lot of mistakes and imagine that marriage can put us back together. But you enter into a relationship with so many needs inside you, and your companion is supposed to babysit you, and you her. It just won't work.

[Steven: You know how American culture is based on happiness?]

Who said that?

[Steven: You did.]

That's true.

[Steven: Where do you think that stems from? Because otherwise –]

Do you have any black friends?

[Steven: Yes.]

How many?

[Steven: I don't count them.]

But if you were to count them.

[Steven: Well, um, one.] *[The room shakes with laughter.]*

Are you guys compatible?

[Steven: Yeah.]

How so?

[Steven: What?]

How old is he?

[Steven: Twenty-two.]

He's no good. Do you have any old black friends?

[Steven: Not really.]

Get rid of this twenty two-year-old, because he's no good for this. Find someone who in his sixties or seventies or eighties, maybe nineties. See how happy he is. If you find someone who is in his sixties or seventies, he can still remember the days when things were rough. And you realize that sure, there are some joys and excitements, but most of these stories that this person will tell you are about pain and sorrow and difficulties. America is about two hundred years old, which is why it can have all these beautiful concepts, such as happiness and success. In two hundred years you can't really test these concepts in a real way, but when you have a culture that has been around for three or four thousand years, when you go to Africa, for example, they also have had concepts such as success and happiness, but African cultures have not been contaminated with the sort of capitalism that exists today. And these cultures are old enough to see how success plays itself out in the long run. And then after a while, a culture comes to realize that when you have a PhD, it doesn't really mean anything, and when you have lots of money, it doesn't really mean anything. Then the culture still talks about the beauty of degrees and money, but also argues that these don't create psychological or spiritual wealth. Degrees and money don't keep families protected, and don't make good citizens in society. With this philosophy in place, when you go to Africa or the Middle East or India, the educational system doesn't promise success. It doesn't work that way. They don't say that when you get a job you'll be happy, or if you get married you'll be happy. These are ancient cultures that have seen a lot of different things, and so they protect people from the illusions that most of us in this class have. These illusions stem from a young culture, which tells us that if you get your formal education, you'll be successful, or that if you get married, you'll be happy. Most cultures don't make these promises. Whether it's a culture or a person, whenever you're dealing with something that's young, you're always going to be dealing with a lot of ridiculous, nonsensical, and childish ideas. But when you're dealing with anything that's young, you're not going to get any substance. So, when you're done with this class, you'll remain a loser. When you get your Bachelor's, you'll still be a loser but a loser with arrogance. No one can save you. You're really messed up. You know, the best thing you can do is just bring me coffee. There is nothing else.

[Lacey: Yesterday you were talking about the Hierarchy of Needs, which need to be fulfilled before someone can reach for Gold. Don't you think that it would be useful for someone who is reaching for Gold to understand the suffering of needing food or water and of the more basic needs, before pondering the greater questions in life?]

Can you ask that again?

[Lacey: Do you think that someone who is profoundly privileged would be able to grasp and understand what it means to be a Jesus or Buddha without having gone through suffering themselves?]

No, of course not. Um, can you ask your question again?

[Lacey: I don't think I can.]

[Dr. Jefferies, who is a professor of psychology at another college, interrupts and give his analysis: Are you saying that in order to go on the journey of self-actualization, using Maslow's Theory, that you constantly have to have the experience of dealing with your physical survival? Well, Maslow argues, forgive me Amir but this is my field, Maslow argues that if you somehow haven't made peace with your ability to survive as an embodied person, if your basic needs for survival haven't been met, you can't go after self-actualization. Your question is that –]

[Lacey: I'm just saying that maybe you have to understand the difficulties of poverty, and not just be a privileged person who is just bored, sitting in

*a room, maybe lazy, thinking What's it all worth? I have everything that I
need –]*

*[Dr. Jefferies: I think you're right. Most people who do not know how to
struggle for survival are very shallow, quite often, unless their family has
forced them into a different situation. We cannot escape our embodiment.
You have to eat, breathe, have clothing, and if you don't have these things
your brain won't let you think about anything else. Unless you've got mas-
sive levels of self-discipline, like a Zen Master.]*

When I started teaching, I was very young. I would invite students to
the house and spend lots of time and energy on them. I would never think
about time, or my energy or capacity because I just had so much. I'm still
relatively young, but as I begin to age a little, somehow time shrinks and
my capacity is stolen from me. When this happens, naturally you don't
want to have a lot of people in your office, regardless of how profound the
questions may be. You become very selective, and you could wonder why
couldn't I be this way when I was in my twenties. Then, I had this wealth
called time, youthfulness, and patience. I wanted to be liked – there are
so many different components that allowed me to entertain all sorts of
people, for all sorts of ridiculous reasons. I'm not quite sure if anyone could
have taught me this when I was in my twenties. Ultimately your real life
experiences and your ability to process and understand, and then put these
experiences into action will tell you how you need to do things.

In regards to the basic needs, somehow you have to find a lot of cracks
in your perspectives about the basic needs, about your stage of privilege.

Can you ask your questions again, but make it personal please? I hate
abstract questions. They make no sense to me.

*[Lacey: What allows a person of privilege to start the journey at all?
Especially if they haven't gone through any real suffering and they have a
happy life?]*

Many years ago I went on Amazon. I bought ten buckets of razor
blades, I think they're called Gillette Three, they got like three blades. And
then I was sitting with like ten boxes of these razor blades, each box had
fifty razors, but then I watched an advertisement. They had come up with
Mach 6 where instead of three blades, it had six blades. I was in a position
of privilege. I had razor blades for the rest of my life. But all of a sudden this
man was shaving with Mach 6. And then I remember touching his skin, his
face, and I couldn't feel anything but smoothness.

If you happen to be in a place of privilege, only an advertisement that is far greater, far more attractive, far more exciting, for more mysterious and enigmatic than what you already possess will entice you. The problem is that we suffer from this thing called habituation. When you live in an environment for a long period of time, it becomes part of who and what you are, which makes it difficult to disconnect, detach, and walk away. One of the difficulties with the New Testament is that you have Matthew, who's a tax collector, which means that he's wealthy. One day Jesus just walks into his place, and he tells a story about the prodigal son. Matthew says, "I'll leave my wife, I'll leave my kids, and I'll leave my business. I'll just come and follow you." Then, as they're about to leave, he turns to Peter and says, "You know, once we follow this man, we can never go back to ordinary life." If whoever wrote these stories had filled in the gaps and had told us about the sort of struggle that Matthew went through, then we could understand the difficulties that these people experienced behind the scenes.

Remember the example we used yesterday about the value of being a virgin, as a woman. This idea is protected by tradition, by religion, by society, by politics, by your parents, where if someone basically says, "Do you want to be intimate?" you'll say, "No, not until I get married." It's a very habituated way of thinking and responding to this particular approach, in that it's created by the world around you. Then all of a sudden you sit next to this man, let's just call him hypothetically, St. James. As you begin to chat with him, he becomes more and more interesting and attractive, and he presents you a different set of advertisements. These advertisements begin to conflict all the stuff that you've been believing in, all the habituations that your parents and your great-grandparents believed in for thousands of years. And then there is an evening after dinner, and for some strange reason, he has the power to exploit and manipulate, giving you a brand-new philosophy of life: "I am far more beautiful, far more attractive than any of the traditions you hold to be true and sacred. Stay the night. Be intimate with me." And then you are.

Everything is about advertisement. But advertisement by itself is not enough, because you have to be in the right place to receive the advertisement. It's no good to just look at an ad that says Mach 6 if I have no money or credit cards. I will have only the desire and that desire will create lots of fantasies, but those fantasies will never come to life.

Do you like James?

[Lacey: I do.]

Do you love him?

[Lacey: I do.]

Like sometimes?

[Lacey: Well, yeah.]

Yeah, that's how it is for all of us. You're very privileged.

[Lacey: I am.]

You have a man. He's sometimes good-looking. You love him sometimes. Sometimes you don't, but that's irrelevant. What if you were to experience the following. Let's say you go to a gathering and all of a sudden there is another man. He has no intentions, and of course you have no intentions. And you sit and you have a conversation. But all of a sudden you stop thinking about James while you're having a conversation with this other man.

The only way that you can sell anyone anything is to break them. Once you break them, you create need. Once they have need, you're the only source through which they can be satisfied. But it won't take place very easily. We've been around for thousands of years so our defense mechanisms are powerful. We'll do whatever we possibly can to make sure we're not contaminated and broken. There's lots of people who are depressed, and a man or a woman walks into their lives and makes all these genuine promises. But if the depressed woman or man gets too close and emotionally entangled, they back away from this person. Now you may say, "They're stupid." That may be so, but their organism has learned that when you get too close to people, chances are they will break you. Why even take that chance? And you just walk away.

You know why this is so messed up, Lacey? Let's just say hypothetically I was relatively okay at my job. I'd have to sell you my age, I'd have to sell you my culture, I'd have to sell you my experience, and I'd have to sell you ideas. I have to compete with your youthfulness, and I have to compete with your gender. I have to compete with your American culture, and I'd have to compete with your American mentality. I have to compete with your concepts of entertainment and pleasure. Do you think I stand any chance? I stand no chance. That's how difficult it is to sell anyone anything that has value. And once you buy into the advertisement, it still has to be protected. Once you leave this class, I have no idea what's going to happen to you. What sorts of conversations you're going to have, what sorts of fantasies you're going to have. I mean, there's a reason why monasteries were created. There's a reason why we have cults. It's like a condom for the mind, which the world cannot penetrate.

[Louise: The other day you said that hope is for stupid people.]

It is.

[Louise: Do you think that there are circumstances where hope is useful?]

I'll tell you a couple of stories. There were two brothers, Prometheus and Epimetheus. Epimetheus was about to get married, but he had also offended Zeus. He was going to marry this woman named Pandora, and so Zeus created a gift. Pandora had a dysfunction, in that she was overwhelmingly curious about things. So Zeus presents a box to this woman, giftwraps it, and puts a sticker on the box that says, "Do not open. Warning." It's kind of like the Garden of Eden story, where God says, "Go wherever you want, except that tree. Don't go there." If you're dealing with curious animals, don't tempt them. So Pandora, being curious, opens the box, and all sorts of evils come out, and the only thing that remains in the box is hope. She closes the lid. The Greeks believed that if you want to know how to live life, make sure hope is not involved. Be realistic and know your environment well.

How many boyfriends have you had?

[Louise: Couple.]

Just a couple?

[Louise: Few.]

Few?

[Louise: Yeah.]

Were you hopeful when you got into them?

[Louise: Mhm.]

What happened when hope lived in time? Space? Realities of life?

[Louise: Expired.]

That is what happens when you put hope to the test. It expires. There was this man in the ancient world named Socrates. He had found hope in Plato. But he knew that the only way that this hope could stay alive and ultimately physically manifest itself, is if he bites Plato really hard. Socrates considered himself to be a gadfly and he saw that Plato is like this horse with wings, but because he's been walking most of his life, he's never really had any use for the wings. Plato doesn't know that these wings exist. Socrates is now in his sixties, which means that he doesn't have much time or energy, so whatever time and energy remains needs to be spent on worthy people. And he only finds Plato. No one else. Just Plato. And considering himself to be a gadfly, Socrates sits on the horse and bites Plato. Usually when you bite someone, they run away and they will never call you back. When bitten, Plato jumps a little and enjoys the jumping.

If I had called you the "n" word the very first night of the class, would you have dropped the class?

[Louise: Probably not.]

You would have. Most of us don't like being abused because when you're abused you're placed in an unknown and unfamiliar environment, and you will have emotions that you don't understand. And we don't do well when our environment is not domesticated because we lose control and power. What was interesting for Socrates was when he noticed, "I bite Plato with questions. I give him emotions he doesn't understand, and yet he comes back for more." So he keeps biting and biting until Plato refuses to walk. He just says, "I want to fly." He bites some more. Until there comes a point where Plato says, "I don't really need to be bitten to use my wings. I'll just use my wings on my own because I know they're there. And when I fly, I can see things."

Every teacher walks into a classroom with lots of hope. The moment questions come up from students, hope disappears. The moment essays are read, hope disappears. The moment even the most insightful student asks for grades and how their essay should be written, hope disappears. The moment you walk past a student on the street who's been in your class for two years, and they look the other way, hope disappears. Hope doesn't do well in the physical life.

Consider Fyodor Dostoyevsky. He breaks down the psychology of Jesus Christ and ultimately argues, "Jesus was far too immature and hopeful. He actually believed that human beings will follow him. He doesn't understand human nature very well."

Next time you want to go out with someone, don't have hope. Be practical and ask: Does he have parents? A car? A job? Money? Does he smoke? Drink? And if the answer is "yes" to the bad ones but "no" to the good ones, don't go in there and say, "I'm going to change him. I'm very hopeful." It won't happen. Isn't that true Elise?

[Elise: It's true.]

Hope has no place in real life. You want hope? Then be alone in your head with your fantasies. But the moment you try to bring these to life, both the hope and the fantasy will disappear.

[James: Sometimes you say that you can only learn when there's insecurity. But if it's the teacher's job to create insecurity, how can those things be compatible?]

First of all, the teacher doesn't create insecurity, the teacher creates a relationship. And when the relationship is created, and when the relationship is strong, then you can handle the insecurities.

[James: But if you have to have insecurities –]

Forgive me. I have this colleague who was going out with this guy for about eleven years, and she said, "Our sex life is really bad. We've been to sex therapy, and we do this and that." When she and I were sitting and talking about all of this, I asked her, "When did they talk about going to therapy?"

She said, "After four or five years."

"So why couldn't you do it before?"

"It's a little too early in the relationship."

You can talk to your companion about spicing things up when the relationship is secure. None of us in the class, when we're in a brand-new relationship, are going to go to our companion and say, "Well, do you want to watch videos and then do it and see how it is?" Because the other person may run away.

A teacher is not going to disrupt your life if there is no relationship. Because once there is disruption, the teacher is there to protect it.

[James: Well, okay. But you say that in order to walk honestly towards Gold, you have to have all these different things, like physical security –]

I'm sorry. No one walks honestly towards Gold. You have no idea what it is you're looking for and why your life is becoming so meaningless. You have no idea why you are slowly plunging into despair and depression and loneliness. I mean it's not like you see something and you're chasing after it. All you know is that the old stuff is no longer working. It's complete confusion and darkness, and there is nothing to look forward to. I mean, Gilgamesh just had King Utnapishtim somewhere in the back of his mind. Where this King is and how Gilgamesh can get there is a different story. All Gilgamesh knows is that he can't go back to his old life.

[James: So it seems then that the things on Maslow's Hierarchy of Needs don't matter then.]

You can't be unhealthy. Your body has to be healthy, you can't be thinking about what your father did to you. You can't be thinking about whether or not you have money to pay rent. These areas of physical life have to be secure.

In the Old Testament there is this notion that God is a jealous God. Do you know what happens when you get jealous? Has Lacey ever looked at another man? Does that inspire jealousy about you? What happens when you get jealous? Are you as welcoming towards her? Of course not – it's payback time! So when she texts you, you say, "No way, I ain't answering her text! I will wait, because it's time for her to suffer now!"

If the Old Testament is right in suggesting that God is a jealous God, you have to ask yourself, what does God care about in the Old Testament? In the Old Testament God is about justice and fairness. God has wisdom, power, and is all-knowing, all-seeing, and all-present. And this is what God expects from people, because He wants them to live in His own image. God wants people to be God, and teachers are no different. So of course teachers are going to be jealous if instead of being in their image, you're thinking about rent because you don't have money. Or if you're addicted to drugs, all you think about is drugs.

For those of us in this class that have been in relationships, you work the same way. Sometimes I walk into a classroom and a student is writing. And I think, "I'm not saying anything valuable or noteworthy." So I say, "What are you doing in the back?"

"I have a quiz next period," or, "My assignment is due."

"Please, then, don't be in the classroom. I don't want to talk to just a body."

So if you want to be on a pursuit towards Gold, first remember that none of us in this class know what Gold is. But also you can't be thinking about your boyfriend or your girlfriend. I mean you can, but you have to do that in your Caesar time, your Rome time. Am I making sense? We're talking about monogamy.

[Ismael: Do you think society would be better if we changed the use of religions, so that some people will pray for more economic status, while others pray for spiritual guidance?]

This question usually comes from a culture that has separated religion from State. If you go to India, there is no separation between religion and politics. When you go to China, there is no separation, and if you go to the Middle East, there is no separation. Because these cultures recognize the fact that there is a part of you that's Gilgamesh, that's sensory, mortal, and with desires. There's another part of you that demands meaning, that's rich and profound. You can't divide this and say, "When you go to your nine to five, pay homage to Caesar, but then when you go home pay homage to God." Because the truth is, in capitalism and consumerism, when you spend that much time in Rome, you're exhausted when you come home. And before you know it, you're like forty years old and you realize you've spent most of your life taking care of things that don't matter. Kind of like what Socrates used to say: "Have you no shame that you spent so much of your time taking care of your flesh but no time taking care of your spirit?"

Western cultures are the only cultures that have midlife crises. There is no mid-life crisis in China, unless they've been infected by Western concepts. You don't have a mid-life crisis in India or the Middle East, this is just a Western thing. A mid-life crisis is where you spend your life, or at least the first forty years, just taking care of your body and you forget that there is this other part that desperately seeks nourishment. Then you get to be forty and all of a sudden you say, "You know I forgot all about my soul or my spirit. I want to do something creative." And then you have to fight against this old life. Your job gets in the way, your wife gets in the way, your husband gets in the way, everything gets in the way and then you just plunge into depression. In a more, say, philosophical or religious culture, something really interesting happens. You know that no one works in the Middle East? No one cares. Indians, in the middle class, don't work. They have jobs, but look. My father went to work at ten, came back at twelve, took a nap for five hours, worked for a half hour and then came home. He did this for fifty years and never got fired. Nobody cares about these things, because people's identities don't revolve around their profession. If you are Indian, when you're born the first thing that you mother tells you is, "You're no good and that's never going to change. It doesn't matter how much money you've got, how much education you've got, how many people you're intimate with, you're just no good." It's beautiful! So nobody takes their job seriously. Really, I'm not joking, nobody takes their job seriously, especially the ways people take their jobs so seriously in the West.

[Ismael: Then why do people aspire to come, study and work in America?]

Americans go to India for spirituality, and Indians come to America for money. That's how it is. Indians don't come here for spirituality because they have plenty of it themselves. Indians come here to exploit the system, to take advantage of it. And the truth is, Indians will remain Indians. They will never change. Americans go to India, they're rich and privileged, but meaningless. So when someone from Africa comes to America, they come with a wealth of religion and philosophy and tradition inside them, that is never going to be lost. So people there suffer from physical poverty, people here suffer from spiritual, intellectual, social poverty. I'm not really quite sure which is better or which is worse. They're both very difficult.

[Denise: Hope and faith – are they the same?]

There is a man by the name of Abu Sayd Abul Khayr. When he was in his fifties or sixties someone goes to him and asks, "When you die and you meet your maker, what are you going to say to him? Because you haven't lived a very religious life, and you haven't worshipped God and Life the right way." And Abu Sayd says, "I know exactly what I'm going to say."

His friend says, "Say it to me now, convince me. If you can't convince me, you certainly can't convince God."

And he says, "I remember being in my mother's womb. It was dark and I had no power. And I said to myself, 'When am I going to be removed from this darkness? When will I go into the light?' And then my mom's legs opened and I came out. But they just wrapped me so tightly in this blanket, I couldn't move my hands, I couldn't move my legs, I couldn't move anything. And all I did was scream and cry. And then I said, 'When am I going to be free of this blanket wrapped around me so tightly? When was I going to be free of gas in my belly? When am I going to be free of the screaming and the crying?' And then it came. I began to walk. And I said, 'At last, freedom has been given to me.' Then my parents sent me to school. And I realized that I can't go anywhere or say anything because the teachers would use a ruler to beat me all the time, because curiosity is not allowed in school. I was again plunged into depression and despair so I said, 'When am I going to be free of my teacher's discipline?' And then I got to be like eighteen or nineteen and I realized, 'Oh no, I'm under the oppression of lust and desires. I love women!' But I didn't want to sin too much so I got married, so I could have sex. I said, 'Good, now I can have sex with this person. No more lust!' But the outcome was children. I was free of sex, but now I am in bondage of caring too much for my kids. I think about them all the time and of their future. And I realize that my oppression hasn't ended.

I haven't been fully emancipated, because I am now focused on my kids. Then I prayed, 'When are my kids going to get married so I could have my life to myself?' My kids got married and left the house, but then I found myself oppressed once again. Now I am in the bosom of old age. I'm sick, I cough, I can't walk, my knees and my back ache. I forget.

"So when God asks me if I've been a good servant, I'll say, 'No way, I never had a chance!'"

So for those of you who may die, untimely, and if there is a God and you should see Him or Her, tell the story to Him or to Her. It's like a checkmate story. God will have nothing to say. He'll send you directly to Paradise.

[Norman: It seems like life is a series of advertisements that create poverty, and then we seek to satisfy those needs. And it seems to be cyclical, like the Myth of Sisyphus. Meanwhile, it seems like the journey towards Gold is the recognition that all of these needs and advertisements are garbage. Why would anyone strive to recognize the futility of these advertisements? It just seems more fun or meaningful to take joy in pushing the boulder up, and then watching it roll back down.]

When was the last time you were intimate with anyone?

[Norman: It's been a bit.]

Two days?

[Norman: No, like a month.]

Do you think about the outcome while you're engaged in the act?

[Norman: No.]

That's why you can have fun. If we actually thought about what we're doing, rationally and objectively, we truly could no longer do it. When you don't understand something well, you invest a lot in it. You create hope and when it doesn't pan out, you feel betrayed and then you get angry and confused. It's true that reflection will ruin almost everything about life, but the nice thing about reflection is that before you make an investment, you will ruin it yourself. And then you actually enjoy it more. There is a man in the book called Tuesdays With Morrie. You can actually watch the movie too, with Jack Lemmon. There is a part in the book where his former student goes to him and they re-kindle their relationship. And in one scene, Morrie begins to cough and he begins to close his eyes, and the student asks, "Are you okay Morrie, are you dead?" And he says, "No, I was enjoying the cough." This is a man who knows he's going to die. He knows there is no hope for a cure. He is going to die. But because he knows he's going to die, and because dying pushed him to reflect intensely about his own life and his own death, he spiritualizes the cough.

You know this journey towards the Gold does nothing for you, except make you self-sufficient. I don't mean that you have God inside you. Self-sufficient in the sense that you know ultimately [Amir puts a cookie in his mouth] the excitement and joy of the taste will last like two minutes. And then it will turn into excrement. That's all it is. There is nothing you gain from any of this, except to know the outcome of almost everything.

[David has brought his father, whose name is also David, to class. Younger David asks: Can we talk about the tools that are useful in understanding things?]

What is that thing that you buy, it's like the thing where you buy steak and this thing turns it into ground beef?

[Steven: Spatula?]

No. Meat grinder. You can't understand, it's impossible. It's not that you can't understand, just let me explain. If only you guys spoke Persian. You're so impoverished.

Imagine life giving you experiences as big chunks of meat. And most of us in this class, they're like stuck right here. [Amir points to his throat.] You know you go to In n' Out and you eat a burger really fast and then you have to push it down with Coke? What the teacher does is slowly brings different components together to make a meat grinder There are all these different parts to the meat grinder and the teacher puts similar parts inside you, glues and bolts them together, then shows you how to turn the handle. And from that point on, you no longer need a teacher. You can grind the experience yourself. But until then, you just have a series of assumptions.

Plato once said, "Women will never have false children. Men, on the other hand, always have false children." Women actually have children but for men, children are their ideas. Their concepts, hopes, fantasies, and faiths. And eventually life will prove these to be all wrong. Students don't understand anything. Look at your father. How can you really understand what it means to be sixty-five? How could you even fathom? Grind the experience. Look at your father. Your sensory experiences will tell you that there are wrinkles, grey hair, and if you know anything about old age, body aches. He has more time behind him than ahead of him. He probably thinks about whether or not he wasted his time on his kids, because it happens to all of us old people: "I should have been a monk from the very beginning. I spent all of my years talking in the classroom to stupid people – for what?" Can you really process that? The answer is, "No." You can't even empathize. Sympathize, maybe, but you will never reach him. Students can never process experiences, it's impossible. You just need to be old.

Even when you look at Plato's writings, there's a tremendous difference between the early writings and the later writings. There are great differences between the speeches that Malcolm X gave when he was younger, and the speeches he gave after he accrued more experiences.

What exactly is it that you want to understand, David? Like what? [Silence.] No, no, really, like what? [Silence.] You want to understand yourself?

You walk into a different stage in life, and you realize it doesn't matter how much you understood the old self, it's irrelevant. Every new stage brings about a different self, a different image of who and what you are, who and what you want. You start from scratch. When your father and I started teaching, we were very hopeful. We never imagined that one day we'd sit somewhere and say, "When am I just going to walk away from this profession?" It's a great job, but you realize that despite the greatness of the job and all the benefits that come with the job, you're actually willing to put it to the cross, nail it, and just bury it. When did this happen?

There are even stages when it comes to language. In Hinduism the first stage of language is called Samaveda, where you just say things. It's like when you're a new teacher and you walk into the classroom with all this fear and stress and anxiety, so your voice quivers a little, and things come out but you have no idea what is coming out. It just fills the space. Then time passes and you gain some maturity and say, "I'm tired of just saying things. I want to understand." So you go somewhere and read tons of books. Now when you walk into the classroom you actually say things you understand. You've met my brother Iraj. He has all these ideas in his head but he's at the next stage, saying, "I teach Sociology and Psychology and they're interesting, but I want to feel this stuff and I can't. I want to feel what made Karl Marx write the way he did. I know what he said but Marx wrote from an emotional center that I don't have! I don't want to just come to class and talk about what he said, I want to feel!" So, for ten years he was okay just talking about Marx. Now he wants to feel Marx, and he can't, so he says, "I understand him intellectually, but so what? It means nothing. I'm like Google!"

So first you learn the language. And then you want to make this language meaningful, so you study philosophy, and then you want to make it into something intellectual and profound. But then you say, "I want to feel it." And you realize that at every different juncture, you're looking for a different understanding, a different processing of experiences. Most of us remain unsuccessful. It's something we talked about last night. It's not difficult to come into the classroom and talk about Plato. Both Plato and Pythagoras argued that math and music are about getting yourself to God. When this ancient perspective is lost, all we have now is calculus and music theory. Math is about order, about discipline, it's about training the mind, the soul, and the body. It's about harmony and balance. Now it's all about grades. You can understand Plato intellectually, but then you will come to realize that it's not enough because you expect more from yourself.

[James: My question is about Daughter of Fire –]

If I may, James. For those of you who may not know this book, it is about a fifty-year-old woman who was a little German and a little Russian. Her first marriage was no good so she divorced, and her second marriage was good but he died. She was somewhat religious, but she got depressed. Her friend told her that there is a guy in India who could help her. He's like this alchemist who could transform metal into gold, and water into wine. Her assumption was, "If I go to India and find this man, I can sit and meditate and I can be enlightened in like two days." And so she goes to India, finds this man, gets trained for eight years and in the introduction of this book she says, "My recommendation to those of you who seriously want to go on this quest: Stay away. Don't go. It's no good."

There is an experiment you can do, David. If time allows, sit with your father and ask him to talk to you honestly about his life, at his stage. I mean really, really try to put yourself in his shoes. If you were to do this the right way, by the time he leaves Oakland next week you will no longer think or feel or behave like a twenty-six-year-old man. You will function like a fifty-five-year-old man. And you know what's going to happen when you do that? Though you're a new teacher you'll begin to think about retirement.

You'll begin to question your marriage. Whether or not you should even have children, whether or not you should pursue a PhD. Whether or not life has any meaning. So it's best for you to stay away. Just appreciate your father and don't ask him any difficult questions

The journey that this woman took is described in Daughter of Fire. It's nine hundred pages long.

[James: Is Irina a bad student or a good student? Out of all the characters in the book, Irina does all the dumb stuff, but she's also the one that's learning. Do you have to do dumb stuff to learn? I mean, when Irina steps

*on the mouse, if Bhai Sahib wasn't teaching in the middle of nowhere,
she'd be damaging things around her.]*

I don't understand.

*[James: Is it possible to teach authentically in society? The argument of the
book is that you have to do dumb stuff to learn –]*

No, no, no. You don't expect things from people with whom you don't
have a relationship. You would mind very much if your woman were
to be with someone else, because you're emotionally involved with her.
You always expect things from people with whom you're involved. And
the more intense the relationship, the more expectation the teacher has.
Which means as a student, you're always going to fail. You need to understand what teachers want to do. You know how God breathes his own
spirit into us? And then says, "You're in my image, behave like me?" That
is what teachers want to do. Teachers breathe their own culture, their own
thoughts, their own emotions, and their own experiences into students.

If David and David were to sit and talk, and David was to ask David
about old age in a very serious way, what do you think David wants to do?
He wants to breathe old age into David. So when David talks, he can talk
like an old man, not like a twenty-six-year-old man. And there is a reason
why David doesn't talk to David in that way. David knows that this David
is stupid! Not stupid inherently, he just doesn't have that capacity. So he
kind of brushes him off and says, "Son, you'll get there. Don't rush into it.
It'll come your way." As a father he's not going to ruin a twenty-six-year-
old life: "Get married, have lots of kids, do a PhD, it's all good. Eventually
you'll realize that it's all no good. It all ends up the same way, but for now
have a good time."

One of the nice things about this book is that it argues the following. If
you fall in love with Bhai Sahib and if he is your God, nothing else matters.
If you don't intensely love something almost everything down here is relevant, and because everything is relevant, everything can push you around.
It is far better for a single person that you adore and worship to mess with
your head than have eight billion people mess with your head. Because if
this is the case, if nothing else can bring you frustration, then no one down
here can touch you! He [indicates Casey] doesn't care what a white man
or a brown man says to him. He cares what Malcolm X and Martin Luther
King Jr. say. Do you know what that means? That means that five billion
people on this planet will never have power over him. Physically, maybe,
intellectually, no. He doesn't care about white philosophy or about brown
philosophy.

Irina has to do dumb stuff because Bhai Sahib wants her to be like him.

[James: What about the people that don't do dumb stuff?]

They don't have a relationship. Do you like the piano?

[James: No, I don't like piano.]

Would you like to learn how to play piano?

[James: Sure.]

There you go. What do you think would happen if your teacher was Beethoven? Would you do a lot of dumb stuff?

[James: Compared to Beethoven.]

What if I was to be your teacher? I've never seen a piano. I don't even know what it sounds like. But if I find one, maybe I can teach you. Do you think I would find you dumb? Of course not. To Beethoven, you're going to do a lot of dumb stuff. You know why? He's a genius at what he does, and he's selling you genius. And because you're a novice, you're going to do stupid things. But if I were to be your teacher, because I'm stupid, I'm not going to have very high expectations of you. All the stupid things that you will do, I'll say, "Genius. Now that is the definition of success." You can never please Beethoven. It's impossible.

[Rebecca: How do you feel about people who say they worship God but only use that to cover their own dark motives?]

Have you ever dated a man who said he loved you?

[Rebecca: Yes.]

Is he still around?

[Rebecca: No.]

It's the same thing. This man who said he loved you, what was he really after?

[Rebecca sighs.]

You know, we have to smell things. Remember Diogenes, the Greek philosopher who hung around with his dog, said, "I don't think truth, I smell it." You have to be able to sniff things really well.

And we'll begin with the container, or the language or the most outer layer of Hinduism from here. About four thousand years ago, a group of people realized that they had to migrate. Unfortunately for them there were two alpha males in their community. These two alpha males were both profoundly charismatic, both had magnetic personalities, and all of the sudden these people that had lived in harmony and kinship for all these years are fragmented by these leaders.

Superhero one says, "Let's go to the South."

Superhero two says, "No, he is wrong, let's go to the North."

And those whose temperaments gravitate towards person number one migrate to the South, and those who gravitate towards person number two migrate towards the North. Those who end up in the South, eventually make this place called India. Those who go to the North, they make this place called Arabia.

India is a very lush country. Food just grows out of the earth. No one needs to work. I'm not talking about now, I'm talking about when it was first created. Exotic animals, exotic trees and plants. Because of this physical privilege, no one had to grab shovels or axes or dig holes in the ground and plant things and wait for thousands of years for things to grow so they could feed their bellies. They had plenty of time on their hands. You know what happens when you have too much time on your hands? You begin to go nuts. So these people would just sit, and to make this more clear let me put it this way.

When I was first created I had no food, I had no shelter, and I had no clothing. And I looked around and realized that I am a tiny worm that lives in Nature and Nature contains many beasts far more powerful than I. So from the moment I would wake up to the time I go to sleep, I am only seeking three things: food, shelter, and clothing. That is who I am, that is my meaning, that is my purpose. There is no religion, there is no God, there is no afterlife. There is no soul. I am a physical man in a physical body. I don't care about animal rights, I don't care about the planets. I am there to kill in order to survive. My religion is food, hunting, killing and finding a cave. Then I realize that life by myself is going to be difficult. I don't love. I don't make friendships. I simply exploit people. People are like tools who help me find food, shelter and clothing because all of my mental space is occupied by these three things. There is no reflection, and by that I mean something that you do when you go inside yourself and you begin to examine yourself. There is no reflection at this stage of our evolution. We think like tax collectors: "What benefits me?" There is no self-examination, there is in fact no self.

Time passes and you and I are able to domesticate animals and do agriculture. You know what that means? It means that if before I had to search for food, and shelter and clothing, I can no longer do that. There is no reason. Animals have been domesticated, so when I'm hungry I just go somewhere, open the fence, grab a chicken or a cow or a pig, slaughter it and eat it. So if hunting took twelve hours, now I have ten hours of empty space. We are not the sort of animals that do well with empty spaces. And for the first time, this thing called free time and free space, begins to torment us. Why? Because when you have free time, you mind begins to turn against itself. Food now becomes something of a luxury: Should I eat a horse or a pig or a cow? And when you eat all this stuff, you say, "Why did I eat so much stuff? What is wrong with me?" When you have the privilege of free time, thought and language and meaning become abstract.

This is Hinduism. You divorce yourself from physical life.

So when you read the Hindu philosophy, you realize that these are the most esoteric, the most metaphysical concepts around. They have over thirty millions gods and almost the same number of meditation postures. Who does that? People who have lots of time.

You don't find social activism, you don't find concepts of social justice. If a Subway truck was to park outside and someone was to bring in five thousand footlong turkey sandwiches, none of us would rush to get a sandwich. There is so much, so you're more than willing to wait.

That's India – the luxury of time, and the luxury of food, shelter and clothing. Those who go to the North find themselves in the desert. There is no food, there is no shelter. It's sand, it's hot, you find one pool of water, and that pool of water is supposed to quench the thirst of a million people. And these million people are all from different tribes, all fighting for the same well.

So those who go to India become Hindus and Buddhists, those who go to the Middle East become Muslims and Zoroastrians. Now when you compare the traditions, you find something amazing. Islam and Zoroastrianism are profoundly physical religious traditions. They are after justice and fairness. They are bring the Philosopher King down here. They say, "People are bad, they need discipline, they need guidance, they need policing." You don't find the same emphasis in India. So if any of you read the news, the Middle East is always going to be in chaos. Why? Because resources are limited. In the Middle East, people are raised and born to be warriors because that is what the desert demands. In India, people are fatalist: "God made me this way, I am in this particular social class, it's my destiny."

How do we make these two worlds relevant to us in the 21st century in Oakland? If you have come from a broken background, you have come from the desert. What you need mostly in life are physical, tangible things so that you can put your physical life back together. If you're angry at your parents, metaphysics will do you no good. You seek revenge, you seek justice, these are physical emotions. If you come from a privileged background, you don't much care about social justice. You want personal justice, you want to put your soul back into harmony. So if you are a desert person, you are filled with anger. Rightly so. Because things were stolen from you that belonged to you.

If you are a desert person the most religious and spiritual thing you could do is to bring harmony to your physical life. You don't need to be like Jesus Christ, you need Moses. Moses is a physical teacher for a physical group of people.

[Steven: I don't mean to interrupt, but I don't know that much about the spiritual teachers, but I was wondering if they had spouses?]

They did.

[Steven: Well does having someone depend on you, someone you worry about, limit you spiritually?]

It's a really good question, and if you look at the lives of most of our spiritual sages, or heroes, there's a few things to understand. First, human beings are able to adapt, in that we modify ourselves to fit our environment. Malcolm X loved his wife, and his wife loved him as well. They were very emotionally attached. Though she wanted him home all the time, there came a point where she realized that Malcolm X's emotions cannot be tamed or domesticated. This is a man that cannot be possessed. And this woman quickly adjusted herself, understanding that Malcolm may be married but he is not emotionally attached to the marriage or the children. He was, in fact, never around. If you look at the Old Testament heroes, David, Solomon, Moses, most of them have three or four hundred wives. And when you go to a buffet, you don't care for any specific dish.

There is physical power, and there is spiritual power. Do you know what happens when you have lots of money in your pocket? You don't care how you waste it. You know why? Because there is plenty more and you can always tap the reserves. When you have spiritual power, remember what spiritual power is. Spiritual power is the following. There is something within you that nourishes you, sustains you, and protects you. You don't need people or anything from the outside, except for the basics of life. Malcolm X is fine with or without his wife. He doesn't see himself as a married man because he is married to an idea. Moses and Jesus and Muhammad are married to ideas, and these ideas become their spouse.

Alan Watts was married a few times. His kids, you can listen to them on YouTube: "That guy was never around. He was an absentee father." And the truth is, Alan Watts never cared. And you know why? Do you know how he saw his kids? He was a Buddhist, so the moment his first son came out, Alan Watts wept. Not weeping because he was in joy, he wept because he remembered what the Buddha had said. "First of all, you can't give your wisdom to anyone. Second, all of life is about pain and suffering." From the moment he saw his son, he realized he is going to scream because he wants to be nursed. Then the screaming will end, and then he will scream because he wants to be tapped on the back so the gas will be released. Then he'll scream because he wants to sleep but can't. Then he'll scream because he wants a bicycle, then a pair of shoes, then a license, then a car, then a marriage, then at the age of sixty this kid will review his life, only to realize that it meant absolutely nothing. That's what Watts saw. You can't have fatherly attachments to your kid when you see your son objectively. Historically, women have never been on the spiritual quest because they don't really need to be, unless you're like St. Teresa of Avila or Bernadette. Most women are quite embodied, and they're perfectly okay with being engaged with life. So unfortunately history reveals that it's always been the women who have been forced to adjust.

The thing you also need to understand is the following. When a woman meets a man who is a little physical but mostly emotional and spiritual, it is true she gets attracted to the physical aspect of this man, but in truth it is the beauty that is expressed through the intellect, the emotions, and the spirit that captivates this woman. This woman likes that all the things inside her that she expresses physically on a daily basis are now seen in this man in a very abstract sort of way. It's like she sees her own image in this man and regardless of what this man does, this woman will never leave him. She knows that the body will come home, but the mind and the spirit and the emotions are always floating around. It's the woman's burden, unfortunately.

A couple more things. When this emotion called jealousy is examined, we find that women typically become most jealous when their man is emotionally involved with another woman. But if you happen to be Malcolm X, and no one can claim ownership to your emotions, the woman has no reason to become jealous, and in fact she doesn't become jealous. If you were a man, on the other hand, you become jealous the moment your woman looks at another man. It's very physical.

Interestingly, in initial Hinduism we don't have a soul. We just have a body and this is the only life we have. Once you die, there is no God to judge you, there is no God to condemn you, there is no God to send you to either Paradise or damnation, and there is only one philosophy of life in the early stages of Hinduism. You are an animal that only seeks pleasure. So before you die, take advantage of your body and all the senses that come from you physical body. Enjoy life, because this is the only life you will get. There is no soul to nourish, there is only your physical body, so nourish it well. If you find a woman to be attractive, gaze upon her, and if you find a man to be attractive, gaze upon him. If there are foods out there that are delicious, eat and be merry, be joyous. There is nothing else in life to do. Just make sure you don't disrupt the flow of society. Every society has its own etiquette and if you happen to live in a monogamous environment, have a wife or a husband, and find entertainments that don't disrupt family life. Your name has significance and your reputation is important, so make sure your definition of pleasure falls well within the social constructs. These are the first hedonists, who say that life is just about pleasure, nothing else.

So this pleasure they argued, falls into three categories. The first category of pleasure is called Kama. Kama Sutra, for those of you in this class who like to have your sex seasoned with lots of spirituality and philosophy and religion, actually comes much, much later. But Kama is about physical pleasure. It's about perhaps smoking and drinking and sexing and maybe playing football or basketball. It's about making sure that your body and your senses are fully married to the physical world. Pick and choose your pleasures carefully, otherwise your pleasures will bring you more pain. There is this guy, Epicurus, who argued that people think that pleasure is a simple thing but it's actually not. All human beings, he argued, desire lots of pleasure and excitement and fun, but pleasure is actually one of the most difficult and complicated things that you could ever do in your life. Because if you can't define pleasure in the right way, you will have sex with the wrong person. That person will get pregnant, that pregnancy will result in a kid, and that kid and that woman and that relationship will hold you hostage. And all of a sudden, five minutes of pleasure turns into twenty years of slavery. And he argued that if you really want your body, mind and emotions to have fun, first think well. Smoking can be lots of fun because you can see Jesus Christ when you're high, but consider what happens when you come down and you are left with a memory. Can this memory fit well into your physical life? Or is this memory of being high going to contaminate the slowness and staleness of the sort of physical life that you and I usually encounter? Do you really want this ten minute high to create an emotional conflict within you because it contradicts your slow and boring physical life?

The Hindus argue that all of us will eventually graduate from the raunchiness of physical life. Kama will only last for so long. You can enjoy getting high for only so long before you become addicted and then you have to suffer a little. You can enjoy watching movies until your eyes begin to hurt, you can enjoy having lots of food until you begin to throw up. There is an expiration date. When you go to school for example, if you want to do a PhD it will take twenty years, and that's a pleasure that has longevity. Zachary's Pizza will fill you up but will inspire vomiting after the third slice. When you drink, you end up puking. After Kama is this next category of pleasure, called Artha. Artha is about power, cultivating the mind, going to school, making money, buying a house and a car. Planning your future in the right way so that physical temptations don't get in the way. Many of you could have stayed home and watched a movie or gone out and had food with friends. But instead you decided to come to class, hopefully to finish this class with a good grade so you can graduate faster and make some money, buy yourself a nice place and a car and have a relatively stable physical life. For those of you who like to read books, it's because you no longer care about drinking or smoking or sexing or video gaming. You like to engage and cultivate the way you think about things. You have entered this stage that we call Artha.

The Hindus argue that both Kama and Artha are very individualistic. However we're born like penguins, in that we are social animals. Eventually you'll sit somewhere and say, "Yes, pleasure is good, money and power are good, but the truth is I want to share myself and my body with another human being. I want to share my money with another human being. I want to share my thoughts with another human being." And then you enter this place called Dharma.

Dharma is about society. Dharma is about you for the first time really becoming a social animal. Dharma is about you getting married, raising your family, being good to your parents, becoming a social activist. For the first time, for example, when you're in this stage in life, when you see someone poor you ask, "Why is there poverty?" Then you help this man or woman. You are a social animal and other people become an extension of you. But they also argue that unfortunately, Dharma also has an expiration date.

So, these three areas in life have one thing in common. They have a point A, which is where they create a desire. The desire turns into a want, the want turns into a need, the need creates infatuation, obsession, love, attachment, and then there comes a point where you might obtain what you wanted. And whenever you're satisfied, boredom sets in and you're no longer as excited. And all of us in this class have seen this happen. We buy a brand-new phone, i7 or i25, or you go out with a brand-new human being, or you buy a brand-new pair of shoes, you buy a gadget and sit there very diligently, looking at the manual because you want to know everything about this thing. And there comes a point where you just throw your phone across the room and say, "I need to eat now." If you have ever purchased a car, you know that you keep it clean for like five weeks, and then after a while you let trash accumulate inside it. The Hindus argue that in these three areas, you may be desperate to get married, and then you will get married, but then you will look into the eyes of your companion and feel absolutely nothing. And then you say, "It's time for a family." And then the kids come and you're happy and joyous and then you say, "When is he going to turn eighteen?" For those of you who suffer from intense, mild or soft depression, you need to understand that these ancient folks have the answers to life. If you are young, you like bodily pleasures and there is nothing wrong with them. They simply say, "Do those things in moderation. Think carefully so that pleasure doesn't ultimately become pain." There is nothing wrong with falling in love as long as you know that this love will ultimately suffocate you. Expect all of these things to dry up, and there is no one to blame, that's just life.

Do not be an American in that when you're ninety, you are made to feel bad for having erectile dysfunction. At the age of ninety, you need to go to Costco and look for tombs and coffins. When you live in a youthful culture such as this, with all these false promises and hopes, you create a group of people who are always going to be depressed, sad, confused and angry. Remember, this stuff was created some five thousand years ago. Drink – just to get a buzz. That's all you need. You don't need to get completely drunk. Get married, not because you love, but because your body demands security. And though they argue that all of this stuff will ultimately turn into boredom, at least you can take comfort in the fact that this is your only life. When you die, all the boredom and frustration of life will go away. You welcome death because when life disappears, no longer will you desire anything. Death is your Sabbath, your resting-place.

But something strange happened. All of a sudden there came a different story or branch of people that made life slightly more complicated, and not in a good way. Forest-folks, as they're walking through the woods and looking at things, say, "It seems that when something dies in Nature, a week or a month or a year later the very same thing that was once alive, but now dead, comes back to life." And they argue, "Is it possible that for human beings, who are also born from Nature, death is not our end? That we come back?" For the first time the concept of reincarnation is created, and death is no longer our salvation. Death is not the final destination because you will come back to life, and this life that you come back to is not going to be fun, it's going to be far more tragic, for a couple of reasons. This is introduced in a brand-new concept called karma.

The universe has a principle. Eventually it needs to balance its own scale, and justice must be served. If you have done something wrong or inappropriate, the scale is no longer balanced, you need to come back so the universe can screw you and balance the scale. So they argue reincarnation means the following. You will come back, and you will forget about the previous existence. Not only will you have the burden of this life, but you will also, perhaps unknowingly, also have the burden of correcting all the awful things you did in the past life. And they argue that all the stuff that you and I did in the past life falls into three categories. There are things that we do physically that create damage, there are things through spoken language that create damage, there are things that we simply think about that create damage, such as, say, you think badly about someone. And when you put this stuff within the physical human life, you realize that in order to survive you have to kill. You may love In n' Out, but a cow gets slaughtered for me, and I'm willing to have a cow killed for me. I love salad, but lettuce is destroyed. And the Hindus argue, you will pay the price for all of this stuff.

Before we go, let me change this reincarnation stuff for a minute, from something abstract to something tangible, visible and relevant. Almost all of us in this class desire to be in relationships, and we do so because for the most part this culture creates lots of social impoverishments. We don't have much of a relationship with our parents, our friendships are rather shallow, and we are emotional animals so we need to connect on an emotional level with other people. Some of you have realized that you keep going out with the same person, so you know that as long as your thinking remains the same, those networks of thoughts will create the same physical environments. In other words, if you like smoking, then there comes a point where you want to have a nice conversation with a man or a woman, but you realize that you were attracted to this person because, very much like you, this person liked to smoke or drink or just have useless casual fun. But then when your life becomes a little serious, you realize that just having fun is not enough. So you break up with this person, but your mentality remains the same. So you give birth to another relationship, you reincarnate another relationship, but it's very much the same as the previous one.

How do we change this? Well, Buddhism gives us all these tricks. It's a difficult philosophy of life but I'll tell it to you nevertheless tomorrow night.

Chapter Four: Buddhism

[Beth: You've said before that Sartre argued that we should be responsible for our emotions and our lives. Is this possible?]

One morning forty years ago, all of eleven of our kids rushed to my wife and mine's bedroom. Apparently, they had made waffles for us. I ended up in the hospital, but I ate the food simply because they made it. It was their first time, and I'm not really sure what it was. It looked like concrete. And the truth is, I couldn't hold them responsible for making such bad waffles. They're just kids. If you were to look at adults who are living as Socrates would say, the "unexamined life," adults are truly like children. The unexamined life does not require reflection, because there is no need. Nothing from the inside pushes someone to reflect, examine or think. Jean-Paul Sartre was French, and during the First World War he was put in a Nazi camp but not in the way that Jews were. Instead he was made to sit in a room and the only thing he could do was write. He didn't write much about war or freedom, in the sense that he didn't say, "Let's revolt against the Nazis." He knew that he was far too impoverished, physically, to revolt against the Nazis, so instead he wrote about the responsibilities that we have in difficult life circumstances. All he knew was that he was given paper, a couple pens, and the space to write.

If I were to tell you that I am a little sick, I would say that when I first got the news I was really angry. It was my right to be angry, because my life was going to be taken away. I could no longer see my parents, I could no longer wash cars, all that stuff. But I could play with this emotion called anger and resentment only for so long. Then after a while I said, "Do I really want to spend the rest of my days being angry, being bitter and resentful of all of those young people who are healthy and living stupidly?" And after a while, I said, "You know, maybe I can do something else with it." And I did.

I don't think the ideas of Jean-Paul Sartre are relevant. Most philosophers are very rich in solitude, self-sufficiency and ideas, and the tragedy is that the rest of us, because we are a consumer society, swallow these ideas the way we consume everything else. The assumption is, "Well, if I'm having a fight with my father or companion or getting an 'F' in a class, then maybe I can handle these emotions differently." And that may be true, but you need a lot of wealth and self-sufficiency, and you need to free yourself from social status a little. When Sartre was put in a room like this, he didn't have to go through the troubles you and I have. Sartre wasn't married, he had no children, so he had nothing to lose. He just had ideas, and I don't think that these ideas are for you. They're just out there for some people who have privilege.

[Beth: So we're not responsible for our emotions or our lives?]

Everyone functions according to their world-view. These experiences create our foundation, and as the Scottish philosopher David Hume once said, "Nobody can go beyond their experiences." You can't do something to which you haven't been exposed to, or trained to do. But this is not responsibility. This is just following habits and routines that are comfortable to us, and it is our "luggage of the known." You do what you do simply because it is known, or familiar.

Another perspective is this. Go to a buffet this weekend with your man. See how well you play with your palette, and the sort of imaginations that come and go. After that, go to another place that only has one or two items on the menu and see how you do then. There is no wiggle-room in a place that only has two items on the menu. Freedom comes only when there is access to a lot of different things, which gives us the privilege of option. If you only have two options, on the other hand, you can either choose this one or that one. That's why most of us can't understand the position of someone like the Buddha, who says, "My wife is no good and my kids are no good and this and that is no good." That's a tremendous amount of power to have. For most of us, these ideas remain exotic. You know how sometimes you go to Mexico, grab a couple of souvenirs and come back? That's what we do. We go to the dialogues of Jesus Christ, grab a couple of ideas, bring them back and spit them out as if they mean anything.

There is another way you can do this. Go home and YouTube Chopped. These chefs receive a mystery basket of a few ingredients, and they have to make something. If it turns out delicious, that's only because they've had a variety of experiences, and that experience allows them different perspectives.

Nelson Mandela lived in a four foot by six foot cell for about twenty years. Who can do that? Only someone who is able to detach themselves from their body and imagine a profound number of perspectives, which is incredibly difficult. Because the truth is, most of us don't like freedom. Imagine you're married to a man and he does all these stupid things. To exercise freedom means that you constantly have to forgive him and turn the other cheek. Do you really want to do that? You can do that for two days or two months, but for twenty years? Do you really want to exercise freedom? So I think the less freedom you have, the better your life is. The more freedom you have, the most perspectives you'll have, and so the more you'll have to put yourself in other people's shoes. And that will ruin your life.

At the same time, there is a man named Hafiz:

Bare qame eshq o roh gadroon nayarad tahamol
Chon mitavanand kesheedan in peekar laqar man

He says that if you look at our organism, we are a bundle of desires and attachments. Most of us function through these desires and attachments and the history that these desires and attachments create. And what we get from Gilgamesh or the Buddha or Malcolm X is that despite being so feeble on the outside, we actually have the stamina to walk away from almost everything in life, including life itself, and be completely okay. And inasmuch as you and I may say that these are wise and profound human beings, in truth they have ruined us. They don't allow us to live a physical life. Love ruins us.

The fewer genuine life experiences you have, the more freedom that you have, in the sense that ignorance truly is bliss. It happens to all of us. Sometimes you express anger, and then you walk away saying, "You know, I shouldn't have done that. I shouldn't have said this," because awareness itself condemns you. The best freedom you could ever have is to not to have any authentic experiences. I've been told that if you touch a butterfly's wing they will stop flying. Whenever you experience anything genuine, you can no longer exercise imagination the way you used to, and you become very grounded. I think you should be very happy not to be free.

On the other hand, perhaps Jean-Paul Sartre is a good guy to listen to in the 21st century. This is a secular and materialistic culture, there is no God and there are no parents. If he says that instead of going to therapy because you hate your father and you have the freedom to look at your experiences with your father in a different way, maybe you don't need therapy. You just have to change the way you look at your father. Don't think of him as a father. Think of him as a young man who had sex for all the wrong reasons, had a child for all the wrong reasons, and then came to realize that he was too immature to take care of anything, so he left you. Instead of saying that your father's a bad man, you just feel sorry for him. And I don't think this is bad, because we're not a culture that says, "God's will be done." We are not a religious or spiritual culture. We are very secular, and we don't have the religious imagination that our parents have.

Let me give you an example. It comes from Rumi. It's just a couple of lines, not very profound. He says that there's a guy who's really hungry and he wants some bread. He runs to the bread-shop, and all he's thinking about is bread. I don't know if you've ever been to the Middle East but what usually happens, or at least what used to happen to us, is that we used to stand in line and then we'd get to the front and the guy says, "How many breads do you want?" And you say, "I want twenty lavash." There is this dough, they flatten it out, there is this pit, this oven, the guy goes inside and puts it to the wall of this pot, and a few minutes later you have your twenty lavash. While standing in line, all that this guy's thinking about is, "Bread, bread, bread, bread." The moment he gets to the front and the guy asks, "How much bread do you want?" he realizes that this young baker is so attractive! And he forgets all about the bread. Like the story in the Old Testament about Joseph, where this person who's been in the desert finally gets to the well and says, "I'm thirsty, I want some water." He drops the basket down to get some water and up comes Joseph in the basket. And what Rumi says is the following, and I suppose you can do this if you live in a very poetic or creative or spiritual or religious environment. Sometimes you walk into a classroom because you want an "A," or because you want three units. But all of a sudden you realize you've been captured into interest by ideas. The grade goes away, school goes away, and all of a sudden you have another interest, which is completely different than your original interest. Rumi argues that you go into a relationship, but it turns out to be really bad, and you went in expecting one thing and all of a sudden God gives you something different. But again, remember that this is not the culture in which we live. Most of us are governed by expectations and the assumption that we actually know how the future's going to unfold. It's like buying a car, because everything in this country comes with a warranty. You don't get that in Africa. You don't get warranty anywhere except the West.

[Norman: For most people, the idea of self-discovery, or knowing oneself, becomes fairly important and relevant. But I have a problem with the way we think of it. So let's say we go off somewhere to learn about ourselves. I think that if we think about it in this way we're wrong, but I think for the most part the way that we understand things is not about the way they are, but it's about what they're not. For example, you need a reflection to see yourself.]

Do you ever find yourself in a mood that demands, say, a specific movie that has emotions that are relevant to you at that moment?

[Norman: Yes.]

And that's the trick. If you know the sort of feelings and thoughts that you want to have inside you, then like a piece of paper, you can put those things inside you and have those emotions. The problem is that I don't think we have the right heroes in our culture. There was a time that most of us wanted to be somewhat heroic, like Achilles or Malcolm X or Mahatma Gandhi, and when you asked someone why they wanted to be like that, they said, "Well, Gandhi is wise, because he knows how to self-sacrifice." What this person is saying is, "I want to become like an empty container and I want to go somewhere and listen to someone like Gandhi talk because when he talks, I am filled with inspiration and a self-image that I enjoy." I think most of these questions have to do with the fact that there is no one in our community that inspires us and allows us to be creative. One of the reasons why the Bible or the Qur'an or the heroes in these books are timeless is because there is something about them that makes us want to be like them. And I don't think it's necessary for anyone to go into a monastery or a cave to get rid of all the stuff that has happened to us in the past. You don't have to cleanse the mind or cleanse your soul. All you have to do is be around something that is tremendous. If that is a little difficult to grasp, think of it this way.

How many of us sit on a daily basis and try to meditate, but get distracted? How many of us try to focus, but instead get distracted? For someone like Rumi, the answer is quite simple. If you really want to become like a magnifying-glass, the moment you fall in love with a woman, ten billion women on this planet disappear and you focus on one. You can be with other women in flesh, but someone else has your soul and your emotions. You don't have to go to sit and meditate. Find an idea similar to what the Danish philosopher Søren Kierkegaard used to say: "I don't want to find an idea that I can think or write or reflect about. I want to have an idea that makes me live with passion."

You don't need to go figure out who you are. I think it's a waste of time. Just imagine how difficult it is to become creative, especially after having a very distracted day. Instead, go home tonight and watch Life as A House or Elegy or Like Water for Chocolate, or any movie that inspires emotions. Instead of sitting and reading the Bible cover-to-cover, which will take years just to create ten minutes of emotions, just watch a good movie and that'll do the same thing for you.

One of the nice things about the religious heroes is that they inspire interesting ideas, emotions and self-images. And so we pursue these things. Just think of yourself as that blank sheet of paper in front of you. You could write all sorts of things on it. You could either write something that other people want to read because it has the power to inspire, or you could write trash. No different than a human being. In this culture what you have, and a lot of cultures really, is a lot of garbage. You go to In n' Out, and there is this kid standing saying, "Buy my CD." "What is it?" "It's rap." "Why do you sing?" "I want to make money." So that's what this culture is all about. And even if your desires are noble, for example if you happen to want to be religious or spiritual, it's not going to happen. Not here.

[Rebecca: How did having kids change you?]

In 1978 there was a mass riot in Iran, and we were in this relatively new town called Gisha. The government was being toppled by the people, literally. And I remember on one occasion a truck came in, stopped, and all these soldiers came out of the truck and started shooting. The truth is, all of us wanted to be in the front to be shot. We had no fear. We knew that even if we were to fall, other voices would carry our spirit: "Down with the Shah! Justice, fairness, equality, democracy!" and all that stuff. Whenever you are able to relate to something bigger than your own time in history, your own gender, your own pathetic thoughts, then it doesn't really matter what happens to you.

There are lots of people who do this. My brother had a colleague at American River College who used to teach computer science. He received news that his mom got cancer, and he was the only person that could take care of her. So he took a sabbatical for a semester, went to Arkansas and took care of this woman. Then he called the campus and said, "My mom hasn't died yet, I need to stay here and take care of her." They said, "Okay, we'll give you another semester." The next semester, the mom was still alive, and the school said, "If you don't come back, we'll have to dismiss you and you'll lose your job." And he said, "Fine, I don't really care." This is a 50-year-old man who recognized that he came from his mother's womb, that this is the woman who nursed him and taught him how to walk. He owes this woman a lot. He lost his job and stayed with his mom for about three years. If you know anything about education, you know that getting a position in a college or a four-year school is a difficult task. It doesn't make any sense for anyone who is on the outside: Why would a man lose his tenure-track position? Love and compassion gave him the power to overcome his own egoism, the fear of not having money, the fear of pursuing another position somewhere out of state. These are frightening things to consider. If you have enough love or compassion inside you, you can overcome a lot of things.

One of the most beautiful stories in the Old Testament is the story of Abraham and Isaac. Abraham is a man with a tremendous amount of love for God, and so when God says, "You have to sacrifice your son," he says, "Fine." No different than the modern hero, Martin Luther King, Jr. He gives himself not only for his own people, but for people in general. It doesn't really matter if his wife or his children or his own life have to be sacrificed, he's more than willing to do it. When you live a small life, then you have no choice but to be fearful of almost everything that comes your way. Those who sit in this class but are not enrolled can walk away from the class at any time, or they can raise their hand and say, "You're wrong," because for them there is no consequence. They're here of their own free will. For you on the other hand, the story's different. If you don't show up to class, I'll just fail you and I don't care about your excuses. So you have a lot of things to consider.

[Casey: Aren't heroes imprisoned in a sense because they're compelled by something much larger than themselves, that they don't even understand? They're locked into a position of self-sacrifice.]

The ideas of freedom and free will have long been in debate in the world of philosophy and religion, and I am nobody to talk about them. Nevertheless, I don't think there is freedom or free will. Everybody in their life gets a buffet of experiences, and they act according to what those experiences have given and shown them. The more profound your life experiences, the more evolved and philosophical, then the more reflective and mature your responses to life-events are.

Tonight you'll go home and be inspired to do something profound, or something superficial. Let's not talk about the causes that bring you to desire something superficial, but let's just imagine that all of a sudden you become aware of two images. Snoop Dogg, who is the most superficial human being in existence, and Malcolm X. See which of these images will win. If you pay attention, one of these images is going to dominate you, and then remove the power from the other image. You and I are nothing but hosts. Things come into our senses and you can either receive them for an hour, or receive them for ten seconds. That depends on the sort of person that you have become through your experiences.

[Andrew: Often, and I don't know if you're being flippant, but you seem to be discouraging people from thinking too much, or trying too hard to follow the advice of the figures we're learning about. This seems to be a hedonistic pathway, in that you're discouraging discomfort. Is there any satisfaction that can come from the absence of discomfort? Is there any satisfaction that could not be classified as hedonism? One of the reasons you might want to study philosophy is to build a coherent synthesis of ideas. For ex-

ample, could reading Sartre be gratifying? I think that could be as gratifying as pleasure.]

Is there anything you care about?

[Andrew: Yes.]

I mean, really care about.

[Andrew: Yes.]

I mean, really, really, really care about?

[Andrew: Yes.]

What is it?

[Andrew: My humaneness.]

Why do you talk like this? It upsets me.

[Andrew: This is what I think about.]

I'm going to ask again. Is there anything you care about?

[Andrew: No.] [Laughter.]

Andrew, when you intensely care about something, it steals your life away. Inasmuch as we say all these nice things about falling in love, and this and that, the truth is, it decays you from the inside. It's a beautiful experience but the idea of living that for twenty years is devastating. That's the answer to your question Rebecca!

People who are pushed into caring for something intensely, maturely, and responsibly turn out to be the Jesus in the Gospel of Judas. They want to die. It's too much. Your idea about caring for humanity is really nice, but it's abstract. It's like Noam Chomsky, who sits in his ivory tower and talks about freedom and equality and all that stuff.

[Catherine: Do you care about anything?]

I suppose, superficially yes, but no, not really. Name one thing that I should really care for, deeply.

[Catherine: Then why do you get up in the morning?]

I get up because my organism wakes me up.

[Catherine: What do you wish or yearn for?]

Nothing.

[Leslie: Don't you even care about yourself?]

No. That's pathetic.

[Norman: What about your mom and dad, sir? I feel like when you care about something, their joy becomes your joy in life.]

Are you kidding? My mom is sick right now. It's not my sickness, it's her sickness. The only thing I'll do is after class, I'll call and say, "Hey, mom, are you still sick?" I can't possibly feel her pain. Caring means compassion, which means being empty and filling yourself with another's emotions. I can only feel her pain for so long.

[John: What would you be willing to say to us about how much or how little you care about your wife?]

I didn't marry because I enjoy intimacy. I didn't marry because I wanted somebody to cook and clean for me, or to give me money. I didn't marry because I was longing for a relationship. Because when you marry for intimacy, emotions come in, habituation comes in, and as you evolve and your desires begin to change, you begin to expect different things from your companion. If the relationship is rooted in intimacy, once you evolve, you won't have the tools to carry the relationship forward, so all these divisions and fragmentations take place. If you do philosophy the right way, you are able to sit in a room like Jean-Paul Sartre and write for ten hours. This is not a man who needs a woman to talk to about his ideas. A piece of paper is his woman. This is not a man who needs to go to the library to read books. His own observations are a library. This is not a man who needs money, and this is not a man who really wants to be in a relationship. Why? Because when Jean-Paul Sartre says something, there is something about his ideas that are immensely beautiful and our organisms gravitate towards beauty. He can find a home anywhere.

The best marriages are done for political reasons. Not for love, or money, or relationship. With a political marriage, there are emotions and attachments of course, but they're more refined. And there is another reason to marry. Most of us get old. And if you don't have the proper history with someone, you will spend your old age by yourself, all alone. You'll end up in a nursing home, especially in this culture.

[David: Can you talk about what it means to be in love with an idea?]

If we were to do this step-by-step and go back to the three categories of love, which are eros, philo and agape, we'd see that you can't first just fall in love with an idea. It's a bit too much, and we are novices. What usually happens is that you go to a place. Let's say you go to a church and someone like Joel Osteen or T.D. Jakes is giving a talk and you fall in love with the way that they are expressing the New Testament. And when you try other churches, it doesn't work, so you realize you can only fall in love with the ideas of the New Testament if they come out of the mouth of T.D. Jakes and Joel Osteen. They become your vehicle.

At this time, the New Testament and Joel Osteen have become one and the same. But then you want a more intimate relationship, in that you don't want to just sit way in the back and listen to him. So you go to the backstage and say, "Can you teach me in private how this is working?" At this stage, it becomes a very intimate setting. Because of this intimacy, it becomes philo instead of eros. And you have to be with this man in philo for, I don't know five or ten years, but after a time, suddenly all the passion inside Joel Osteen that drives him to stay home and read the New Testament for sixteen hours a week – this passion now lives inside you. The way he weaves in and out of ideas lives inside you. This is agape. All the stuff you love now lives inside you and that's how it ought to be. You become autonomous. That's like the Kingdom of God that Jesus talks about, that's the Light of Muhammad, that's the Promised Land, so to speak, perhaps Atman in Hinduism. That's the Buddha-seed in the Buddhism. That's the Tao in Taoism. If we were to go back to Andrew's questions about caring, if any of you in this class have ever been moved to write something inspirational or creative, care for those moments and protect them. It's almost an impossible task. It takes so much out of you, to be mindful and aware of your environment, who you want to talk to, the sort of emails and texts that come your way, the sort of emotions that you entertain. You have to dismiss most of them if you want to keep that seed alive inside you.

Rumi, the Persian poet, says that you have to be a gambler if you really want to understand this stuff, in that your only addiction should be another gamble. Win or lose, that's not your business. You gamble because there is nothing else to do.

The truth is, I don't know how people fall in love. It's a mystery. I don't know how someone becomes a Jesus or a Malcolm X. We don't know. I know that this is a "how-to culture" and everyone's looking for a way to get to this other place, but I don't think there is a way. This is like everything else that's out there. You can play basketball forty hours a day, but there's a good chance you'll never become a Kobe Bryant. Just as some people are geniuses in basketball, football, hockey or baseball, you have to be a genius in the spiritual game too, I suppose, or in philosophy. Your own effort by itself is not sufficient.

[Maria: Is spirituality real or are we just animals?]

For our age it's not necessary to use the word "spiritual," and I think it's better to use terms like being "creative," but in a healthy way. People can be destructive and creative, and I don't think it's a bad idea to be healthy and creative.

The problem is that all of us in this class have had moments of creativity. And that ruins us. All of us in this class have been devoted to our companions, but you go somewhere to get a cup of coffee and all of a sudden something about you jumps out and says, "I like this person and I don't really know why. Though I shouldn't be thinking this way, this person inspires me." There is something powerful in us that wants to jump out. Sometimes it whispers, "Creativity, freedom," and all sorts of things, but other times it shouts. We try to tame it because, especially as adults, our lives are very domesticated. We create a noble life in which we wake up at six, feed our kids, read a book, take a shower and go to work, come to class then go home. We can pay attention to a thousand things in a single day, but the moment you become intensely creative and focused and passionate, you're paralyzed. Your wife or your husband complains, your kids say you've abandoned them, you lose your job, your boyfriend leaves you, all sorts of things happen just because you've been inspired, in any way. That power lives in all of us. To take care of that is devastating. For the past ten years of my life I've been telling people, "Don't do philosophy." Just be content with these moments that you have. You can consider them to be Grace, like gifts from the heavens, these tiny moments that you have once in a while where you sit and write poetry. Because if you become a glutton, where you want more and more and more, you will paralyze the other parts of yourself and your life. Now if you want to call it spiritual, you can. You want to call it creative, you can. It doesn't really matter; playing with semantics is a waste of time.

Even the times when you wake up and say, "Why am I married? Why do I have children? Why do I even care for my kids, who are really out of my control and out of my power for the most part? Why do I love them?" When you really think about this stuff, in a healthy, mature way, without romanticizing these emotions, but objectively speaking, these things are not worth the love that we give them. They're not worth the money or the energy. I'm not saying you should abandon them, but it's something that my sister tells me all the time, especially when kids turn adolescent. "All this money, all these different activities. In the end, they're idiots!" These days, it'll cost parents half a million dollars to get your child through their Bachelor's, from zero to about twenty three. When you really think about it, you get what in return? For any of us in this class, if you have saved any money, you know how you want to spend money. You invest this money in a business that's not going bankrupt. Now imagine you have a child. This investment is in the middle of where? This investment lives in America, where capitalism, consumerism, the Beyonces, the Snoop Doggs, and the weed reign. You have no way of protecting this investment. Not to mention that biologically and psychologically, because these kids want to be explore life, they will rebel against you because they want to be autonomous. They want to figure things out on their own, and that desire to discover things for themselves will also destroy everything you've given them. Now, why would anyone have children? It's the politics of life. Rationally, it doesn't make any sense.

Now, I'm just giving you a man's perspective. I don't know how a woman is, but I'm sure that if a woman were to employ a good amount of reflection, she'd come to the same conclusion. Relationships are stupid, having children is stupid. You need them, don't get me wrong. You need them. But you also need a good amount of detachment and education, as to how you should look at your kids.

[Catherine: But why do you need them?]

If you're attractive and have come to be relatively self-sufficient, where in young age, middle age, and old age, men will come your way, there is no reason for you to imprison yourself to a single man or woman. If you have enough money, there is no reason. If you have a good, healthy dose of self-image about yourself, you don't need to. Having none of these needs puts us in a position of privilege. However, if you are fearful of getting old, getting ugly, and being lonely, you need a man or a woman. And the funny thing, Catherine, about life is that it doesn't allow us to be in a position of privilege for too long.

Jiddu Krishnamurti was a man who didn't believe in God, didn't believe in the soul, didn't believe in reincarnation, and to be honest, he didn't really believe in anything. He had been sick most of his life and I remember when he was on his deathbed in Ojai, he was moaning and groaning because the pain in his body was consuming him. He looks at his doctor and says, "I wonder what wrong I did in this life or the past life." If you read sixty years of his work or listen to his lectures on YouTube, this is not a man who talks like this. But life pushed him into poverty. He had no physical strength, his mind and spirit were agitated because of sickness, and all of a sudden, in a condition of immense poverty, he says things that he'd never said before. All of us, at one time or another, are moved into this position.

If you have the courage of Robin Williams, and you've been on the center stage of life and addicted to the center stage for the past fifty years, and life is slowly being taken away from you and being on the bench watching other people act out is not what you want to do, there is nothing wrong with suicide. Robin Williams lived a very full life. I think if you've lived a full life, exiting from life is not a problem. If you have lived a good life, but not a full life, then you will continue with your life.

If you were to examine a love relationship, what exactly does love do for you? It puts you at the top of Mount Everest, and there is nowhere higher to go. In love, you become like Abraham, but an Abraham who is willing to sacrifice himself to love. Whatever your companion may want, you say, "Okay." It's the ultimate self-sacrifice. But no one can live on the top of Mount Everest for too long, because eventually you have to walk down. Though this is a very basic way of looking at love, it doesn't matter whether you love ideas, women, men or music, eventually you have to come down. If people were to examine the progression of love, how love plateaus, and slowly forces you to come down, they wouldn't invest all this time and energy in these love relationships that eventually go nowhere. I think the best way to do it is to walk into love very self-sufficiently. You know how sometimes you walk into Safeway and you have a list and you don't deviate from the list? Imagine you have a list. "I want a man to have these particular qualities and these particular attributes. Any many who's here for my looks, dismissed."

Let me put everything that we've said within the context of our good friend the Buddha. [Amir takes an Oreo from the package and waves it in the air.] I have never in my life seen this. It's my first time, tonight. Oreos Thin. They bring about curiosity, awe, fascination, mystery, they are indeed an enigma. I don't care about anything else on this planet, except Oreos Thin. And I will try, in a very cunning way, to find a way to stretch out my arms, grab one or two or three and put one in my mouth and see how it tastes. [Amir eats an Oreo.] Delicious. Everything that is new is delicious. Everything. But remember, this deliciousness lives in space and time. There is a birth, it lives out its life, and then there is an expiration point.

The problem is, they're too sweet and if I have one more, I will throw up. They're sickening me. They're dead. And this is what the Buddha argues. In every part of life there is a newness, this newness ages, and then you no longer care. Think about the car you bought. Think about the cell phone you bought. Think about the shoes and the purse that you bought. Think about the book that you read that once inspired you, but now bores you. Think about the guy or the gal that you enjoyed. In the end, we become indifferent, and we just don't care. It gets old, it gets stale, and it's dead. According to our good friend the Buddha, [Amir laughs], life is bad.

The Buddha says that all of life is about pain and betrayal and suffering. Before this guy actually becomes the Buddha though, let me tell you the four stages he experiences. But it's only him that goes through this stuff. Not me, not you.

All of us in this class have parents that care about us. They protect us, they send us to school and they give us money and a car. Then they will see that we have reached an age where we need to get married, so we get married. Then we come to an age where we say, "We should have children," so we do. Then there comes a time where we say, "All this work for this? Really? Is this what my life amounts to? Marriage and children and house? This is my kingdom? A lousy husband or a wife, and a couple brats as kids?"

And then instead of being outward, you turn inward. "I want my life to be more than what I see." And this marks the spiritual, or the creative stage of our life. Our wives and husbands no longer satisfy us and we don't much care about our children. I mean, we do the best we can to alleviate their suffering and confusion, but still, we are more detached at this stage in our life. We become religious. We read lots of books, we renew our vows with God, with the Bible, with our spiritual friends, we begin to fast and pray, we begin to read all these fancy books. We stop drinking and smoking. When you see a woman and you only think about her body, you catch yourself and say, "No, this is not something I want to think about." You may have a dream of Jesus Christ or Moses, or this or that.

But then the Buddha tells us that there is another stage. If you happen to be one of the geniuses on this particular path, you say, "It's not enough to read books. It's not enough to talk to my friends. It's not enough to go to church. I really want to feel this stuff. I want to be seasoned and consumed and transformed once and for all. I don't want to go back and forth, I really want a good understanding of what it means to be a human being." He has no physical life because like Gilgamesh he no longer cares about his kingdom, his wife, his kids, his parents, and he longer cares about meditation and religion, about fasting and praying about having out-of-body experiences. None of those things matter. Why? Because eventually he'll be pulled back into his physical body and the body is the prison of the soul. And the Buddha knows this. You could have a beautiful dream, and that dream could inspire you for two weeks, but eventually what's going to happen? You will forget and other things become interesting.

This is a man who says, "I want to season life with spirituality." I don't want to be pushed into forgetfulness. I'm not going to allow life to breathe life into me, because if that were to happen then life would have power me. I want to be in a powerful position where I can baptize life. I will tell life when something gets old, when something gets sick, when something dies. I am going to breathe life into life. I want to have power over life. But he knows, where he is in life, the way he understands and experiences himself, he doesn't have access to this other world. He gets depressed and confused. But ultimately he accepts his place in life. There is nothing more to experience in the spiritual life. A dream, an experience. There is nothing to experience in the physical life. Sex, children, parents, money, drinking, smoking – all these experiences dim with the passage of time. Here he says, "I want something that stays real and true," but he knows he's not yet mature enough to have this in his life. So he just says, "I am just going to go sit somewhere. If life has anything to offer me, I'll be open to it. If not, I don't want to go back into life. It's not worth it."

While he's contemplating death, there are four stages he goes through, after which his name changes from Siddhartha, "the physical man," to the Buddha, "the spiritual human." He begins to understand this thing called "sensory perception," or the world as human beings experience it through the five physical senses. You could call this the plagiarized life, cheating to finding meaning. As long as your senses are healthy and active, life is going to bring you meaning. Images are going to come in, you're going to look at a woman or a man, there is inspiration or repulsion; you go to a buffet and your tongue will tell you if the food is good or bad; or you hear music and your ears will instinctually tell you if this is something that you want to listen to or not. And the Buddha argues that as long as you and I live through "sensory perception," the world has us, kind of like The Matrix. But once you understand that the world is temporary, nothing but a movie full of images that come and go, then the Buddha argues that you'll no longer want to attach yourself to or have a relationship with these images. As you pass over "sensory perception," you fall victim to depression, grief, and dread. If you're able to accept the confusion and anxiety and the fear, somehow if you're lucky, Grace will walk in and something will happen to you, which he calls "intuitive perception." Instead of looking out for answers, you'll look in for answers. Self-sufficiency. If that's a little difficult to grasp, think of it this way. If a person has no food in the fridge they have no choice but to go to Safeway, but if a person goes home, opens the fridge and has all sorts of ingredients, then there is never a reason to go to Safeway. W. E. B. Du Bois – his fridge is full. He just writes. Jesus talks to people for no more than an hour-and-a-half, two hours max. This is a man whose fridge is full, who can keep his own company, and who doesn't have very many needs from other people. "Intuitive perception" means you are nourished by yourself from within. Next time any of you sit somewhere and cry, next time you sit somewhere and play music or write poetry – that is what we call "intuitive perception," and you can't claim ownership to it, because it doesn't belong to you. Your senses have been shut. Your past has been shut, or if they haven't been completely shut, you use them as sources of inspiration. Something oozes out of you, then you sit back and say, "This is really good stuff!"

When you fall into "intuitive perception," in which your ego, your personality, your past and desires are no longer at play, the Buddha says you fall victim to this third stage, which we call "the end of desires." Desires come from the self, from a human being who has been socially constructed. Desires come from the five sensory perceptions. Sometimes you're sitting with a full belly, and yet you're slowly being pulled towards the fridge. You want ice cream because ice cream is in your head as a memory, as an experience from twenty years ago. This experience comes to life in your memory, and then your memory begins to govern your body, emotions and intellect, so you go to the fridge and take a couple of bites only to feel sick. "Intuitive perception" means that not only do your senses shut down, but your memory too becomes irrelevant.

So when you're reading the Gospel of Luke and JC is sending his disciples away to heal people, the first thing that he says to them is, "Be as gentle as the doves as clever as the fox, and if someone should ask you a question, don't forget that you are never the speaker, but the Father within you does the talking." In other words, if someone asks a question, and you want to show off, and you want to reveal how spiritual and insightful and intuitive you are, it's all about you and your ego. It is you wanting to come out and tell people how great you are and in those moments you need to shut up. If any worthy question comes your way, you need to be only a conduit or vehicle. But for the Father within you to speak, you must have elevated yourself to a very mature stage in life.

Now that you have "intuitive perception" and you are governed from within, and to some extent your self, ego, and desires have little say, the Buddha says you enter this fourth stage in life called ananda, or bliss. You live in Paradise and accept all sorts of things. You understand why people do the things that they do. For us, today, being non-judgmental is a very difficult thing to do, but not for someone who understands human nature, culture and condition. The Buddha doesn't say that only poor people suffer, or only black people suffer. The Buddha argues that every human being will suffer, regardless of race and gender and social status. Why? Because newness, oldness, and death apply to everyone. And I'm not talking about physical stuff. Even ideas become boring.

For those of you that have questions about gender issues or politics or this or that, just put your questions within the context of the Buddha. It doesn't matter the issue, because if that issue lives in space and time, even if you fix it, new issues will arise. One of the best things that protect relationships is that the husband and the wife will never get a chance to look at each other and say, "Are you happy with me? Are you happy with yourself?" For the longest time in our history, nobody had enough money to pay rent. Nobody had enough food in their fridge, and people had twenty kids because they had a big plot of land that needed to be worked. So the less privilege, the more protected your relationship. The more free time, the less protection, because then you begin to question.

Once you understand this stuff, this is what he says about life. We call this the Four Noble Truths. A couple things about the Noble Truths. In some of the Sanskrit texts, the Buddha argues that these Noble Truths are not for those that live in the Iron, Bronze, or Silver stages. They should only be expressed to those with "golden" or "noble" souls, for those that are questing to be in the Gold.

[Leslie: Is it possible for someone in the Iron to skip these stages?]

It is possible, but they have to be protected by this man named the Buddha, symbolically speaking. We'll talk about that in a minute.

So for those of you that have golden souls, here is the First Noble Truth. All of life is painful. Every time you have a desire, you're looking for a birth, and a brand-new self. And once that desire is obtained, that self gets old, that desire gets old and we move onto something new, something different. Life is suffering because nothing escapes death. No physical thing, no emotional thing, no intellectual thing. Eventually everything gets old, and then sickens us. There is another reason why life becomes immensely painful for us. For the past fifty-some-odd years, anytime I look in the mirror, I see myself. Every time I see a wrinkle, I kind of get a little depressed. The assumption is that I am my body, and so I am attached to it. Because of this, the way people look at me and judge me defines who and what I am. Because of my body, and because of the way people look at me, all these emotions are created inside me and I entertain those emotions. So I will forever try to keep this body young. I will try to make it look really good for people because my assumption is, I am my physical body. The next reason I suffer is because my perspectives about life are limited. I imagine that I am my history. I am Persian, my parents are this old, I'm a teacher, I'm a man, I'm a this and a that. My life experiences have created emotions inside me and sometimes I sit back and have regrets and desires. These regrets and desires make me depressed and I become anxious and fearful, imagining that I am also my emotions. But in fact emotions are like waves; they come and they go. They are not me.

You need to understand how difficult this stuff is. For those of you who are black and really don't enjoy people calling you the "n" word, instead do this. Inspire people to call you the "n" word. Deliberately train yourself so that you don't allow anyone from the outside to create an image inside you with which you identify. You are above all of that. For those of you that may have emotional or physical difficulties, what the Buddha argues in contrast to this youth-centered, self-involved culture, is this. If your emotions are not you, if your history is not you, if your body is not you, but you are only an empty vehicle which the wind enters then leaves, then never identify yourself physically or emotionally with anyone.

And there are tons of stories where students are tested. A man goes to this teacher and says, "I want to follow you. Am I qualified?" The first thing the teacher asks is, "I need to borrow your wife for a couple of weeks. Is that possible?"

And the student says, "You want to borrow my wife? And do what with her?"

"That's none of your business. I want to know if I can borrow your wife."

And the man says, "Of course not."

And the teacher says, "Well, you're married to your expectations, your history, your tradition and a set of beliefs. This path demands emptiness and depression so that something from above can come down. You're not yet qualified."

This doesn't suggest that you and I should put ourselves in harm's way, but what the Buddha is suggesting is that if you want therapy, go back to this man from three thousand years ago. Beautiful therapy: your father doesn't define you, your mother doesn't define you, your girlfriend or your boyfriend doesn't define you, your looks don't define you. Inside you there is this free spirited organism, which sees the body and its history as a cage and it desperately wants to fly.

The Second Noble Truth is that the reason why life is so painful is because we're attached to all sorts of things. We're attached to our bodies, our minds, our emotions, our expectations, we're attached to everything and when you're attached you expect. And when you expect, you have to defend the things over which you claim ownership. And when you claim ownership to things, you aren't being generous, open, or giving. You're always going to hold back. And the Buddha says, "There is nothing in this life that you could own. If even your body or your emotions aren't you, what does this say about the rest of life?"

The Buddha is not a life-friendly human being. He doesn't give us a set of ideas that inspire a happy, joyous, pleasant physical life. This is a man who will ruin your life if you take him seriously.

For those of you in this class who have a good amount of money, and once in a while you're able to part with your money by giving it to charity or a homeless person, you're not attached to the twenty dollars you give away. You're not attached to time that other people take from you, because you know that there is more. The Buddha argues that if you have fallen into this "intuitive perception," if you're guided from the inside, then you have lived a profoundly full life. And if you've lived a full life, it's like having a million dollars in your pocket. You're more than willing to give a hundred away. It's not even a dent. If you have lived a full life, you will no longer be attached to any part of life at all. You have lived like a god, and there is no fear of death.

Remember that attachments come from physical, emotional and intellectual insecurities. Attachment comes from our desire to domesticate our environment, protect our future, and know that we're not going to get hurt. These are all legitimate concerns, so next time you have a difficult time in relationships do not just take the Buddhist approach and jump right into yet another relationship, saying, "I'm going to be detached and I'm not going to expect." You're not in the intuitive stage, and that approach is not going to work out well for you.

The Third Noble Truth is that, though everything we've talked about is somewhat gloomy, dark and pessimistic, the Buddha argues that there is a way out of this, which is the Fourth Noble Truth. He says, "If you really want to live a full and happy life, there are eight steps that you have to follow." I'm not going to give you all eight of them, just do that on your own time. I'll give you the ones that I think are interesting.

The first is having the right images in your head, or thinking about things in the right way. You can call it meditation, you can call it concentration or focus, it doesn't really matter. What does this mean?

The passion that comes from the newness of things will go away. The sorrow that comes to you, as Shakespeare would say, "the slings and the arrows of this world," will also diminish. Nothing down here will last. Many of you in this class have fallen in love. You have been devastated and broken by love. It is true that it took you maybe a couple years to get over it, but you got over it. And then time passed, you ran into the person, and you had been able to examine the situation and say to yourself, regretfully, "How could I have been so stupid to dwell on this experience for two, three, four, five years? That experience and the memory, it was like a vulture sucking my life away."

Right thinking means this. With the birth of every new experience, with the birth of every joy that comes with every new experience, see next to it a tomb because soon this experience will be entombed and you will bury it because it will no longer be relevant, exciting, or inspiring for you. So if you have found a book, and that book is exciting, man, get yourself consumed with the ideas and the joy and inspiration, because should you go back and read for the second time, you'll be far too reflective, and far less passionate about it. You want to understand, not feel. So make sure it's the right feeling and the right emotions and it's the right thoughts. Remember, he argues that inside every person there is a Buddha-seed. As you'll find in one of the Gospels, the seed can either be sown on a ground that is hard, where it'll eventually die. You can put it on a good ground, but kill the seed through alcohol and drugs and stupidity, which the Buddha calls "negative behavior." Or you could give it "positive behavior," because this Buddha-seed has the power to blossom, to give you insights and intuitive perspectives about life, comfort and this thing called the "Kingdom of God." And so you nourish this seed by thinking about life the right way and acting the right way. If you are getting together with someone because of sex, know that because of the way we are designed, though this person may grow on you, the root of the relationship is sex. Don't build a house on it, and then expect this house to eventually become a home. It won't work out. If you're going out with someone for sex, be mindful and aware, and when you become aware, you will not expect very many things out of this relationship except sex and sexual pleasure.

This is not a man who romanticizes any part of life. He's very clear that everything down here that human beings touch, as Dante would say, turns into dust. So you won't get too happy and you won't get too depressed.

Next is right livelihood. Making money. Depending on how serious and intense you are, if you are on this path of understanding and finding where the Kingdom of God and the Buddha-seed are, you can't work at Home Depot or Zachary's Pizza or Gap or a tax place or the writing center or Kaiser. At least not at the novice stage. There was a tradition in ancient China of feet-binding. It ended, I think, about a century ago, and might still exist in some parts of China. For some strange reason, Chinese women who had very small feet were considered majestic and divine, and thus attractive. But what would happen is that a fifty or sixty-year-old woman would have small feet, but they would have difficulty carrying their weight. Or there was a show on TV twenty-some years ago where women who would always wear high heels because of social status and because of their work, and after a while they came on TV and said, "We have so much difficulty just walking because high heels are bad for our feet."

As a novice, anything that distracts you from tending to your soul, spirit or creativities could hinder your growth. You can work at In n' Out and there is nothing wrong with that, but you will treat your customers really bad. Then you will come home and punish yourself for not having finished school and as a result you have to work a job you don't like. If you really want to do this the right way, your physical life has to be in harmony with your spiritual life. If that is a little difficult to grasp, I'll give it to you this way. You've experienced this if you have ever been touched by another human being, in the sense that you've been in love. But if you have no idea how this other person feels about you, the longing and the yearning and the frustration and the anxiety and the stress, sometimes even the anger becomes so much that you sleep with another human being just to relieve the pressure. But because someone else has your soul or heart in their hands, you can't enjoy pleasure from the flesh. If you have a soul that's been inspired, the Buddha argues, and you want to have a noble soul, make sure you find a noble job, or something that speaks to your innermost.

When you are not a novice and when you are, to some extent, a graduate, something amazing will happen. Let's say you have all these beautiful experiences and you've attained the intuitive stage. This stuff called "organon" is now inside you and this harmony will eventually become "canon," or the law. When this organic stuff now lives inside you and you're fully aware of it and it's been active through your own work and effort and mindfulness and awareness, the best place for you to work sometimes is In n' Out. Why? You're going to get a lot of stupid customers but you know how to baptize emotions that run short. Now you can practice forgiveness and compassion and control anger.

And then there is dharma, a set of teachings. Because they are very demanding, the teachings initially create a prison. It's kind of like piano. You have to read the notes and approach the piano in a certain way, but when you graduate from this stage you turn off the lights, close the books and improvise. The lessons and the notes and the other things that the teacher has been giving you all now live inside you. But before any of this stuff can happen, you need to have a good amount of desire, which will turn into interest, that will then turn into infatuation and obsession. It begins as love in the sense of eros, where it's very physical. Then it will turn into philo, where you will worship this person who is teaching you. Ultimately through this person you will gain autonomy, and you begin to worship yourself. Not the self as a history, not the self as a body, not the self as a set of emotions, but the self that has the power to be completely empty, so something from above can be poured in.

[David: Is that why in the movie Monsieur Ibrahim, this teacher can work as a grocer even though he's very religious, and a philosopher, and all those things? Because he's advanced?]

Teachers come in a variety of forms. There are those who are loud, those who are quiet, there are those who are butchers. There is no one way of being a teacher. What they all have in common is that they have this thing about them called Beauty, and I think if you were to get to know them a little, they would make a home for you, and they would also give you a set of teachings. If you're talking about Monsieur Ibrahim, one of the things you need to consider is that teachers don't usually assume the role of a teacher. They usually enjoy being invisible.

Another thing is this, something that we haven't talked about yet. In Buddhism, when you become a teacher, or when you tap into this intuitive part of yourself, somehow you will begin to have magical powers. There is an account of a woman named Betty Eadie, who had a near-death experience and then wrote about it in this book called Embraced by the Light. She wrote this account after she had an experience where she was pronounced dead, but then saw all these spiritual beings and was completely transformed. When she came back to life she had the power to see how people are from the inside. In Buddhism this is called "past incarnations." In other words, the Buddha can look at you and see why you are the way you are, why you have addictions and habituations, and he also knows how many lives you have lived and why in this particular life you have all these issues. And then he can give you the right remedy.

[David: How can Monsieur Ibrahim be both a teacher and a grocer?]

I don't know what your definition of a teacher is. If you are this thirsty and this cup [Amir holds us his coffee mug] could quench your thirst, and if I'm carry a ten-gallon bucket on my shoulder, then I'm not going to say to you, "I have ten gallons and you have to drink all of it." The truth is, what I have to give will damage you. Because of where we are in life, we have to be given the right amount of things. Most of us should be glad, as Dostoyevsky would say, that Jesus Christ is not our teacher and that the Buddha has not come back to guide us. They have too much to give us and that's not what we want. I just want my relationship to be fixed, I want my sex life to be better, I really just want to make more money, or I just want black people and white people to live well together. I mean, these are what I want but the Buddha gives me things that I can't handle. He wants me to look at humanity at large, at the human condition. That's not what I want. We have this idea that teachers are a one-size-fits-all, and that's not the case. Teachers give different things to different people because people have different needs and capacities. In the movie Monsieur Ibrahim lives in France, he is from Turkey, he runs into a tiny boy named Momo whose mom has died and father has killed himself and he's got no money, he's got nothing. The only thing Monsieur Ibrahim says is, "I don't need any friends, I just need my Qur'an." Why would you want to talk to people when you can read the Bible? Why would you want to watch raunchy movies when the Bible can create the proper images in your head? Why would you want to drink when the Bible can get you high? But give the Bible to someone who's not at the proper stage and they will become an atheist, and the you'll have to spend twenty years giving them religious components before you can give them the Bible again.

[Casey: I read somewhere that Buddhism is an extension of Hinduism in some ways. Is that true?]

Yeah, that was Huston Smith. He was stupid but he's dead now so we should be kind to him. But I don't think anything is an extension of anything. Let's just say the Buddha's parents were Hindu, but there comes a point in this man's spiritual evolution where Hinduism no longer works for him. Afterwards, he becomes the fountainhead of a new tradition where they say, "If you're awakened, your name becomes the Buddha." But it's like saying Malcolm X created "X-ism." "X" is short for ex-smoker, ex-this and ex-that, but X is also for the enigma. He belongs to a mystery – you can't define Malcolm X. You can't tell him that he's black or white or blue or yellow, that he's Muslim or Christian. Sure, Siddhartha or the Buddha had some ideas about Hinduism, but the truth is, Hinduism failed to nourish him and like every good student, he walks away from the whole thing and says, like Moses, "If there is a God, I want to see him." And this is the way God revealed himself to the Buddha: There is no God, there is no self. He's really just doing the Ten Commandments in a really creative, spiritual way. No graven images of anything, you can't worship the images in your head, and you can't even speak of it.

[Lester: Jainism as far as I understand it is a, well, you just said that there's no extensions of Hinduism, so . . . What is Jainism?]

There's a guy whose name is Mahavira and a lot of people say that he didn't really exist because his life was very much like the Buddha's. He left his parents, he left his wife, and he left his kids and renounced everything. In some time, when he became enlightened he said, "I just don't want to harm anyone." Kind of like when Albert Schweitzer was a young kid, his prayers would be, "I don't want human beings to suffer. I also don't want flies to suffer. I want horses to always be fed," and that's what Mahavira's all about. Make sure no one suffers because of you.

[Lester: And how's that different from Buddhism?]

It's not. All of these traditions are saying the same thing in a different way. If we spend this entire six weeks just talking about Hinduism, we would have covered all the traditions. But because we are such a literal sort of people, if someone labels themselves a "Christian," they will say, "You know, I signed up for a World Religions class and you never mentioned Jesus Christ."

[Tyler: So –]

Who are you?

[Tyler: I'm Tyler. I was here maybe six months ago.]

Oh that's right, Tyler. It's good to see you.

[Tyler: And you. I'm getting the sense that we are sematic people, and you are talking about developing perceptions in the Noble Path and the Noble Truths. When we define the sangha, and we're to be aware of socially conditioned identities that we attach to, how do we discern what is "right" for one sangha is actually what the Buddha would talk about? The communities of choice would ideally be something that could bring out this intuitive perception. How do we check in with ourselves, where we get to that place where we're really a bit more sure, apart from the social identity from which the sangha is teaching us?]

Can you say this differently?

[Tyler: How do you determine what's right in a sangha?]

How can you make sure that you're not being deceived?

[Tyler: Yes.]

You can't.

[Tyler: There's no method?]

You can never know. Someone asked this question last week. No one knows. I think the best way that we could answer this question is the following. I'll tell you a story.

There was a woman and she had grown tired of dating these losers so she called her friends and said, "I'm not going to date anymore. I'm just going to get myself outside, and then go back in when I'm ready." When she was out, she created a list of qualities and attributes she wanted in a man. It's like when you look in your fridge, see what you have and what you don't have, and then list the things that you don't have so you don't spend too much money on things you don't use. And so after two or two-and-a-half years, she calls her friends and says, "I am ready. So if you think that there is a man out there with these qualities, have him give me a call. Just give him my number, you don't need to ask me." So this Indian guy calls her, and she was white. They go out on a date to this really fancy restaurant and she took her list with her. And as the date was progressing, she cheated. She looked at her list, and she would ask pointed questions, and then he would answer them. What she didn't know, is that this man had also taken a break from dating. He also had his own list. Things meshed really well on the date, and two months later they were married.

The first thing you need to ask is, "Why would people create a list?" How does someone create a list for shopping? Well, you open the fridge, and you have no illusions. You don't create fantasies, that the milk is not there, but you say, "Well, I see milk there, so I don't need milk." You actually realize that there is no milk, no cheese, no bread, no lettuce, and you put the list together and go. And when you have the list, and when you're on a budget, almost every aisle in Safeway disappears except the lettuce, cheese, and milk aisles. Sincerity deletes most of the inessentials.

Two months into the marriage, the woman doesn't feel well. They go the hospital and she takes an MRI, and it's found that she has MS. Six months later, she can't walk, she can't hear, she can't see, she can't do anything. She takes pills and the pills that you take when you have MS just expand your body. One day this man is giving her a bath and she looks at him and says, "I'm very, very sorry for having destroyed your life." And he says, "I have never been with a more beautiful woman."

And I say this for the following reason. You have to have been a very, very self-serving, self-deceiving student for a long, long time until you just say, "I am tired of this game I play with myself. I really want to understand. I really want to know." And when that happens, no one can ever deceive you, it's impossible. Ultimately, the best measurement is your own clarity of what exactly it is that you want. If you want someone to play the father-figure for you, you'll be deceived. If you're after power, you'll be deceived. If you're about showing off who and what you are, you'll be deceived. One of the remarkable things about Malcolm X is that he was really sincere. He didn't want the microphone, he didn't want the power, and he came back from his pilgrimage as a solitary man. You have to be very clear as to who and what you are, and what exactly it is that you want. Why are you reading these books? Why are you asking these questions?

When you're very clear and when you find someone who you find to be spiritually or emotionally or intellectually beautiful, you'll give yourself to this person completely. But if you're walking around having childish needs and fantasies about "wanting to become spiritual," or "intellectual," I think you'll fall.

The mark of a good teacher is to bring to your attention that this is not about what you think it is. Good teachers usually just push you away. How old are you?

[Tyler: Forty-eight.]

I have this eighteen-year-old friend that wants to date older men. I think she will like you. I mean, she's not very mature, but she's very attractive. Would you like me to give her your phone number?

[Tyler: I'm ambivalent.]

You're "ambivalent"? Is that like a "yes" or a "no"?

[Tyler: It's impartial. I don't know.]

The answer, Tyler, is no. And it's no because you're not in the baby-sitting business at your age. I mean, sure it'll make you feel good that you're relevant and significant and visible, that an eighteen-year-old would show interest in you. But the eighteen-year-old needs a lot of work to think and feel like a forty- or fifty-year old woman so that you can build a home together. For someone's who's wasted a lot of time, as all of us in this class have, sure the eighteen-year-old may be very attractive, but all pleasures that come from pursuing intimacy are the same, and with some age and some clarity and some observation you'll realize that the eighteen-year-old is nice, and she can be your therapist perhaps, but when it comes to an actual relationship, it's a different story. That is what clarity is.

I had a friend who had a taste of what this spiritual stuff is all about, like Buddhism and Hinduism, and she got frightened because it began to seep into her life and the sort of organisms that we are, we have a tendency of seeking domestication, so she got rid of all that stuff. I was there when she approached this teacher who had come from Kazakhstan, she turns to him and says, "I really want this stuff. I'm just afraid." And the teacher didn't try to calm her fears. He looked at her, and we were all there, and he said, "They'll get worse." But it's interesting how she came back. She wasn't as open. She knew the consequences.

Some of the pointers are that if someone says that they're a good teacher, they're usually not. And teachers usually come without having a name, without having a face. In other words, you don't really know why you're attracted to them, you don't really know why you're interested in them, and you don't really know why you want to be around them. The most interesting teachers are the most vulgar ones, and they're usually about ninety years old.

[Rebecca: Do you think it's a waste of time to try and disprove something that isn't able to be proved, like Kant and how he spent a lot of years of his life?]

Immanuel Kant comes around the 18th century, also called the Age of Reason or the Enlightenment, when feelings and sentiments were less valued. Though he was also a very religious man, whatever that may mean for 18th century folks, Immanuel Kant prized rationality and reason above all things. David Hume was an atheist and he wanted to prove that there is no religious self and that there is no God. I think Kant was an idiot, to be honest. I think most of the Western philosophers are idiots, no offense to my Western friends. When you have something that's valuable, I don't think you force others to buy it. Instead, people should grow to appreciate what you have, and then they can receive it. Immanuel Kant is one of those people who is forcing others to buy his ideas, which primarily revolve around, "David Hume's wrong because of A, B, C."

When you go to your own gatherings and see someone who's very mature, who's experienced war in Serbia perhaps, you see this. It's true that old people like young people are passionate when it comes to war and all this stuff, but just watch someone who's really tasted the war, who's sat back and observed the mayhem and all these emotions. Usually this person just sits and watches people like dogs biting each other with conversation. When someone approaches this person directly, then he or she will say a few things, and what this person says is going to be very different than what the other people in the gathering say.

There is a really good movie called The Last Castle. Robert Redford plays a captain who does something wrong and ends up in prison. The person who is running the prison is sitting in a room above the yard where the inmates are, and he looks at a guard and says, "I want to show you the difference between maturity and immaturity." A fight is created between two inmates and then two gangs jump in. Everybody's shouting and screaming and hollering except a captain, Robert Redford. This captain stands back and watches the whole thing, refusing to get involved in the fight. He knows that emotionally, we are far too easily contaminated. You look at someone, they have gorgeous face and emotionally they trap you. Someone says beautiful, flowery words and they trap you. Someone says a few things about Rumi and they trap you.

It is best to stand on the outside and just watch, and when someone wants to come and seek advice, just see where they are. One person will seek advice, and the best reply is, "Listen, you're just a tax collector. You're not really here to really know what I'm saying, you're doing it for your own benefit." But then there is another guy who comes and asks for advice, and then you should give him advice. Good teachers are like that. They don't give that which is valuable freely, and you'll find the same statement in the Gospel of maybe Matthew, "Don't give that which is holy unto dogs." Most of us are dogs, in that we want to lick the bones, eat the meat then walk away from the whole thing. And Jesus says, "You know what, if you have really worked hard for something, it has a tremendous amount of value." And a person who has experienced life fully, observantly, and reflectively, is not going to get emotional about anything, unless it's worth their time. I think that's the reason why these people have so few students. They're not ready to lower themselves for others.

[David: Can we talk more about "right images"? How do images, on the outside and on the inside, affect our thinking?]

Is there a food that you don't like, David? That makes you vomit? [David nods.] What is it, so that I can make it for you next time?

[David: Cauliflower.]

So, when I say "cauliflower," what happens to you? When I say "cauliflower," images come up in you. Images go back to your experience. You have no idea how it happens. I say, "Cauliflower," you think back to when you were like ten, your girlfriend shoved this cauliflower down your throat, you almost choked to death, you hated her, she beat you up, you killed her, you served time, then you got released so every time I say "cauliflower," all that stuff comes up. Right?

[David: Right.]

Now, when all those things come up, there are all these emotions connected to cauliflower. Emotions fall into two different categories: pleasant and not-so-pleasant. Do you know why you have those emotions about cauliflower? Because it's rooted in real life experiences. You have a palette, you have real taste buds, and because of this there are no illusions or self-deceptions. You don't yet have a soul and because there is no soul, there is no tongue, and because there is no tongue, there is no palette, and so you don't have taste buds. And because there are no taste buds, you are more than willing to consume all sorts of things. When you begin to see glimpses of your own soul—or whatever word you want to use, consciousness to spirit to creativity and so on—you realize how you got this particular soul. And when you get this soul, you will know how it makes you feel, what it makes you think about, and how you are with other people, whether you laugh or cry, whether you read or you write, whether you're quiet or you're noisy.

So when you think of food, you don't think about cauliflower. When you think about food in regards to your soul, you don't think about Snoop Dogg. It's the same thing.

Forgive me, I know all of you are close to vomiting when I talk about love. But you know when you love someone, it seems that only that person's image can bring about joy. All these other images do absolutely nothing for you. In fact, all these other images make you angry and you say, "I see all these useless people. Why can't I see that useful person?" And I think whenever something about you has gone through a very genuine experience, you will know what the right or the wrong images are. No one needs to tell you. If you have experienced me, for example, to be a relatively boring or uncreative instructor, I think it's impious of me to sell my teaching style to you. I can't do a good job of selling myself to you because I've left a very bad taste in your mouth. And I can say all these things about culture and tradition but it won't do anything.

But to answer your question in a very simple way, I'll just give it to you like this. Imagine, for some strange reason, that you have fallen in love with piano, and you want to be a really good pianist. You ask your teacher, "Well, how did you become such a good pianist?" "Well, you know my father spanked me, and then I had a teacher for about eleven years and that teacher slapped me on a daily basis. And then when I got done playing piano at his house, I would come home and play another five hours of piano. And then my father would wake me up at two in the morning and say, 'Play some more.' And then I was consumed by it, and then I began to fall in love with it." And then he says, "David, do you want to learn how to play piano?"

"Yes, yes."

"Do you smoke?"

"Yeah."

"How much?"

"Well, every day for like ten hours."

"Well, listen, you can't smoke if you want to do piano. Do you watch TV?"

"Yes."

"How many hours?"

"Twenty hours."

And he says, "Listen. If you really want to become a good pianist, you can't smoke, you can't drink, and you can't hang out with your friends. You just have to be preoccupied with piano. If not physically, then emotionally. If not emotionally, then intellectually." People who go on diets or do rehab or anything really, what they have in common is that if you really want to be good at anything, you have to be on a diet. If not physical, then emotional, if not emotional, then intellectual, if not intellectual, then spiritual. You can't do anything without a good diet. It's impossible.

If you want to do the stuff that the Buddha talks about, you need to understand that for the past twenty-six years, you have lived a very physical life. You have lived a lot of Iron stuff, you have lived a lot of Bronze stuff, you have lived a lot of Silver stuff. You think about sex a lot, you think about money a lot, you think about relationships a lot. And so, the Buddha is about you becoming self-sufficient. Not having sex. Not needing power. Not wanting power. And being okay with not being in a relationship, because now instead of having a relationship with a human being, you have a relationship with books, with your teacher, with ideas, with your emotions, with crying and longing and frustration and anxiety. And it will be uncomfortable because this is very new stuff for you. And without a community, that is, without the Buddha protecting this seed that was planted inside you, you won't get anywhere. It's impossible.

Anyways, do you have any other questions? John, Norman, Catherine, Jess, Maria, Ricky, Steven, Ismael, Elise, Lester? Anyone? Well then, if you could please come up and grab a slice of this Serbian dessert. Even if you don't like the way it looks, just grab a slice, eat it in front of everyone, and then go home.

Chapter Five: Taoism and Confucianism

[Andrew: Is war inevitable?]

Yes. Any other questions? Did you think otherwise?

[Andrew shakes his head.]

Good job.

[Andrew: Why do we start wars?]

It's mostly about domination and aggression. You know there hasn't been a century where there hasn't been a war of sorts. It's okay.

Early in his life, Freud was religious because his father was religious. After a while though he couldn't understand religion. If religious ideas are so profound, he asked himself, why do people never try to apply them? And if they do apply them, why do people always come up short? After many decades of studying human behavior, he argued that most of life, especially war, is not about religious ideas, but mostly about power.

[David: Can we talk about St. Teresa?]

No. We'll finish Taoism and Confucianism tonight so that when we come back next week, we can talk about Judaism, Christianity and Islam. But if there are any other questions or interests, go ahead and raise them.

[Lacey: Can we talk about self-expression, and what it means to express yourself and find good ways to express yourself?]

It's a complicated question because the concept of the 'self' is in itself an enigma. If you're going out with someone and your intention is in Iron, sex and drinking and entertainment, it's not very difficult to fill the space while you're sitting having coffee or pizza. You can find almost every topic to be interesting. Then when you go to a different stage, you want to express yourself not so much through the physical pleasure, but the mental and intellectual pleasure, let's just say going to school or taking a math class or a psychology class and you want to talk to someone about how interesting the ideas in the classroom are. And though the conversation can carry you maybe for an hour or two, eventually you'll grow tired of the conversation. And then if it happens to be a man who's attracted to your physical body, he's going to listen to your nonsense about psychology and eventually take you home because that's what he wants to do. When you get to the Silver and you want to talk about commitment, you're going to be asking very pointed questions. You may use some sarcasm or humor, but only as a mask, and it won't be the undercurrent of your conversation. You want to know whether or not this person is worth hanging around. By the time you get to the Silver stage, you have to some extent understood the importance of time and energy, and you want someone to respect you in a different way, not the sort of way you wished to be respected in the Iron, someone who can move your body through music or sex or drinking. When it came to the Bronze, you also wanted to be entertained, but intellectually, and in a superficial way. When it comes to the Silver, you're very clear. You've done a lot of pleasure and power, and now you're looking for a man who's going to be with you for say the next twenty years, and a man who's worthy of you having his children.

And then there is the Gold. The problem with the Gold stage is that it takes us a long time to figure out what exactly we're looking for. Pleasure, money and relationships, fail us. Inasmuch as these things are healthy and necessary in many ways, when you begin to see yourself differently, through for example an illness, a mid-life crisis, or the tragedy of a parent passing away, a different set of questions arise and now the difficulty is that this confusion can't be expressed because there are certain experiences that are missing, or that haven't ripened yet. And this confusion has a lot of anger in it: "How could I have spent twenty of my years doing A, B, C, D, only to realize I don't have anything in my pocket?" So one of the difficulties with most of us, especially when it comes to relationships, is this. We meet people at the Iron. Physically, there are lots of people who are attractive. We know the world and the language of Iron. You take his hand and go to a party or bar, or you go see a movie. We also, to some extent, know that when it comes to Bronze, expression is not very difficult either. You come to this class and find someone to be somewhat attractive, and you know the language. You take the same classes and you go to a coffeeshop and read the same books. Now, the problem is, if you should meet someone in Iron, and should you evolve to Bronze, you're going to be talking about school and they want to go out drinking and smoking and having lots of fun. And you say, "Listen, I'm on a time-constraint." As long as the relationship lives in Iron, it will remain harmonious and balanced and you guys will continue to confess your love for each other. But the moment you walk into Bronze, there are going to be all these cracks in the relationship.

Now it's not your fault or his fault, that's just the way things are. You use different languages as you move through the stages. When you come to the Silver, language is again different. Often in Silver, couples want to see who has more power in the relationship, and eventually one will submit. And that submission will create a lot of resentment and anger in the long run. When you get to Silver, you speak the same language: "Are we ready for marriage? Are we going to buy a house? Is it going to have a backyard or a front yard? Are we going to have a car, minivan or big van?" Those ridiculous questions. So it's not difficult expressing who and what you are in Silver either. The problem arises when you're in Silver but you meet someone in Bronze. And you want to tell this person that you're ready for a commitment, but for them it's all about power. There is no equality here.

These are physical languages in Iron, Bronze, and Silver. You don't have to be very educated to be able to communicate with people. Some difficulties will exist, and the 65% divorce rate is an indication that despite our language being physical, there is still a lot of confusion. And if you meet someone in Iron, and if both of you do not go up to Bronze, there are going to be problems.

Then you're talking about Gold. [Long pause.] There is no way.

In these three areas of life, you get to know yourself by going outside. But when you're on this particular journey, the assumption is that all the things that you were looking for were going to satisfy you, because these three areas have Beauty in common, a sense of aliveness. But they're just short-lived. And then you say, "I want something that is relatively permanent." And in this day and age, when we're told that we should be on this quest to figure out who and what we are, that becomes the Gold. The problem is that you have to disconnect from all three areas. And you have no idea what's happening to you in the midst of this journey. It's like a psychological earthquake and you'll go to people in these three areas and ask for advice, but they won't understand you:

Ahtashast in bonge nal ye nist bud
Har ke in ahtash nadarad nist bud

In the three physical worlds you are full of things but when you want to go on a sincere quest, you become like the reed flute, and the problem with the reed flute is that it becomes hollow from the inside.

Whenever you experience moments of emptiness and boredom, you can fill it with something, whether it is drugs or movies or entertainment or a book or children or your companion. But when you get to this fourth environment, slowly something inside you has gotten rid of all these different things. For the first time, you feel a nakedness about you. And we have no idea what to do with it, because that's not the way that we've been functioning for most of our lives. This is a shock.

When this happens you're not going to be rational. Depending on how intense this is, you could either be emotional once every two hours or you could be emotional every five minutes. You won't be dependable and your promises will become no good. You won't be able to commit because you have no idea how you're going to be. Despite all your intentions to keep yourself together, you're going to fall apart all the time. There is going to be confusion and this thing called "homelessness." In the previous three areas, you could find a home. But here, there is no home. It's like when you fall in love, and the guy isn't there and though you really want him you can't have him, so you go to other men. But for some strange reason, though you can find companionship in their physical body, what you really want is an emotional, spiritual and intellectual home, which these men can't give to you.

Confucianism is all about the three areas of physical life. Don't try to get to Gold, he argues, because it's nearly impossible. You have to detach yourself from too many things, and when I say "detach" the truth is, you don't have to do anything. Things come off of you. Whenever you find a human being who is being hollowed from within, or has been hollowed, try to listen to the sort of purgatory they are trying to express. But Rumi is saying that you should never pay attention to what they are saying, but instead look at the heat or the longing or the yearning or the frustration or the anger that is behind their expression. That's the only thing that matters.

So there is no way to express yourself. You just have to wait twenty years. It's like any other thing that we're beginning to learn. It just takes a while for you to become proficient, that's all. It's like crawling then walking.

Someone in this class emailed me over the weekend and said that we spoke about being broken in the "right way," and they wanted to know what that means. Let me just quickly say what that may mean and I'm just going to wing it, and I'm probably wrong, and then you guys can take this stuff home and figure things out for yourself.

For those of you who are in Iron, you like to have fun and there is absolutely nothing wrong with this. The problem, if you were to stand outside of your life and look in, and then examine and study what is happening, you realize that this is a place where physical desires arise. You have the five senses, and the five senses have only one function. You see something, and they're looking for something attractive so that they can bring it in. And once it's brought in, attraction creates interest, and if you nourish these seeds then slowly you become obsessed with the object of your desire, and then you pursue it and then you obtain it, then you hang onto it for a while, and then it just dies. You lose interest, that's all. For those of you in Iron, if you want to know how your next high is going to unfold, you don't have to be Yahweh. You can just look at the mapping, and then before you even begin to open this pursuit, you know how it's going to end. You're going to find yourself bored and you'll want something different. So next time you go into something, when you understand this well, next time you want to drink or smoke or have sex, you will have lots of sex and drinking and smoking, but now your understanding has given you a conscience. In the back of your head, you know that this is going to be a failed attempt. You can have fun for twenty minutes, but you'll end up screaming at yourself, "How could I be so stupid to do this, yet again?"

In Bronze, you sit in a class, become anxious about the grade and the future, and this class, like every other class, will eventually come to an end. Every brand-new car that you've bought will become old. Anything that you can obtain down here will eventually suffer the same fate. It will get old and you will want something different. The way the desires play themselves out are no different than those in Iron. And we haven't even talked about capitalism, which produces so many physical desires inside us, especially in Iron and Bronze.

In Silver, again, I have no doubt that many of you have been in relationships, for all the wrong reasons but that's beside the point. You looked at someone, and physically they're attractive. Now you want to see if they have any power, if they're educated, have money or savings or a home or a car and if they're emotionally broken or intellectually mature. It's about power. And then you find them attractive. And then you hang out with them and eventually you say, "They've been in Iron and Bronze, now they're capable of a relationship." After some months, you want to get married and the poor guy or gal says, "Yes." And then of course you get married and it's fun! It's like anything else down here in that every brand-new desire is fun. You sit and talk about decorating your home, how many kids, what sort of car and eventually you'll look at this man or this woman and realize that there is nothing going on. There is no juice. Lights are out, and there is no power. And now, you can't leave the man or the woman, so you say, "So honey, you look mighty fine tonight. Do you think we're ready for a family?"

And he says, "What do you mean?"

"Children, you know, those tiny little things."

"I think so."

"I know you, you know me, I love you, you love me, let's do it!"

And then these tiny beasts are like tornadoes. They walk into your life and destroy everything.

No matter what you do down here, age usually bring maturity, maturity brings conscience, and conscience itself introspectively whispers, "I'm stupid. This is no good." You may take a lot of classes, have lots of degrees, money, houses, friends and books but then you say, "So what?" You may even try to have a fling, but in the end you realize that nothing really works for you anymore. You have understood that down here, you will be broken and betrayed. This is what the Hindus call the "ocean of illusion." This is how samsara, or pain and suffering, is created. It's not created by God, but by our own misunderstanding of things.

When you realize that there are going to be lots of cracks in relationships, lots of cracks in money and power and lots of cracks in just casual entertainment, the question now is, "What exactly can you do to make yourself relatively happy and sane?" And the answer is, "Nothing."

That is what I mean by being broken in the right way. When you get broken by pleasure in Iron, Bronze, or Silver, you should really understand why it has betrayed you, and understand why power doesn't do much for us in the long run, and why relationships in the long run will leave us empty. It doesn't mean you should walk away, but just have a good understanding. And then the next time you do something, you're not governed by greed or false thinking, imagining that if you do something different, something magical is going to happen to our life. Nothing is going to happen.

[Norman: Is the understanding achieved organically, or is it the teacher who makes you reflect?]

It can happen in all sorts of different ways. It can happen through your own reflections, but usually because of the way that we are, there has to be a very powerful shock to your system. I personally believe that it's much better to have a teacher who like a jackhammer breaks you. And remember, when you become defensive or angry, these – the Iron, Bronze, and Silver – are the stuff that's coming out. It's not like you have any idea about what is right or wrong or ethical or unethical, we don't know any of that stuff. We're just reacting to what's being done to us.

If someone has a truckload of asphalt, and they are jackhammering the back part of a road, you can be rest assured that once the concrete is removed, they're going to pour the new, better-quality asphalt. Another nice thing about being broken by someone in Gold is that it could create a sangha for you. They are your home. But that doesn't mean that you shouldn't go back to these areas, should you belong to them, it just means that if at any time you should find yourself in despair, you can always run here.

[Norman: So because of the rarity of people that actually possess Gold –]

Yeah, it's no good.

[Norman: Well, most people are not going to have a shelter to actually run back to. So they might be broken, but there's no comfort being offered.]

This is, for us, relatively new. In other words, for the past many thousands of years, the mass population have always been protected. They've always had a very busy life, working in the fields from sunrise to sunset. They sit together and talk amongst each other, and have a very strong, familial environment. It's only in the past century or so, with the coming of urbanism, big vast cities where all of us are strangers, where we are pushed to reflect. And now it's in our pop culture. Everybody wants to be enlightened and figure out who and what they are, everybody wants to be happy, and the truth it, that's never been the case. In no century, with the exception of the last two, do people want a job that is an extension of who and what they are. Look at your grandparents, or even your parents. Our parents didn't have a job that was an extension of their soul. They didn't have a soul because our parents only had one function, which was to have a job and put food on the table for the rest of us. It's only today: "Oh, I don't like this job and I don't like this companion and I want something that makes me happy." But the truth is, nothing's going to make you happy. Just be satisfied with the poverty that lives inside you.

The difficulty, Norman, is that we create a lot of history in Iron, and it's the history that devastates us. It's not very difficult for you to live in Montclair Village, but if you have hood mentality and hood emotions inside you, you're going to contaminate the woods. What makes this journey difficult is all this baggage that we carry. If you happen to find a very young teacher, he or she may have the stamina and energy and stupid hopefulness to say, "Oh yeah, I can get rid of all this stuff." But if you find someone like Jackie Chan in the movie Karate Kid, the story's different. The movie is about an old teacher who never even says, "I'm a kung fu teacher." Only when he finds a really good student does he train him. Until then, no one knows. Teachers remain invisible, because teaching is really a difficult task. Add to it the fact that in this culture there is no etiquette for these things, which adds another layer of complexity.

[Thomas: What is innocence, and how do you get it back?]

Chon ke sad amad navad ham pishe mast

When you have a hundred dollars in your pocket, you also have five dollars, you also have twenty and fifty and ninety nine, because you have a hundred. But if you only have ten dollars, you don't have fifty or sixty or seventy dollars. In Iron, you have ten dollars but you think that you have a hundred, so when it comes to spending a hundred you realize that you don't have it. In Gold, you have a hundred. If that makes any sense.

[Rebecca: What happens when someone reaches the Gold stage?]

There is a saying in the Zen tradition, "When you're hungry you eat, when you're tired you sleep, and when you're thirsty you drink. "Most of us eat because we're bored, we drink because life is difficult, and we sleep, well, we can't really sleep because we're filled with anxiety and dread. So there you have it. Good luck.

[Long pause.]

We will start Taoism. There is a guy whose name is Lao Tzu. Like the rest of us, he was actually hopeful that he could teach people things, could actually transform them and bring about social justice. But then he realizes that teaching is no good, people are no good, and teaching and people don't really have a good relationship. So he decided to leave China and education, and tradition has it that before he was about to leave China, someone asks him, "Can you write down your wisdom?" He says, "It's not going to be any good," because as we talked about, language is layered with meaning, so if you should find someone in Iron and this person has 5% intellectual curiosity, they're going to read a profound book, then they're going to find a woman or a man, take them to a coffeeshop and dazzle this woman or this man with lots of sayings and this woman is going to say, "My God, I have found a sage after all." And this woman is going to have sex with this man, fall in love with this man, only to realize that this man is like what you read in Corinthians, "He's just a gong, hollow on the inside but makes lots of big sounds."

So he said, "It's best for me not to write anything, but if this is the only way I can escape you, I will write a book called the Tao To Ching, or the Book of Life."

The very first lines of the book say, "If you're looking for truth or reality or happiness or Beauty, you're not going to find it, and especially not in language. Even if someone was to express it, it wouldn't be the real thing." And then he goes on in the next eighty chapters telling the rest of us how ridiculous we are and how we can't get anything right. Also, I will leave the sexual elements of Taoism aside. It's very profound, but we won't talk about it.

[Steven: Why?]

We're short on time, and it's not also really my place to talk about it, for a very simple reason. Someone who's in Gold has the right to talk about what you need to do with your body and what you need to do with another's body as a tool to have a glimpse of Gold. For those of you that are interested in this, and I don't recommend any of you doing this, but should you desire to play with this stuff, there is an old man whose name is John Butler. All you have to do is go online and search, "Philosopher John Butler." When he was thirty, he and his wife had a farm and they wanted to change the world and he used to have a lot of people on his property, and once in a while they would gather and they would meditate. On one occasion, he said, "At a certain point I realized that I was comfortable meditating with this other woman." Let's call his wife Janet, this other woman we'll call her Janice. Butler said, "For some strange reason I felt comfortable sitting with Janice," and as they were sitting and meditating, he said that something about him opened up, and he saw an image of himself that he had never seen before. The only thing that was left for him to do was to nourish that experience some more, which meant that he ultimately was intimate with Janice and he saw a beautiful image of who and what he was. He eventually left his wife, we don't really know what happened to Janice, but the point I'm trying to make is, since many of us are curious and these ideas are like fire that we play with, it's best not to approach them or even know about them. For those of you that are curious you can just Google this stuff, buy books on Amazon about Taoism and sex. But keep in mind, just in case you want to play with this stuff, Butler left his wife. You will do the same.

We don't know how teachers are made. All we know is that teachers begin like us, ordinary and mediocre. Then something about them opens up and they begin to be hungry for something. No one knows what they're hungry for. They become attracted to a certain set of ideas. That attraction creates attachment and desires, longing and yearning, curiosity, interest, they eventually become infatuated, they get obsessed, they fall in love with an idea, they go on this rabbit-hole quest, and no one knows how they're going to end up. Some kill themselves, some go mad, some don't reach the destination and ultimately just give up and accept their capacity, and others reach their capacity, which is Gold.

According to Lao Tzu, teachers possess five qualities, the first of which is that they are like water. Water is symbolic in the following ways. Many of you know how draughts come to be. In draught there is no rain, but more importantly, there is no snow. When the mountaintops don't have any snow then in the summertime there is no snow to melt to give the rest of us water. To create snow, first there must be a dark, gloomy, and thunderous sky, and from these stormy clouds come these tiny white things. But remember where the snow is coming from – not sunshine, but a horrific environment. In the New Testament there is a saying: "Do not give that which is holy unto swine." So if the snow falls, and if it falls in Oakland, it disappears after a minute. But if the snow falls in Yosemite, it stays there for weeks and months because it is protected.

The snow lands, and then teachers become like ice that sits on the mountain top. Ice is symbolic of a teacher, of someone who climbs a mountain and sits on the mountaintop, all alone, having removed himself from everything that we call life. How they get there, no one knows. How they are willing to stay at the very top of the mountain, no one knows. But when they turn into ice, they become hard and nothing touches them. Complete detachment makes for a very cold and depressed human being. But this is not social depression. This is not the depression that is the outcome of being betrayed. This is a willful, chosen path of depression. You've come to realize that nothing in life gives you value, so sit on the mountaintop. Here, sometimes teachers look and feel absolutely indifferent. Not the indifference you and I feel because we are bored or depressed. These are people that are filled with life, and yet they don't care about anything that life has to offer them. Because of this, the mountaintop can be a very lonely place. For those of you in this class that want to understand how it feels, go back in your own life and bring memories to the foreground, memories that were immensely painful and troublesome, where you wanted to talk about your difficulties to someone but you were misunderstood and eventually gave up. And you simply had to think and feel about this stuff on your own, because you had no one. That's the ultimate seclusion. That's your monastery. No one enters and you can't leave. The only thing that can melt this ice is the sun.

In all these three areas of life, Iron, Bronze and Silver, desires are created, effort is demanded, expectation comes afterward, and then disappointment. We struggle to make our expectations come true, and we make a tremendous amount of effort to make our dreams and our desires on these three different levels come true. Most often of course, we are met with complete failure, for the following reason. Rumi in his book the Masnavi argues that when you look at a tiny pebble, or tables and chairs, if you break them open like a physicist you would realize that there is an aliveness inside the rock and wood. The nucleus is dancing, revolving around something. Even a piece of rock desires to be happy. And Rumi argues that it doesn't matter who you are or what your nature is, what you really want to is to go way up there, and to experience the sun. Down here, on these three physical levels, we have glimpses of the sun by having sex, but the only problem is, the sun sets after ten minutes. Money and power set after maybe an hour. Relationships ultimately set after a decade, but they will set nevertheless. Regardless of who we are or our station in life, we are questing towards the sun.

Finally the sun hits the ice, and then the ice slowly melts. When the ice melts, it no longer sits on the mountaintop. The Return is when the teacher becomes water and slowly comes down. Why is it that Malcolm X simply can't enjoy living in his ivory tower called the psyche? Why is it that the folks who understood a few things about life don't simply stay home and enjoy their lives? Why do they go into society and deal with the burdens of people? Because that is what teachers do. Teachers only have one function: to submit themselves to the sun. They melt and begin to exercise this thing called compassion. Remember most of us in this class can't really do that. I know that some of us go through difficult times and we try to be forgiving and compassionate and generous to other people, and we can do those things for maybe five minutes, but eventually they'll go away. I'm talking about something that has become part of who and what we are. And this genuine compassion, symbolized by water, is subtle. Next time any of you go to San Francisco, sit by the ocean. Go when the sun is out, when there is no wind, and look at the water. The calmness of the water is immensely deceptive. It's eloquent, it's soft, it's gentle. And the funny thing about the ocean is that it tempts you. As you jump into the water and swim, something about you says, Go further, go further.

Next time any of you go to the woods and see a pool of water on a trail, know that the only reason this pool of water is created amongst these gigantic stones is because one drop of water is added to another. You would think that these drops of water would have no impact on the solid ground, but despite being subtle, and gentle, these drops have the power to crack things open and destroy them. So if you're wondering why Socrates gets condemned and crucified, or Malcom X, it's because despite their subtlety, they have the power to destroy. The power of water is invisible. It's alluring, and attractive, so we gravitate towards it. But we have no idea what it will do to us.

As their freeze melts and as they come down, teachers exercise compassion in different ways. Water has always been the symbol of baptism and purity, for example in relation to the Christian notion of sin. For those of you in this class that may want to go home tonight and make yourself a sandwich, the first thing you'll do is wash your hands. You know that the meat, lettuce and tomatoes and bread are clean, and you don't want to contaminate these ingredients with your dirty hands. You wash with soap and water because you're keenly aware that your hands are dirty. But water is only good for those who are aware that there is something about them that demands cleanliness. Remember the saying, "I am not here for the righteous, but the sinners." "I don't like the educated, I like those that don't know anything." "I don't like the arrogant, I like the humble." What is it that the righteous have? False pride and assumptions. The righteous are full of themselves.

As the water comes down, the water meets people in the Silver area, people who are filled with the worries of relationships, having a wife or husband and having parents. So when the water wants to fill them, the water realizes that they are full of stuff already and there is no space for water. According to Lao Tzu, water is not in the business of aggressively fighting those who are full of things. Instead, it simply goes around them. Teachers can fit almost any psyche and temperament, and they don't want to force anyone to do something that they don't want to do. To see this in action, when you go home today, grab a piece of cardboard, run some water on it, and place your finger right at the very center of their piece of paper. Water is not going to stand there like Mike Tyson and fight your finger, but instead it will just go around your finger. Water doesn't pick fights. Like a good judo master, water uses your power against you in ways you never imagined.

Kierkegaard, the Danish philosopher, argued that it's easier to teach a Muslim how to be a Christian than to teach a Christian how to be a Christian. In other words, a Christian has assumptions that they know what Christianity's all about. A Hindu or Muslim or atheist has no ideas about what it means to be a Christian and because of this, they are ready to receive. So for the people in Silver, they already know what their meaning and purpose is so they have no time for water. They may entertain water, but eventually they are passed over by water. Should, on the other hand, someone in the Silver ask, "How can I use your Wisdom Tradition to fix my relationship?" then because it is fluid, water has the capacity, the potential and the power to walk into the life of someone with a relationship and give this person nuggets of wisdom to put the relationship back together, if it's meant to be put back together. Nevertheless, no one in Silver quests to become the water him or herself, but they want to use water to fix where they are in life.

Water passes the Silver group of people and comes to the Bronze group of people, people who are about money and power. And water tries, to some extent, to convince them that perhaps there is another way to find fulfillment and happiness. When Andrea came to my class some years ago, she said she had money problems. And my suggestion to her was, "There are all these ridiculous people that go to school, all these ridiculous people that get degrees and teach. You can be one of them! And while teaching well is extraordinarily difficult, there will be ten minutes out of the five hours that you're in the classroom where you can feel excited and inspired. And those ten minutes are extremely valuable."

Compassion does not discriminate. The only thing compassion sees is brokenness, pain, incompleteness, and dissatisfaction. Passing the people who are already full of themselves, eventually water comes down and hits the flat land and finds those who are depressed, down, and homeless. Usually when someone is homeless, there is a ditch. In this ditch there is no pleasure, money nor power. In this ditch there is no husband, wife or family. There is nothing. Water can only be contained in this ditch. And water just sits in this ditch. Remember what we said last week: a flashlight's only purpose is to find a dark place. Water, or a teacher, is only looking for someone who's broken. It doesn't matter whether they're broken through pleasure or money or a husband or a wife. They're just broken. They have a big hole inside them. And what this person tries to do is to say, "Listen. It doesn't matter if you were broken through Iron, Bronze, or Silver. What you need to understand is how to remain broken in a very healthy way." All of us in this class walk around saying, "Yes, I'm a sinner, I was born a sinner." But our commentary on that verse is just conceptual. If you confess to being a sinner without longing and yearning and weeping, that confession doesn't make you a sinner. You have to feel the sin inside you, and that feeing allows you to reach up and ask for help.

If a human being is not broken in the right way, then they don't have the proper hole inside them. And if there is no proper emptiness inside them, they can't hold water. If this is a little difficult to follow, look at it this way. The only way Socrates can have Plato follow him is that Socrates needs to break Plato. He needs to create a void inside Plato. That space has a good amount of longing and yearning that says, "Please! Only the person that broke me can put me back together." And Plato follows Socrates, and only Socrates – for ten years! Matthew follows Jesus – why? Jesus creates a spiritual hole inside Matthew. Without emptiness, teachers have no function. Teachers can do things that seem violent and aggressive; they create negative impacts; depression; loneliness; isolation; and self-examination that leads to further isolation. Because the bigger the hole inside you, the more of the teacher that you can hold within.

This emptiness, the second component of Taoism, happens to be the quality of both a student and a teacher. But the emptiness that the teacher has is very different from the emptiness that the student has. The teacher becomes empty before Life and exercises humility before Life, and waits for Life to fill him or her. The student doesn't have that capacity yet. The student waits for the teacher to fill him or her, because they don't live at the top of the mountain just yet.

For those of you that want, to some extent, a better grasp on emptiness, go back to the times when you've been immensely depressed. For those of you that get really depressed and there is no sangha or home, you're going to be in really bad shape, and sometimes it may take you five minutes, sometimes five hours, sometimes five decades to overcome the depression. When you wanted something, but you couldn't get it. Lots of anger, resentment and jealousy, and how it made you aggressive and dominating, sometimes even violent. The student has no choice but to feel those emotions. The teacher doesn't have those emotions. It's like the cross scene in the Gospel of Mark: "I give myself to you," is what he says to God.

There are different kinds of emptiness. If I was to come to class on Monday and talk about money, what I'm trying to do is try to create a need inside you. And that need is going to try to translate itself as, I'm poor and somehow I want to be more wealthy. And when the class is over you're going to go somewhere and think about how to make money. Without a need, there is nothing to be satisfied. Or do this. When the class is over if you have any cups or containers, go and fill them up with some soil. And when it's full, try to put more soil in it. You will realize that when there is no room, it can't hold any more. To receive anything, there has to be a good amount of emptiness. It's need that creates emptiness.

Just as there are physical needs that create physical emptiness, emotional emptiness and intellectual emptiness, also there are spiritual emptinesses. Hugh Hefner, even though he is dead, he tries to create physical void. Donald Trump creates void in regards to power. If you have a brother that has gone to Berkeley and has graduated and you're still at Laney, every time you see your brother he creates an emptiness inside you. The point is that all these different stages of life creates their own unique emptiness.

But we're talking about Lao Tzu, who is concerned with the spiritual condition. One of the difficulties of emptiness is that there has to be a relationship for this emptiness to be created. We're talking about someone who is in the business of breaking people in order to create spiritual void.

The nice thing about religious, or spiritual void, is the following. There is this passage in the New Testament: "You should first seek the kingdom of God, and everything else will be given unto you." If you want to put that to test, think of it this way. If you long for intimacy, how much power does money and marriage have over you? If someone with water-qualities creates a void inside you, you won't much care about the emptiness that is the outcome of emotional problems, like your father, mother or boyfriend. Or the physical desires: I want a wife, a husband, kids. A strong enough spiritual void has the capacity to swallow the physical voids.

You know what happens when you're really hungry and you go and eat food. You eat like an animal. Remember what happens you're really hungry for a relationship. It takes only two weeks to fall in love. You eat the other person like a pig, then you throw up love, and you realize all that you have in the end is sickness. The emptiness, or sin, that's created inside us by spiritual teachers, in this particular case Lao Tzu, is that if there is a good amount of emptiness inside you, water from the mountaintop will fill you. You can call it the Kingdom of God, or you can call it an image of yourself that's very close to perfection. It's the same.

Think of it this way. There is this Zen teacher around the 14th century. There was this girl who goes to her parents and says, "I'm pregnant!"

And the parents say, "What! Who touched you?"

And the woman says, "That monk over there!"

And the parents go to the monk and say, "You did this to our daughter? You're supposed to be a monk!"

And the monk said, "Oh, is that what she said?"

"Yeah, that's what she said. The child is yours. We're going to give you the child."

"Okay, if that's what you want." The monk doesn't complain, accepts the will of God, and so the child grows to be twenty and this woman can no longer contain herself, so she goes to the parents and says, "You know, I lied to you. The monk really wasn't the man who was intimate with me. It was this other fellow." And so the parents go to the monk and say, "Our daughter told us that you're not the father. This other guy's the father."

And again the monk says, "Oh is that so? Well, here it is," and hands over the child.

The point I'm trying to make is this. It's not that the monk doesn't know how to love. It's not that the monk is not attached. It's just that monk can play with the various facets of life, the comings and the goings. The openings of some curtains and the closing of other curtains. There is a tremendous amount of power in being able to live in poverty, in being broken, in emptiness, in not knowing and not having and being okay with confusion.

The third component of Taoism is formlessness. Because compassion does not discriminate, it has the ability to take the shape of any container. If you look around this room you will see bottles and cups. The liquid in the bottles doesn't care about the size of the container. Teachers, i.e. water, i.e. compassion, have the ability to put themselves into any container, shape or form. So as a white man, listen to the Dream Speech. Whether you're white or black, old or young, it will move you. There is a young kid named Hazrat Inayat Khan who came from India and died at the age forty-four. He was a teacher of his own order, or school. "Hazrat" is also "Hazur," which means "someone who is always present." He didn't write but he went around and talked, and people followed him and collected his talks into a 17-volume set of books. In one of his books, he says that a mature human being, when he is around gay people, becomes gay. And I doubt very much that he is saying that he engages in homosexual behavior, but rather temperamentally he understands. When he is with a Jew, he becomes a Jew. When he is with an atheist, he becomes an atheist. Water fits the shape of its container. Teachers work with people, so they fit all types of people. It's a one size fits all. It is irrelevant whether you're young or old, straight or gay, male or female, because these concepts have to do with the physical entity. The human soul has no gender. So one container becomes a Muslim, one container becomes gay, and another becomes an atheist. The only important thing is that there is someone who is broken. But being broken by itself is not enough. You must also no longer have any anger or confusion inside you. In other words, you can't resist when the water comes down.

There are lots of social and physical elements in Iron, Bronze and Silver that inspire desires, until we realize that we no longer want to be touched by the desire for pleasure, or money, or even your companion. It's like being in a relationship and meeting someone on the side and thinking, "I don't want my husband to touch me, I want this other person to touch me." What you're saying is, "I no longer want to be formed or shaped or cooked or put in an oven by the elements of these three environments." Lao Tzu argues that if you really want to be formed the right way and if you don't have access to Life itself, just find someone who has access to Life and they can shape you. Remember what we have in Buddhism, the reason why you and I suffer. First we have a physical body and our physical body has senses, and those sense create emotions.

Those emotions create relationships.

Those relationships create history.

That history gives us identity.

But if there is no self, as Buddhism argues, then there is no identity.

If there is no "identity," there is no history then all the emotions that hurt us so much don't really belong to us.

If that's the case, we are free.

I have a friend who is going through a difficult time. His wife left him. The truth is, he doesn't want to stay in the relationship either. The only problem he has is that he has eleven years of emotional history with this person. He doesn't want her, but the truth is, he still closes his eyes and thinks about this woman. Imagine if you were a really good Taoist. You could be with someone for twenty years, and sure you will miss them, sure there will be some sadness, but they are not responsible for your identity. Do you see how difficult this is?

You all write. But all your essays have been shaped and formed by the classes that you've taken; the fear of the grade that is related to the class; the fear of your future; the expectations of your instructors; their subject matter. Lao Tzu doesn't care about any of that. He doesn't care about how we've been shaped or formed by society. He doesn't care about any of the things that you have on the inside that have been shaped by your parents, by your friends, by your ex's. He doesn't care about the way that your brain has been formed by the books that you've read, by the people you've talked to, by the conversations that you've had. None of those things matter for him.

Formlessness is coming to realize that all of your educational accumulation and information do you no good. If you realize that, you will no longer talk about the information that lives in your head. In fact you won't even talk because language for the most part is very socialized. Language only contains components of your limited physical life experiences. Lao Tzu doesn't care about any of that stuff.

Formlessness means the following. Imagine a marker, and we have given it no meaning, we have given it no shape, we have given it no purpose. It has no identity or value. It just sits there. Now someone will pick this marker up, perhaps from the physical, Iron stage, and says, "Wow." [Amir writes "Wow" on the board.] Which means, "Wow, look at how attractive that man or woman is. I would like to be with them." That's the shape, value, and identity given to the marker at this stage. The marker is picked up by yet another human being who happens to be in the Bronze and this person too says, "Wow." But this time "wow" means, "How could I have wasted so much time smoking and drinking? I'm thirty-five, I should have finished school." This "wow" has a lot of regret, it's like baptism. And all of the sudden you realize that the value of this marker has gone up slightly. Then you get someone who is in Silver and walks into his kid's room and finds the kid smoking and says, "Wow." There is a tremendous amount of fright and care and compassion as the father looks on and sees the potential addiction that will come to the child. It's given another value, another identity. Now this is all the physical. Then comes Lao Tzu who lives in the Gold stage, transcends all of this stuff, and says, "Wow." He looks at another human being, and says, "I see the kingdom of God inside you. I see that underneath all of this junk there is a genius." This has to do with awe and worship.

So Lao Tzu argues the following. Instead of allowing people like me, people who write books, people like Dr. Phil, people like Oprah, society and all of its branches, to shape the way you think and feel, why not just open yourself up to Life itself? Allow Life, capital L, to shape you? Realize the futility of the Iron, Bronze, and Silver, and become an empty container. Like the Buddha, sit under the tree and say, "If Life has anything worthy to give me, let it give it to me, otherwise I'd rather die." And remember the Buddha doesn't come back and tell us information. Moses doesn't tell us information. Muhammad doesn't give us information. What they all give us is the spirit of Life, the very marrow of Life! The stuff that transforms us, bothers us, troubles us! This is a completely different set of educational tools!

So you can either be in a relationship and have a man or a woman fill you up, but because you don't understand how this stuff works, you have some foreign object from the outside filling you up, then they will lose interest or you will lose interest and then you will become empty. But that's not the spiritual emptiness. This sort of emptiness creates a lot of anger, hatred, vengeance and violence. Lao Tzu argues that if you allow the Gold, Life itself to empty you, you will be depressed, you will be lonely, you will be isolated, but you will have no anger towards any specific human being. You will want no answers from any books or human beings. You want answers from Life itself, i.e. God.

Then there is the fourth component, being childlike. Being like a child is having no idea where you came from, who you are or where you're going, and you're okay with this. You have no desire to hang onto anything that's superficial, such as name, age, profession, gender, thoughts, emotions, or body. As adults we seek security, permanence and stability. Children like to open things up and break things because they are able to suck the marrow out of life, in each moment. Children have a difficult time playing with adults, but when children see other children, they come to life. Remember what Gilgamesh had said about society: it's always the place of contamination. Whether you're small or big, young or old, you've been contaminated. I'm not really quite sure how you and I in this classroom can apply all the stuff that lives in children: curiosity, awe, worship, innocence, trust, faith. For those of you that have very young children or nieces and nephews, here's an experiment you should perform. Stand them on a dinner table, one of those long rectangular ones, and put them at one end, and tell them to run towards you, and that you will catch them. They will run across the table and jump to you, because this is what children do. They quit their jobs and they just jump. Children have no idea what monogamy is. Children will have fun with anyone who can show them fun because children don't create an emotional history with anyone. Adults are not like this! Children get sucked into the moment, and something about them opens up and blossoms.

And there is the last component in Taoism called being creative. Don't do anything that doesn't allow you to express your own creativity. And the truth is, you and I cannot claim ownership to our creativity. It doesn't belong to us. It comes when it wants to and leaves when it wants to. Creativity means that you don't do anything that doesn't move you. If you're not moved, don't move yourself. Just sit there, like the Buddha. Sit under this tree, because life has nothing to offer you. If Life finds you worthy of making you profoundly creative, then fine. If not, death is much better.

When you have completed these five steps – possessing the qualities of water, emptiness, formlessness, childlikeness, and creativity – you will get to this place called wu wei wu. It's like the story I shared with you about John Butler. He's sitting, meditating with this woman, who happens to not be his wife. For some strange reason their bodies begin to touch, they begin to be very, very intimate, and he doesn't condemn it, he doesn't judge it, he knows that this is not his doing, and he submits himself to the will of life. He can't go back to his wife because he has seen something very magical about himself. And then, after the second wife, he lives a solitary life.

A quick recap. We are flatlanders. We live in the city, and everything for us has been organized. We know where the Safeways and Costcos are. The city will give us anything we want. Lao Tzu argues that you need to get yourself to the mountaintop, and it's going to be a very lonely and difficult journey and once you get there, you will not be able to fall in love, or enjoy yourself in conversations or at parties. You'll be a recluse, even though you may live with people. It's like one of those steps that the Naqshbandi Sufi have, hadbad anjuman, where you live a very solitary life even though you live under a roof with fifty or sixty people. No one has access to you, and no one can get to know you. And even if you wanted to tell people who and what you are, the truth is, you are beyond description. Once you get to this particular place, you fall into the Return stage. You turn your back to the sun and you face people who have difficulties in their relationships, or money or power, or sex, alcohol and drugs. And eventually you realize that even those who have difficulties don't even want a remedy, they just want to talk about their difficulties. So you're only going to be looking for ditches: those who no longer want to talk, those who no longer want to do anything, those who are depressed in a very, very healthy way. They simply sit and they pray for someone or something to walk into their lives and fill them with something. Aristotle argues that our nature as primitive novices is to put any new experience into old, familiar categories: "Is this about sex? Is this about power? Is this about romantic relationships?" But Lao Tzu argues that the people in the ditches are beyond categorization.

You either get emptied by life, which takes a long, long time, or you get emptied by a teacher, because he or she happens to find you at the right place, and they gut you alive. And if you have the capacity to receive, they will give. If not, you will walk away and remain broken.

In formlessness, look at who you are and study all the forces that live in society and inside you. All these forces shape who and what we are. We are not the creation of God, but rather the creation of society. If you are the creation of society, you are going to pursue society's definition of happiness, and be defined by the media and the books we read. But Lao Tzu argues that the only worthy pursuit or form is the one given by Life, or the teacher.

The most popular rendition of the love story of Majnun and Laylee is given by Nizami, but there are lots of people who have told these stories. Majnun means "intoxicated," or someone who's in love, and Leylee comes from the same root as "Lilith," which means "dark," or the creator of confusion and chaos. So this woman creates chaos inside this man's head. He's fallen completely and madly in love with her and he doesn't know what to do. He wants to marry her but he can't. He's stranded in the middle of nowhere and the woman is somewhere having a great time, and in the middle of his despair this man runs into a deer. He looks at the deer and says, "I know you're here not as an animal, but as a messenger. I know you know where my woman, Leylee, lives. Give her this message:

Eh sareban ah aste ran kharam janam miravam
Van del khod dashtam aram janam miravam

Tell her that a long time ago, before I had met her, my heart was in my chest. The moment she revealed herself to me, she took my heart with her. Tell her that without her, I'm homeless." And the deer runs to Leylee and tells her the story of Majnun. The deer is like the teacher. Since you can't get to Leylee, this woman that is a symbol of the Beloved, God or Truth,

you have to use a mediator. This person connects you to what you're looking for. All of us in this class have done this. If you have drank, the bottle
becomes the mediator, because in drinking you quest after freedom – freedom from thinking, or from feeling. Or you're bored and the fridge becomes your tool towards freedom.

[Norman: About the story about the monk. Why wasn't he bothered?]

You know, Norman, I have children. I doubt that I'm going to see them
married, and I won't experience what it means to be a grandfather. I have
no idea what they're going to do with all the things that they will inherit.
And the truth is, I'm not doing it for them, I'm doing it for me. And should
they take the things that I have, so be it. The point I'm trying to make is the
following. You can't claim ownership to anything, not even your own emotions or desires or passions. They're not yours, they're like gifts that come
to you. And the forces that bring these gifts to you, it's their right to take
these gifts away. They don't belong to you.

Is it not true that sometimes you kiss me in greeting? Would it be
wrong of me to expect a kiss from you every time you and I depart? Do you
think that expectation would create frustration and anxiety? Of course it
would. Do you kiss me because you're gay? No. And even if you were it'd be
okay, because you are moved by something. We shake hands, we embrace,
you go your way and I go mine, and that's the end of it. You don't go home
a write a book about it, you don't say "He kissed me because he wants to
be intimate with me," none of those things exist. You're moved by the moment, and when the moment leaves, the chapter closes, and it's done.

This monk raises a child and happens to be a really good monk. I mean,
image all the diapers that you have to clean, imagine all the time that he or
she awakens you at night and you have to put your own frustration aside.
This is a weak, tiny entity that needs your help. You have to be imaginative
and creative to survive the way that this monk does. It doesn't work well
for us ordinary people. It creates a lot of chaos, because you want to be
generous but you say, "Ah, he's not worth it, what is he going to do with the
money?" There's all these paradoxes that you and I fall into.

*[Norman: So the monk is like a happy Sisyphus. He's perfectly alright with
rolling the boulder up the hill, even though he knows that it's going to roll
back down. Is that quality something that we can obtain?]*

Imagine that you really want a Tesla. And you keep reading about it
and writing about it and dreaming about it and fantasizing about it. You
just don't have the money to get it. If you're okay with the fantasy, that's

fine. The problem is, we become greedy. We actually want this fantasy to become reality – that's where the problem is. I don't think we can be content with the fantasy. There is nothing wrong with the fantasy, but we are gluttonous.

It's like the story of the young man who finds a young woman attractive. But just looking at the young woman is not enough. He creates these plans, and the plans actually work and he's finally holding her hand. But that's not enough because he wants to kiss her, and a few months later they kiss but that's not enough. He wants to see her naked and then he does but that's not enough. He wants to be intimate with her and he is, but that's not enough. He wants commitment. So he has it but that's not enough – he wants children.

We are not content with the fantasy, and the truth is, all of life is fantasy. The only worthy pursuit is making sure that your fantasies are never realized. Just fantasize about money and power, but make sure you never get these things, because if you do then boredom will set in. Remember the Buddha said that all things will only serve to bore and betray you.

[Elise: Can we talk about grief?]

I was talking to the bank this morning and all of a sudden as I was taking notes, the ink in my pen ran dry. I became anxious and I told this woman, "Can you wait please?" And then she couldn't hear me, so I became a little angry. Then I was looking for a pen and I found one, but it soon ran out of ink. I realized that I have suffered a loss. But then I found a different pen, and I could very easily overcome my grief. It took ten minutes.

But this morning my wife told me that she's leaving. I have like thirteen kids with her and we've been together for about twenty-seven years. I have assumed the role of a husband – mowing the lawn and picking up the trash, being pushed around. I like that. I've also grown accustomed to my kids telling me, "DAD! Where's my ice cream?" They're like the mini-version of my wife. My wife is leaving me for another man, which makes me feel really lousy. What does he have that I don't? I know what he has, and it has nothing to do with his body. He has what's called "newness," and that's all he has. And in newness, he's a mystery, an enigma. But I know something that my wife doesn't know. Do you know what that is? Every new thing will get old. And she's a little too old to create a twenty-year history with this man. I'm going to wait, and she's going to knock on my door, maybe not tomorrow, maybe not next week, maybe not next month. But I assure you, there will come a time where she looks at her kids and looks at her life and she will say, "I've destroyed twenty-seven years of marriage for this? A set of uncertainties?" She's going to knock on my door. I've never needed her, and I will simply say, "No."

Grief is about attachment and history, but mostly about loss. But the truth is, what exactly have you lost? The problem is when you start your relationships [Amir points to Iron, Bronze, and Silver] on needs, someone on the outside has power over you. The nice thing about this is that every good teacher ultimately wants you to be a teacher. Self-sufficiency. The fear of death, for example, it's a big loss. You won't see your kids, you won't see your parents, you won't see your this and you won't see that. But what if you have come to realize, kind of like Malcolm X, that life has nothing to offer you anymore? What are you going to lose? You have lost everything long before you die!

Grief is about liking things a bit too much, and they're not worth liking at all. We are animals where once we eat something, we have to excrete. Whether it's food or relationships, books or money, it doesn't really matter. Things have to come out.

What you're saying is, "I don't want to excrete things." Well, then you'll just feel constipated.

But honestly, these people are no good! Lao Tzu. They tell us not to be human: "When you suffer a loss, don't grieve." "When you're in a relationship, don't be attached." There's a physical body! "No, that's not you." But I'm creating all these emotional histories with people! "No, that's not you either. Always be empty." Who can live like this?

[David: Can we talk more about homelessness? Are there any productive or useful things that can be done in homelessness?]

Have you ever seen homeless people? [David nods.] How do they look?

[David: They look bad.]

How do they smell?

[David: They smell bad.]

Their clothes?

[David: Their clothes are bad.]

Do you ever talk to them? [David nods.] How do they talk?

[David: They talk bad.]

Do they have relationships?

[David: No.]

So they are . . .

[David: They're bad at relationships.]

So when it's really hot, do they feel good or do they feel . . .

[David: They feel bad.]

When it's really cold, are they enjoying themselves or are they feeling . . .

[David: They're feeling very cold.]

And?

[David: And bad.]

And when they're sick, do they have anyone to take care of them? [David shakes his head.] And that must make them feel really . . . [Silence.] Bad! Do they have friends? [David shakes his head.] So they must feel very lonely. [David nods his head.] Hm. Imagine you're homeless by Lakeshore, which is the hub of California. And yet the homeless person gets dismissed. Do you think that a homeless person sometimes says, "I'd like to be like them?" There is this scene in that movie, Into the Wild where he's literally homeless. He doesn't want to go to school, he just wants to live in the wild but he stops by this restaurant and suddenly imagines a different image of himself. A man, clean-shaven, hair combed and wearing a suit and tie. He's having dinner with wine, he's laughing and having a great time with people. But all of a sudden he finds that socially-constructed image of himself rather disgusting, and he moves away very quickly. He finds a home in homelessness.

If you want the answer to your question, just look at any homeless person. That's how you will look on the inside. With the exception that you're homeless because you chose to be homeless. Most of us become homeless because of the Fates, the slings and arrows of life where you lose your job or your home or your wife leaves you or you just go bankrupt or you get sick and tossed out. But these people remove themselves from life. They become homeless. And if they remove themselves from life and do things the right way, they won't be jealous or angry or resentful. That's the only difference.

There is this man that you guys should meet. He usually walks on College and Ashby by Café Roma. He's a white guy with blue eyes, beard, he usually wears a green plastic raincoat. He's a really nice guy and there's something about him that screams, "You need to respect me," and the truth is, everyone does. I don't know what sort of a man he is, but he's quite interesting.

That's homelessness.

[Josh: Someone that has a comfortable life but chooses to be homeless –]

Do you have a girlfriend?

[Josh: Yes.]

Did you have one before?

[Josh: No.]

This is your first one?

[Josh: Mhm.]

Hm. Have you ever thought about leaving her?

[Josh: Maybe, yeah.]

May I ask why?

[Josh: Um.]

Why would you want to leave her? She's no longer your home. You and I have done this homeless business for a long, long time, but on a very small scale. You have a brand-new phone and it works relatively well, but iPhone 25 is out, and I want to get that. Someone would ask, "Why would you want to get rid of your old phone?" You say, "I don't know. I've just got the money and I want to do it." You've become homeless in regards to your cell phone. Approach it from a place of privilege. You buy a watch, you buy sneakers, you buy a different car, you change your job, and every time you walk into something new, that new thing demands that you spend time getting to know it really well. It's like moving from one state to another. You choose to be homeless in all these different ways. In this particular case, you choose to walk away from anything that gives your body pleasure in a superficial, stupid, callous or childish way. You move away from putting information in your head, as if it means anything, like "Let me memorize the entire New Testament." "Let me read Noam Chomsky so when we go out I can dazzle people with my intellectual prowess." Some people just walk away from those things, on a bigger scale.

[Josh: What level of the Iron, Bronze, Silver, Gold are they on?]

I don't think you can think about it that way. Usually what happens is, for example, you no longer care about sex and instead you want to go to school and get a degree. [Amir points to the Bronze level.] There comes a point where you say, "This, Iron, is no longer enough." In fact, it gets to be a little boring. When you can predict how things can unfold, you begin to lose interest. Maybe the first hundred women or men will feel good, but with the one-hundred-and-first woman, something about you opens up and says, "I just don't want to do this anymore." If you've been in Iron for five years it's going to be difficult to psychologically adjust to the discipline that school demands. But if Iron becomes disgusting enough, as Darwin would say, you will adapt. It may take you some time but you will adapt. Iron and Bronze are about your individual happiness and pleasure so by the time you get to Silver, which is about relationships, you can't just have intimacy whenever you want. It's not going to work that way. You can't work seven days a week, fifteen hours a day, and keep a companion around. Again, you have to adapt. The point I'm trying to make is this. Every time you leave a stage, there is grief, loss, confusion and anger. Every person in this room who's ever been in a relationship knows that there are moments when we say, "If only I could be alone. If only I could be single. There is freedom in being single. Then I could use my freedom to do something else." All of us go through these emotional crises, and we have to wait until the tornado goes away and the storm dies down to be able to adjust to these new stages.

I really don't know which is best, to be in a mediocre relationship and have lots of friends, or to fall in love and have this grand experience, but be lonely. There is a poem that Rumi has:

Roh sar baneh be baleen tanha mara raha kon
Tark man kharab shab gard mabtala kon
Maeem o moj soda shab ta be rooz tanha
Khahee beea bobakhsha khahee boro jafa kon
Az man goreez ta toh ham dar bala neejatee
Begazeen roh salamat tark roh bala kon

Someone goes to him and says, "Is there something that I can do for you?" He says, "Listen. I am like a virus. Don't catch what I have. Go rest. I've been in seclusion for most of my life." So even Rumi complains about these things. If you read the very last book of his, it's a very strange thing. The book is dedicated to a man, Hassan, who doesn't speak well, doesn't think well, doesn't know how to read or write, he's just a stupid man. But

Rumi says, "There is something about this man's soul. I worship it." And he dedicates this last book to Hassan. You have to understand what a desperate place Rumi is in. People's eloquence and social etiquette are not enough. How they look, what they have, and how they say things is not enough. He needs something more. And what he needs can only be found in a single human being in a town of three thousand people. How could you consider this man to be happy? Read the Gospel of Judas. Jesus says, "I want to die, this place is no good. People are stupid. Even the gods that they have created are stupid."

[Beth: Is there anything besides brokenness that makes someone ready to learn?]

I honestly don't know what makes anyone ready to learn. There is this story from Rumi about a man who says that he's ready to have a tattoo on his right arm, of a lion. Lion, of course, is symbolic for Truth and being a student and all this stuff. So very proudly he walks to this tattoo shop, looks at the tattooist, and says, "I'm ready to get a tattoo." The guy looks at him and says, "Are you sure?"

"Yeah!"

"Well, what do you want?"

"I want a lion!"

"Whoa, lion, ooo, okay."

Remember the symbolism: the tattooist is like God or a teacher, the one who goes to the tattoo shop is a student, the student's desire is the lion, which means, "I am here to find God and Truth and all that stuff."

So the tattoo artists says, "Fine, let me just get my needle and put some stuff in it and stick it to your arm." The needle gets to the man's arm and the guy says,

"OH!"

The artist says, "What? What happened?"

The guy says, "This is so painful! What is this? I'll sue you! Can you do a different part? What part are you doing?"

"The head."

"Don't do the head! Do something different!"

So the artist does a different part and the guy says, "Ah! AH! What part of the lion is this?"

"The leg."

"Don't do the leg! Do something different!" So the artist does a different part and the guy says, "AHHHHH! IT HURTS! What part is this?"

"The tail."

"No tail! Do something different."

And ultimately the tattoo artist says, "This is ridiculous. I've never seen a lion that has no legs, no head, no tail. That's not a lion – get lost!"

And the point that Rumi is trying to make is, who in this class doesn't want to be happy? Who in this class doesn't want to know right from wrong? Who in this class doesn't want to be touched by something grand? All of us do! But the moment something is given to us, and we genuinely and intuitively know that we are about to leap out of our skin because it is so beautiful, all of a sudden we say, "Wait a second—what is this? Because, you know, when I'm going home, I can't function well. It's painful."

"Okay, so what do you want?"

"Give me something smaller."

"I don't know, go find it yourself. There is nothing smaller – this is it!"

Ultimately if you want the lion, regardless of what part of the lion that you want on your arm, the needle and the ink have to go inside your skin and it can never be deleted—it's lifelong. These stories suggest a very profound thing. That if you really want to understand something, be careful who the tattooist is. Be careful what sort of an animal you want. Because once the ink gets inside your skin, you can't get it out.

Who has the capacity to endure a lion? None of us in this class have the capacity for all of the lion, some people are just okay with the tail. At least it's a part of the lion. Some people are okay with the teeth, some people are okay with the mane, some people are okay with the eye. But to have all of it, that's beyond our capacity. But the problem is, there is this saying by Hassan Kharaghani, "I am ready to learn, but you have to give it to me in a way that I accept." It just doesn't make any sense. It's like going to a therapist and when things get tough and he's trying to really get inside your emotions and experiences, you say, "Listen. I really respect you, but don't go there. That's too painful. Let's just play with the silly stuff." "Well, you're here to get the whole truth but nothing but, and now that we're almost there," but you say, 'No."

Teaching is like dating. You date to see who you can hang out with, you date students as well. Teachers do that to see who has the capacity for what. And some people are good for one date, some people are good for two dates, some people are just not good. Some people are just okay with the tail and remember, tail has no eyes, so they like the experience but when it comes to achieving clarity through their own work, they say, "No, it's too much."

[Norman: What role does curiosity play in one's ability to be a student?]

I remembered the poem that I couldn't remember the other night:

Goftam del o deen bar sar karat kardam
Har cheez ke dashtam nasarat kardam
Gofte toh ke bashee ke konee ya nakonee
Un man budam beeqararat kardam

Why are you in this room?

[Norman: I have no bloody idea.] [Laughter.]

Curiosity is the most basic element of your quest. But curiosity by it-self is no big deal. Curiosity is a hit-and-run. Like you see someone who's old and you say, "Hmm, I'm going to get there?" It's something to be curious about. If a class is interesting, it's a good thing to be curious about. But it has no longevity. The only difference between Casey and someone like Malcolm X is really quite simple. Curiosity infected Malcolm X to the point where he became obsessed and ultimately fell in love with the idea of justice, of what it means to be a human being. For Casey, it's just a pit stop. Almost everyone can make you curious about something, but curiosity doesn't create a permanent relationship. If you want a permanent relation-ship with this stuff, it has to live inside you like cancer. And eventually you have to be able to live with it. You became curious because you just walked into a class. Should you go home and do something stupid, that curiosity means nothing, except that once in a while it helps you feel guilty about what you've done.

Let's say, for example, you like this class. The task of this class is quite simple. Sure, it's here to make you curious, sure it's here to create interest, sure it's here to make you infatuated with ideas, sure it's here to have you be obsessed with ideas. But it's also here to have you fall in love with ideas, but that's not enough. You need to change your major to philosophy. But that's not enough. You need to stop drinking and smoking because you need to have very sober thoughts about life. But that's not enough. You also have to put your own life on the cross and see it, observe it, and examine it. In other words, love makes you poor and you have to be okay with that. Now, that is called a committed relationship.

The seed was curiosity, but it's only a seed. It means nothing. If you happen to be married, you have to go home and fake it to your wife. That's how it is.

On to Confucianism. First I'll make Confucianism really easy, and then we'll make it complicated.

[Ismael: What have you not complicated?]

I went to this bar last night to get myself drunk. It was crowded, maybe two hundred people. This young couple came in, maybe in their midtwenties. We had to wait in line to get our drinks and our boneless chicken wings, and these two people embraced one another, and kissed for like a half-hour, in front of everybody. It took me back to when I was five, when I used to do those things. They were in love and they didn't care about the public, because they were beyond their judgments. It was like they lived on an island all to themselves, it was like their own Garden of Eden, despite all the serpents around them. They lived in a bubble. I went to them, because they were in front of me and I told them a few things about the cycles of life. And I could do that because one of them was my former student.

The point that I'm trying to make is this. I have no doubt that this couple, when they observe the rest of us nonchalantly looking past our companions, make judgments about us and rightfully so. Life is short: "Why are these people together? You don't like your wife or your husband or girlfriend or boyfriend. Just leave them, go somewhere and have a good time with somebody." Passion complicates everything that's passionless.

So Confucianism. Society can be made harmonious in five ways. There are social roles that people should play, and we should never transgress against these roles. In other words, life is like a dresser. Everything has its own special drawer, its own unique function in society. The role of men in traditional society is to make money, buy a house, buy a car, find a woman, give her some kids, make sure she takes care of the children and the house. Women shouldn't play men's roles and men shouldn't play women's roles either. Men are supposed to be masculine and women are supposed to be feminine. End of story. Men should respect women's role, and women should respect men's role. Remember, do not apply this! This is about three thousand years old when there were villages of less than a hundred people. There were no urban societies, no technology. These traditional values do not have a home in modernity. In three hundred years we have undone ten thousand years of tradition, and now everything is just confused.

So point number one is that the family consists of man and woman, husband and wife. The woman receives, and the man gives. Number two: Children must, at all times, obey the wishes of their parents. Children don't have rights. And why should they? What have they done? Are they like Google Maps, do they know where they're going? Do they have this razor-sharp reflective ability where they can discern good from bad and right from wrong? Those of you in this class who are over the age of twenty-five, you're here only for one reason. Your parents were lenient with you.

They should have been harsh with you, and now, instead of being at Laney College at the age of 25, you'd probably have your Master's or PhDs from Stanford. Parents have been around the block a couple of times. When they say "Don't drink, it's bad for you," don't say, "I want to experiment with it." Just don't drink. Period. And also, you have inherited your parent's last name and reputation. Don't mess it up. You don't want to ruin your parent's reputation because then when they want to sell stuff no one will want to buy it. If they want to marry off their son or their daughter, no one will want them because you have tarnished their name. Parents have knowledge, not so much Wisdom, but knowledge of physical life. If you can make coffee at the house, don't waste your money buying coffee outside for $2.88. Every one of us carries our parents' reputation. Not today because our parents have been ruined by their parents, and so on, but I'm talking about 3,000 years ago. So you come to this class with no reputation and no name, and even if you do have a name and reputation there's nothing in it. But it's okay.

And no one just has one child. People have twelve kids. The younger kids must always respect the oldest kids. When I go to Roseville every weekend my brother, who is just a year younger than I am, takes off my shoes and massages my feet, then washes them. And then he rubs my fingers, and then gives me money for allowing him to do all this stuff for me. The point I'm trying to make is, when you're young, you must have a good amount of respect for your elders.

So the first three commandments are this. The first: in the house, the wife and the husband must play their appropriate roles. They must also be profoundly respectful towards one another, because they're modeling relationships for their kids. Two: the kids respect the parents through their actions, thoughts and language. Third commandment: even if the parents are out of the house, the kids have to respect one another. Once you've been disciplined the right way, you take these practices into society. This means the following. If, for example, Casey is older than me, culturally I am burdened to respect him even if he was to say, "Amir, you are a cameljockey, you man from the Middle East. I will say nothing back."

Do you see what happens to the sense of self? It goes away. Do you know what happens to the emotions that most of us Westerners carry? "Oh, I was hurt, oh I was this, oh I was that." Even if all those things were to happen to you, you would never voice them. The culture wouldn't even allow you to entertain them within yourself, in the privacy of your own thoughts.

Imagine a husband and a wife having a fight, and ten minutes later guests come in. If you're unruly and untamed, you're going to leak out these frustrations and your guests are going to say, "Are you guys okay?" You won't see too much of that, at least in comparison to the West, in India or in China or in most parts of the Middle East, because people know how to contain their emotions.

Finally, you have an emperor, and emperors used to be, well, anyways, respect your government, or anyone who has power over you. Now as extraordinarily problematic as all this is, still, that's easy Confucianism, just the social and ethical philosophy of Confucianism. Now let's get to the messy part of it.

Mandate of Heaven. Every human being is destined for something. Every human being has the Kingdom of God within. The ultimate task of every human being, in Confucianism, now I'm not talking about the casual way that Confucianism is usually talked about, which is a social and ethical philosophy of life. We'll just make it a little more esoteric and spiritual like the other traditions. Every one of us in this classroom wants to find a way to have sucked the marrow out of life before we die. We want to look ourselves in the mirror and say, "Mine has been a life well-lived." If you are a believer in God, you want to say, "God's will has been done through me." If you have been like Khalil Gibran, very creative and poetic and gentle in spirit, you want to say, "I've always been guided by my creativities in life. Regardless of how difficult my physical life has been."

For the Mandate of Heaven, you don't allow society to create you. You don't allow social desires to create you. You don't allow your friends or their judgments to create you. You must always lift your head and gaze towards the heavens, represented by the Emperor, the sun-god, the teacher. If you go out with a drug dealer, eventually you'll become a drug-dealer. If you go out with a professor, you'll eventually become a professor. If you go out with a CEO, you will eventually become a CEO. If you go out with the Mandate of God within him or her, you will eventually desire to be like them.

Once you have found the Mandate of Heaven, once you have found what the spiritual voices are telling you, how you need to live your life, how you need to spend your energy, two things now live inside you in harmony. The masculine and the feminine. The yin and the yang, the husband and the wife. You know that you need to pay rent, that's the masculine part, the discipline part. But you also have this feminine part that says, "If you need to make money, you can't work for the city. You can't work for In n' Out, unless you are passionate about making burgers." The yin and the yang must be complete inside you, and must live in harmony. There are times when the creative part of you, the spiritual part, realizes that the spiritual part has been taken to Rome and must live amongst the Romans. Caesar is the king and this creative part submits and says, "You know what, your will be done. Make money. Lie. Cheat. Whatever you need to do. But when we go home, whatever wealth we take home, it goes to the creative part of life."

There is another way you could look at this, and I think this is a much better way. If you haven't figured out the Mandate of Heaven, in other words, if you haven't figured out who you are, don't get into a relationship. You will find yourself the wrong companion and your children will suffer because you will break up. Find someone who is also creative. Find someone who also has the yin and the yang playing inside them harmoniously. Remember what we talked about in these stages. Your language may be the same in Iron, but the moment your meaning or purpose begins to change, you define happiness as going to school whereas your companion is about sex and drinking. In Silver it may be about you and I having a family whereas you only want to go to school or you only want to make money. Should you meet someone in Iron or Bronze or Silver, should you form a relationship, it will bust because you're approaching the relationship through needs. The Mandate of Heaven tells you to get to the Gold, and if you're not there, at least know the function of the Iron, Bronze, and Silver. Make the appropriate choice.

Children. One of the most awful things that anyone could do is to bring about children. Sure, some of us get lucky, but for the most part, they turn out losers. The story in Confucianism is that if a harmonious man and woman get married, they know a lot about discipline but they also know a lot about creativity. They know a lot about the masculine and the feminine forces and so they can both be content. When these two people come together and create a family and have children, they don't want their kids to only study business because this kid will become lop-sided. In other words, repressed emotions will eventually leak out in a negative way. These parents want their kids to not only study business or stats or math or history or geography, but also the creative arts. They know that every child lives in the physical as well as the spiritual world. And so Confucius argues, when you have a good man and a good woman coming together and having children, that becomes a good family. If your next-door neighbors have done the same thing, then you have a harmonious village. If every village lives in that way, you have a harmonious state. If every state lives that way, you have a harmonious country. He doesn't say, "Pick up arms and fight the enemy." There is no enemy, except the fact that people have not realized the Mandate of Heaven. They don't know who or what they are.

[Andrew: How does Confucianism lead to social stability, and is it worth sacrificing individual liberty for social stability?]

There are many unknowns in life, and unknowns are no good. It's good to live a domesticated life. You may not love your husband or your wife, but at least when you go home, there they are, with the pizza ready. There is no chaos. Even if it's a bad marriage, you know what you're walking into and with the passage of time, you know how you're going to adapt to this mediocre relationship, and there's nothing wrong with that. What would happen if you're in a marriage and it happens to be mediocre, and all of a sudden you fall in love with your neighbor? You're going to create a lot of unknowns in your life. Those unknowns are going to impact your life, your husband or your wife, and it's going to impact your children.

Confucius argued, "Listen. Life is too short. We impact one another in mostly negative ways. Make sure that no new or untested information comes into your life. It will ruin and devastate you. All of life is about stability, that's all it is. Don't tell anyone, even women that they're free. Men have to earn money and be out in society, and women have to get pregnant, raise their children, and take care of the house. End of story. Don't tell men to be pianists or artists, they're out there to make money, to bring food home, and to eat. Children have only one function. Not to figure out their passion, but life is difficult so get a good job that makes good money so that they can support their parents in old age. No sex before marriage, and no love before marriage. All of you in this class have been burdened by going to a restaurant that has a menu as thick as the Bible. And what do you do in the end? You look at your companion and say, "Order whatever." We always like going to a place that has two or three items on the menu. It doesn't create unnecessary desires. You're free. You just take your cheeseburger and you eat it and you go home – it's finished.

[Beth: How do people discover what their Mandate of Heaven is?]

Imagine a humongous rock that's sitting, and all these people or entities are looking at this rock and they say, "You know, you're just so ugly. Change. Become something different." And this rock says, "No, I am what I am." And there are these drops of water that look at these entities and say, "Have no worries. We'll fix the egoism of this rock." Ten times every day these drops hit the rock and after twenty five thousand years the rock is now a beautiful oval-shape that contains water.

The message of the story is that none of us really know what the Mandate is. We keep trying things, and I think that's why we keep trying things, even relationships. We keep trying because we are not completely happy with the image that we have, or this image of ourselves that we've created through our relationships. And I think it's nice that we get broken and depressed, and it's nice that we live in the dark. When we feel these things, it shows that things aren't working. We don't know.

If you remove religion from a culture, what you have are secular emotions of depression, loneliness, anger and frustration. If on the other hand religious philosophies are re-injected into a culture, there will still be depression, but religion always argues that physical life is no good. For example, as you read in Romans, a man goes to God and says, "Look at my riches," and God looks at this man and says, "Everything about you is always seen as wretched rags before my eyes." Life, everything that we possess down here eventually becomes no good. So depression becomes part of life and it becomes very sacred because depression helps you pray. But when you make a culture very secular, when you get depressed you seek therapy. And therapy goes back to psychology, and psychology goes back to Sigmund Freud, and Sigmund Freud is all about making you fit into society, which Freud argued is sick itself. How can someone be healthy in this framework?

One of the things that Fyodor Dostoyevsky argued was that we need magic in our life. If there is no magic or mystery, life becomes stale. That's why relationships and new things are so tempting, because they hold magic inside them. This cell phone does something that that cell phone cannot do. This man does something that that other man doesn't do. LSD does something that LDS doesn't do. We are seekers after magic, because magic brings us to life. One of the nice things about being broken the right way is the following. Imagine for a moment that you're unhappy with your man. Now he's an idiot, and most men are. You say, "If I change to this other man, things will be different." The only thing that you're saying is, "I know my man relatively well, and he's a little boring and lifeless, there is no mystery or magic to him. I come home, there is dinner, there is a movie, that's it. Do I really want to do this?" So you look for the magic inside another human being. Now the nice thing about being broken is that whether your man is John or Jack or Giovanni, eventually the magic will go away. If you look at your man and say, "He decent. He's 51% relatively good," you'll keep the idiot.

When you don't understand things well, you keep playing with fire. You keep texting, which creates fantasy and these fantasies create magic. But for someone who really understands, say, the Fourth Way (and no one really does), or another really substantial philosophy of life, the end result is what? All external paths lead to the same place: boredom or despair. Instead of looking for the magic out there, look for the magic inside. And you don't have to be religious. Learn how to play music. Do poetry. Wait for inspired moments so poetry can ooze out of you. Become self-sufficient and stop depending on other people to create your magic. But for that to happen, you need someone to lift you from Iron to Bronze, and then from Bronze to Silver, and from Silver to protect you in this desert of nothingness. Once this person gives you a glimpse of a few things, then you can go back, but you will do something interesting. Instead of wanting Iron, Bronze, and Silver to give you magic, you will inject magic into them. You'll become a really good cook. The only thing you need to do, is not be in a rush. This is about a ten- or fifteen-year process. As long as you have the patience for that, you'll be fine.

All of you in this class have heard the story, it comes from none other than . . .

[Class mumbles in unison: Rumi.]

There you go! It's about a man on the ground looking for something, and his friend Ismael says, "Hey what are doing?"

And I say, "Looking for my key!"

"Where is it?"

"It's around here somewhere."

So Ismael looks with me and after two hours Ismael says, "Where exactly did you lose the key?"

"Well, I think I lost it inside the house."

"Inside the house? Why are we in the backyard then?"

"Well, because there is more light out here."

The truth is, going inward and figuring out what the Mandate of Heaven or the Kingdom of God or the Buddha-seed or the Light of Muhammad is a difficult thing to do. Most of us find it easier to go outside but even when we go to outside, we go to the wrong people who entertain us in all the wrong ways.

Editor's Appendix

Professor Sabzevary often recites Persian poetry, usually amidst the most inspired and troubling ideas. These poems are often interpreted but rarely translated, yet even without translation, these poems convey much of the unspoken background of these lectures. Professor Sabzevary provides an immigrant's perspective of the American culture, which he often compares to the traditional narratives that now compete with modern cultures. In addition, this poetry demonstrates his obvious facility with the 3,000-year-old Persian religious and poetic traditions, which are being placed, not without some conflict, within the context of the comparatively young, secular Californian community college system. Regarding the translations themselves, the syrupy beauty of the Persian tongue is lost in written form, even moreso once transliterated then translated into English. Nevertheless, to give more meaning to the ideas that underlie these recitations, below are rough literal translations as well as a brief history of the poems from each chapter.

Chapter One:

Introduction to Religious Philosophy

(1)
Morde ye am meeravam bar rooye khak
Zendeh garden jan ye jan bakhshe pak

I am like a dead body, roaming a dead, dusty world
Grant me Life, You who are the Giver of Life

These lines are found in the opening poem of Fariddudin Attar's 12th century *Mantiq ut Tayr*, the overall synopsis of which Professor Sabzevary relates at the beginning of the Gilgamesh lecture. In addition, when describing how Enkidu sacrifices his innocence to cure Gilgamesh's corruption, Amir relates a story central to Attar's epic poem. These particular lines close a long, ecstatic description of the difficulties of various Prophets, the beauty and tragedy of the relationship between the divine and the human, and the feelings of deadness that accompany the quest to find meaning in life.

(2)
Ma boron roh nanagereem o qal roh
Ma daroon roh benagereem o hal roh

We don't look at the outward form of speech
We look within people, at their inner condition

Like many of the Persian lines recited in *Introductory Lectures on Religious Philosophy*, this couplet comes from Rumi's *Masnavi ye Ma'navi*, a 13th century six-volume poem that is often referred to as the "Persian Qur'an." God speaks these lines after Moses sees a shepherd praying unlawfully. Moses, known for his strict adherence to the law, criticizes the shepherd for his unusual prayer. God in turn apprehends Moses, telling him that the intention behind the prayer is more important than the language, eloquence, or intellectual exhibition of the prayer.

(3)
Buyad gereftarm shavee ta ke gereftarat shavam
Az jun o del yaram shavee ta ke khareedarat shavam
Man neestam chon deegarun bazeeche ye bazeegarun
Aval be aram toh roh vangeh khareedarat shavam

You must be taken with me before I am taken with you
Become my friend from the depths of your heart and soul, then I
will consider how your friendship benefits me
I am not like the others, who just play games for the sake of the
game
First fall into my trap, and then suddenly I will buy all that you can
sell me

This poem was written by the 20th century Iranian poet Rahi Mo'ayyeri. Though this could have romantic or political undertones, Professor Sabzevary gives a moving interpretation that instead introduces the initial dynamics between teachers and students.

(4)
Agar bar deedey Majnun nasheenee
Be qeer az khoobe Laylee nabeenee

If you could see the world through Majnun's eyes
You would only see Laylee's beauty

The Middle Eastern tale of Majnun and Laylee has a long history, but the most popular rendition comes from the Persian poet Nizami. The plot of Majnun and Laylee is similar to the relationship between Romeo and Juliet, as both stories describe lovers that long to overcome political boundaries. Professor Sabzevary gives a more thorough history of the names and symbols in the "formlessness" section of the lecture on Taoism. However, unlike the plays of Shakespeare, the story of Majnun and Laylee is used to illustrate religious and philosophical concepts, such as the relationship between a student and teacher or love's ability to transform the human psyche.

Chapter Two:

The Epic of Gilgamesh

(1)
Eshq ostrolab asrare khodast

This line, again from Rumi's *Masnavi*, is found within the following couplets:

Ausheqee peydast az zareey del
Neest beemaree chon beemareey del

Elate ausheq ze elatha jodast
Eshq ostrolab asrare khodast

Ausheqee gar zin sar o gar zun sar ast
Auqebat ma roh bedun sar rahbar ast

Love is found through heartache
And there is no sickness like heart sickness

The sickness of love is different from other diseases
As love is a star-map to God's secrets

Love, whether romantic or Divine,
Guides us towards that which is holy and sacred.

Like all philosophical poetry, these lines beautifully describe the conflicts that define the most significant moments in our life. Love is universalized in these lines, meaning that romantic love provides a brief glimpse into love of the Divine. Though at first a flattering interpretation of affection, it also means that our affections are not in truth aimed at the supposed inspiration of these affections, but rather inspired by God. Like most religious and philosophical ideas, these lines draw the reader inward, encouraging them to feel more for their soul than for the world around them.

(2)
Be omre kheeshtan ta yaddaran
Ze hejrat naleh o afqan bar lab

For my entire life, for as long as I can remember
Life's journey has only caused moans of pain to escape my lips

As stated in the lecture, these lines are from the 9th century Sufi philosopher Abu Sayd Abul Khyar. The lecture's interpretation is more moving than the literal translation, as the interpretation describes Gilgamesh's lament for his dying friend, Enkidu. Enkidu's death allows Gilgamesh to see the futility of physical life, a cornerstone of self-knowledge that is slowly revealed through life's frustrations and failures. This lament, according to this poem, is lying dormant in each of our hearts, waiting for a traumatic life event to bring these cries of the soul from our heart to our lips.

Chapter Four:

Buddhism

(1)
Bar qame eshq o roh gadroon nayarad tahamol
Chon mitavanand kesheedan in peekar laqare man

The pain of love cannot be endured even by the heavens
When the heavens cannot endure this pain, how is my pathetic body
supposed to suffer this pain?

These lines are from one of the most renowned Persian poets, Hafez. Unlike Rumi or Attar, Hafez is more celebrated as a literary figure as opposed to a religious figure, but in the 14th century the lines these two categories are blurred beyond distinction. This poem shows how love, unfortunately, can overwhelm all the instinctual comforts that psychologically attach us to the surrounding world.

Chapter Five:

Taoism and Confucianism

(1)
Ahtashast in bonge nal ye nist bud
Har ke in ahtash nadarad nist bud

The cries that escape from the reed flute are not wind, but fire
Whoever does not have this fire has never truly tasted life

This couplet comes from the opening lines of the *Masnavi*, which contain perhaps the most well-known images in Persian poetry. In the opening verses, Rumi uses a reed flute as a metaphor for a human being who is longing to once again feel complete. According to this poem, this sort of emptiness is filled with psychological torment, isolation, and passionate despair. When a person is in this state, each of their expressions is filled with a plaintive longing, similar to the emotions evoked by reed flutes.

(2)
Chon ke sad amad navad ham pishe mast

When a hundred comes, ninety is with us as well

This epigram from the *Masnavi* is an aside in a four hundred line exposition of the complicated relationship between faith and effort, described in the form of a dialogue between a lion and a hare. The preceding line provides the Islamic context:

Name Ahmad name jomleh anbeeast

The name of Muhammad contains the name of the other prophets

Together, these lines are similar to the phrase, "Seek the Kingdom of Heaven first and everything else will be given unto you." Both argue that if a person first struggles to understand themselves, then the desires of physical life can be seasoned with a profundity that would otherwise be absent.

(3)
Eh sareban aheste ran kharam janam miravam
Van del khod dashtam aram janam miravam

Oh, leader of the caravan, go slowly because my life is leaving me
With your departure, you will be taking my heart with you

These famous lines are spoken by Majnun, describing the agony of separating from his beloved, Laylee.

(4)
Roh sar beneh be baleen tanha mara raha kon
Tark man kharab shab gard mabtala kon
Maeem o moje soda shab ta be rooz tanha
Khahee beea bebakhsha khahee boro jafa kon
Az man goreez ta toh ham dar bala neoftee
Bogazeen roh salamat tarke rahe bala kon

Go and lay your head on the pillow and leave me alone
Leave me because I am drunk on Love, wandering around in the night
I am alone with dangerous waves, from night to day
If you'd like you could be kind, or you could abuse me
Avoid my company if you don't want danger
Choose the safe path, and leave the path of dangers

This poem comes from the *Divane Shams*, the collection of inflamed poetry that Rumi wrote upon the final separation from his teacher, Shams. As the lecture indicates, the poem, among many other things, describes the dangers of love and recommends that the reader stay away from the path of love and separation.

(5)
Goftam del o deen bar sar karat kardam
Har cheez ke dashtam nasarat kardam
Gofte toh ke bashee ke konee ya nakonee
Un man budam beeqararat kardam

My heart and soul live inside everything you do
Everything that I had you scattered to the wind
Because of who you are, no matter what you do
My very essence will remain restless

These couplets again come from Rumi's *Divane Shams*. In comparison, the *Masnavi* is a sober work, more known for its teaching stories and explication of the journey towards self-knowledge. However the *Divan*, written upon Rumi's separation from Shams, is helpless, lonely and intoxicated poetry that shows the psychological dimensions of submission, testaments to the incredible weight and pressures that the human psyche can endure.

CPSIA information can be obtained
at www.ICGtesting.com
Printed in the USA
FSHW011249130820
72946FS

9 781933 455495